Entrepreneurship and Small Business
Management in the Hospitality Industry

The Hospitality, Leisure and Tourism Series

Butterworth-Heinemann's Hospitality, Leisure and Tourism series of books is aimed at both academic courses and management development programmes. The series represents a planned and targeted approach to the subject and the portfolio of titles provide texts that match management development needs through various stages from introductory to advanced. The series gives priority to the publication of practical and stimulating books that are recognised as being of consistent high quality.

The Series Editor

Professor Conrad Lashley is Professor of Leisure Retailing, Centre for Leisure Retailing at Nottingham Business School, UK. His research interests have largely been concerned with service quality management, and specifically employee empowerment in service delivery. He works closely with several major industry organisations including the British Institute of Innkeeping, J D Wetherspoon Scottish and Newcastle Retail and McDonald's Restaurants Limited.

Entrepreneurship and Small Business Management in the Hospitality Industry

Darren Lee-Ross
School of Business, James Cook University,
Australia

Conrad Lashley
Nottingham Business School,
United Kingdom

AMSTERDAM • BOSTON • HEIDELBERG • LONDON •
NEW YORK • OXFORD • PARIS • SAN DIEGO •
SAN FRANCISCO • SYDNEY • TOKYO
Butterworth-Heinemann is an imprint of Elsevier

Butterworth-Heinemann is an imprint of Elsevier
Linacre House, Jordan Hill, Oxford OX2 8DP, UK
30 Corporate Drive, Suite 400, Burlington, MA 01803, USA

Notice
No responsibility is assumed by the publisher for any injury and/or damage to persons
or property as a matter of products liability, negligence or otherwise, or from any use
or operation of any methods, products, instructions or ideas contained in the material
herein. Because of rapid advances in the medical sciences, in particular, independent
verification of diagnoses and drug dosages should be made

British Library Cataloguing in Publication Data
A catalogue record for this book is available from the British Library

Library of Congress Cataloging-in-Publication Data
A catalog record for this book is available from the Library of Congress

ISBN: 978-0-7506-8448-4

For information on all Butterworth–Heinemann publications
visit our web site at www.elsevierdirect.com

Printed and bound in Hungary
09 10 11 12   10 9 8 7 6 5 4 3 2 1

Working together to grow
libraries in developing countries

www.elsevier.com | www.bookaid.org | www.sabre.org

ELSEVIER   BOOK AID
              International   Sabre Foundation

Contents

Preface

Entrepreneurship is a fascinating practical and academic area of study. As a phenomenon it is has been around in one form or another since the earliest civilizations including the Mayans, Ancient Greeks and Romans up to relatively more recent times of the Renaissance (15th and 17th centuries), Industrial Revolution (18th and 19th centuries) throughout the 20th century up to the present day.

Interestingly, the number of entrepreneurs and establishment of small firms has dramatically and uniformly increased globally over the most recent 10 years. Reasons for this include globalization, liberalization of labour markets and enactment of entrepreneur-friendly government policies such as removal of barriers to competition and other trade restrictions. The prospect of starting one's own business is not as daunting as it used to be. Free advice and start-up grants are now available from a variety of sources including government agencies and non-profit organizations. These initiatives have helped a booming small to medium-sized sector create more wealth than firms at any other time. This phenomenon can also be said of new and emerging economies, ethnic groups within larger host nation states and indigenous entrepreneurship. The latter developments are particularly pertinent to the tourism and hospitality industry as many nascent nations are recognising the role entrepreneurism plays in economic development and the alleviation of poverty and dependence on public subsidy for citizens.

However, environmental enablers of entrepreneurship are only one side of the story and this is where the more academically oriented perspective of the phenomenon begins. Essentially, it is argued that entrepreneurs have certain characteristics and which predispose them to behave in a particular way. 'Risk-taking' and a 'desire for achievement' are often quoted as being key necessary traits. In reality, the picture is rather more complicated, for example, some individuals may have been 'pushed' into self-employment by virtue of redundancy. Many of them could hardly be described as being risk-takers yet there are many examples of resounding business success. Equally, there are those spectacular failures who not only possess the appropriate internal characteristics of entrepreneurs but have been 'pulled' into the field because of its perceived intrinsic benefits.

Beyond this question is the fundamental role entrepreneurs play in the economy in terms of employment and wealth generation. Indeed, small businesses are the backbone of the tourism and hospitality industry and, depending on which statistics one uses, represent somewhere between 75 to 95 percent of all firms globally in this sector. It would be reasonable to assert that the incumbent entrepreneurs are industrious, multi-talented, creative and innovative. They work hard, weather significant hardships during business start-up and bear all of the risks involved in making such a personal sacrifice.

The aims of this book are:

- To explore both the complexity of entrepreneurial theory and practice applied to the tourism and hospitality industry. It does this by exploring some key theoretical concepts and grounds them in a number of practical real-life scenarios;

- To move back and forth between strategy and operations in order to illustrate the linkage between the two areas and explain how both perspectives are necessary for entrepreneurial success;

- To engender a sense of enthusiasm about the field by not only discussing some of the major challenges and opportunities but by providing the knowledge and skills required to start a small business and drastically improve the chances of sustaining it successfully.

The chapters of this book invite readers to ponder their reading through a series of reflective activities. This allows them to both think actively about themes, concepts and issues and then apply them to a number of suggested scenarios. Authors have deliberately designed the book to actively engage readers as *reflective practitioners*. Reflective practitioners are required by modern hospitality and tourism organizations. The term describes managers who are able to complete physical tasks as well as reflect and think about their actions. Reading this book, therefore is intended to be an active process whereby readers think about the practical implications of what is being communicated. The authors are informed by the work of Kolb who suggests learning needs to engage actions as well as theorising and thinking.

Kolb (1983) states the most effective learning as involving all aspects of the learning styles. They must reflect on actions undertaken – see how these reflections fit with theories – consider how they might need to alter future actions, and then act.

For the purposes of this book, and for future activities, we suggest that the process of learning needs to move through the stages outline on Kolb's model. Active experience needs to be followed by reflection including the critical evaluation of the experience; and consideration of how these experiences inform or adapt theoretical understanding; and how this might inform future actions. Traditionally this is shown as a cycle, however, it is more accurately a series of spirals where the process of acting, reflecting, theorising and deciding of future actions leads to new learning situations leading on from the past.

Chapter 1 discusses issues of historical and contemporary context of entrepreneurship concluding that the global field is vast and continuing.

Some definitions are explored concluding that entrepreneurs are difficult to classify given their diverse backgrounds. Some key attributes of entrepreneurs are explored including the ability to spot the opportunity and develop it into a sound business proposal. Issues of personality and environment are discussed. The quaint notion of running small hospitality firms 'risk-free' is also introduced.

Chapter 2 scrutinizes entrepreneurship through a cultural lens discussing and defining indigenous and ethnic dimensions and how they impact upon small firms. The key developmental role of entrepreneurship amongst indigenous societies is discussed together with an outline of the main differences between indigenous and ethnic entrepreneurship.

Chapter 3 evaluates the meanings of the term entrepreneur, comparing and contrasting 'growth' and lifestyle entrepreneurs in terms of their origins and motives. The overriding pattern of small business ownership and its impact on hospitality and tourism provision is then considered.

Chapter 4 considers the notion of creativity in an entrepreneurial context and its relationship with innovation and how it impacts on the entrepreneurial process. Emphasis is placed on the lifelong commitment to idea generation in small hospitality firms along with some important techniques to develop and enhance creativity within the individual. Ultimately, the relationship between creativity and 'mystery' is debunked and the ability is advanced as one that can be learned.

Chapter 5 defines innovation as a systematic logical exercise designed to harness creative ideas and bring them to a successful entrepreneurial conclusion in the marketplace. The chapter then discusses its role in the entrepreneurial process and identifies its relationship with creativity. Opportunity spotting and the subsequent development of business ideas is then introduced and the importance of a methodical systematic process of environmental scanning and strategic and tactical planning is emphasized in this context.

Chapter 6 explores the term 'feasibility analysis' and how it applies in maximizing the chance of entrepreneurial success. Porter's Five Forces is identified and applied as a suitable model. The prevalence of intuition and gut reaction are discussed and their weaknesses identified when planning to launch new hospitality ventures. The chapter proceeds by outlining the role and importance of research in entrepreneurial success.

Chapter 7 identifies the inherent advantages family firms have over non-family firms whilst recognising the roles of key individuals in the family firm. Some of these include commitment, resilience and long-term stability. The impact of conflict on small family businesses in the hospitality industry is outlined. The process of business transferral is discussed along with the many accompanying challenges faced by entrepreneurs and second-generation successors.

Chapter 8 discusses hospitality and hospitableness in the context of small firms. It also introduces the notion of attractiveness of commercial hospitality to owners/managers. The linkages between commercial homes and hospitality businesses are evaluated. Tensions and dilemmas inherent in commercial homes are also outlined.

Chapter 9 addresses the need for producing and working to a business plan described as a working document designed to assist planning with sense and realism, and through which to monitor performance against desired objectives. The key activity of writing and presenting an effective business plan is discussed together with the role of feedback and iteration during the process.

Chapter 10 deals with the entrepreneur as leader and identifies the behavioural attributes of entrepreneurial leadership style. The changing role of the leader/entrepreneur as hospitality firms developer is explored. The assumption that successful entrepreneurs and sound leadership naturally go together is discussed and challenged. Major theories of leadership are explored as a basis for effective leadership. The chapter then introduces some major intrinsic entrepreneurial characteristics said to detract from effective leadership. An entrepreneur's understanding of organizational culture is then identified as key for effective performance in small hospitality firms.

Chapter 11 outlines the major issues involved in the discourse of small entrepreneurial and lifestyle hospitality firm growth. The strengths and weaknesses of growth models are outlined together with a discussion of the major components of expansion strategies for small hospitality firms. 'Good fortune' is explored and the role plays in entrepreneurial success. The chapter then discusses the major challenges or barriers faced during growth stages of firms.

Acknowledgements

This book is dedicated to my wife Amanda for her intellect, patience and support – the brightest and the best.

Darren Lee-Ross

CHAPTER 1

Context, Theoretical Perspectives and Definitions

After working through this chapter you should be able to:

- Understand that defining entrepreneurship is problematic but hinges on an interplay between key personal attributes and appropriate environmental opportunities
- Recognize key changes in the macro environment enabling increased entrepreneurial activity
- Define small firms and identify their key characteristics and distinguish between entrepreneurs and owner/managers
- Identify the contribution of small firms and entrepreneurism to the service and hospitality sectors of economies

INTRODUCTION

Most of us have an intuitive understanding of what entrepreneurs are due to much publicized activities of characters such as Richard Branson (Virgin), Anita Roddick (Bodyshop), Bill Gates (Microsoft) and others. The international hospitality industry of course has its own icons such as Charles Forte, Conrad Hilton and Ray Croc. Indeed, some of these figures have almost reached superstar status appearing on reality television programs and having cameo roles in movies. Therefore, it would be reasonable to suggest that most of us would link entrepreneurship with a particular personality trait or type and many writers have sought to do so (for example, see Hornaday 1982; Timmons Smollen, and Dingee, 1985; Lessem, 1986; Gibb, 1990; & Wickham, 1998). The likely ones here are 'charismatic' and 'extrovert'. However, these characteristics are too simplistic to provide an adequate description of what constitutes the entrepreneur. Definitions of entrepreneurship emanate from several disciplines including the 'great person' school; classical and neoclassical economics; psychology; sociology; and management

1

(Yeung, 2002). Other researchers have sought to explain entrepreneurship by linking it with national culture (for example see, Shane, 1995; McGrath, MacMillan, and Scheinberg, 1992; and Mueller and Thomas, 2001). Others including Meredith, Nelson *et al.* (1982) and Zimmerer and Scarborough (2005) have focused on the entrepreneurial environment. Therefore understandably, one single universal definition of entrepreneurship is problematic given its multidisciplinary nature.

Many writers agree with Kirby (2003) and Chell, Haworth & Brealey (1991) who state respectively that:

> *'there is no agreed definition of. . .what constitutes. . . entrepreneurship'*
> *(p. 10).*
> *'there is still no standard, universally accepted definition of entrepreneurship' (p. 1).*

Baumol (1993) goes further suggesting that:

> *''Any attempt at rigid definition of the term entrepreneur. . .[should] be avoided. . .because whatever attributes are selected, they are sure to prove excessively restrictive, ruling out some feature, activity, or accomplishment of this inherently subtle and elusive character''* *(p. 7).*

However, if we stay with the idea of popular media icons, especially fictitious ones such as Dell Boy Trotter and Arthur Daley from UK television programs 'Only Fools and Horses' and 'Minder' in the 1990s it becomes fairly obvious that any definition must necessarily include elements of both the individual and the environmental opportunities present.

Excerpt from 'Only Fools and Horses' BBCTV, UK, 1983

1. Del Boy has just sold a number of broken lawnmower engines to his brother Rodney and business partner Mickey Pearce via an auction. Both Rodney and Mickey do not, as yet, realize that del is the vendor:

Del: I never thought I'd get rid of 'em Rodney but you know me, 'He who dares wins'.
Actually, I've made a tidy little profit.
Rodney: What are we gonna do with 'em.
Del: Why don't you do what I did. Find yourself a couple of right little plonkers (idiots) with cash on the hip.

Up until the end of the last century many definitions failed to consider the key role played by the environment upon entrepreneurs and entrepreneurial success and vice versa. Definitions tended to fall into two exclusive categories, one featured personality traits and behavioural characteristics of (for example, see Hornaday 1982; Wickham, 1998). However, others looked at the environment for situations where entrepreneurs were likely to develop and thrive (see Meredith, Nelson and Neck 1982; Zimmerer and Scarborough, 2005). Essentially, the area of entrepreneurship necessarily involves more than just a simple enquiry of who the person is and what they do or the environment. The phenomenon is a complex amalgam of both the individual and opportunity. Common sense suggests that any definition of entrepreneurship should include both dimensions by considering what Shane (2003) refers to as the individual–opportunity nexus. Given the above, it would seem reasonable to define the entrepreneur as:

> '. . .one who creates a new business in the face of risk and uncertainty for the purpose of achieving profit and growth by identifying significant opportunities and assembling necessary resources to capitalize on them' (Zimmerer and Scarborough, 2005, p. 3).

Just as entrepreneurs are difficult to define so too is identifying a typical one as they come in all shapes and sizes from different educational, cultural and industrial backgrounds. However, using data from over 35 countries, Minniti, Bygrace and Autio (2006) help us to provide a composite picture of the entrepreneur. He or she is likely to:

- Be based in a middle income country;
- Survive in high income countries;
- Be opportunity-driven as success if necessity-driven is less likely;
- Not offer new products or services;
- Own businesses likely to have limited or no growth potential;
- Be between 25 and 34 years (early stage entrepreneurs);
- Be a man;
- Have post school or graduate qualifications; and
- Be more likely to have confidence in own skills, know other entrepreneurs, be more alert to unexploited opportunities and less likely to let fear of failure prevent them from starting new business.

Adapted from: Minniti *et al.* (2006, pp. 10–11).

Key point 1.1

Defining entrepreneurs is difficult as they are a composite of variables. These include personal traits and characteristics and environmental enablers. Some argue that entrepreneurial success stands or falls by the right person being in the right place at the right time.

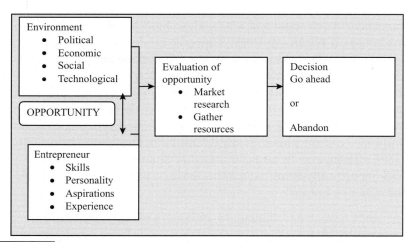

FIGURE 1.1 *Entrepreneurial process of creating a new business venture. Adapted from: Schaper and Volery (2004).*

Using our above definition and type, entrepreneurs and entrepreneurship may now be understood as a certain individual or individuals ('copreneurs') engaged in the process of creating a new business venture as shown in Figure 1.1.

A key element here is the entrepreneur as the person who identifies an opportunity. The propensity for being able to spot a gap in the market is a difficult and complex area to describe. So too is identifying a sustainable competitive advantage setting the idea apart from the competition. Several authors have identified various specific traits (Hornaday, 1982; Timmons Smollen, and Dingee, 1985; Lessem, 1986; Gibb 1990; Wickham, 1998) believed to play a role in this regard, with locus of control, need for achievement and risk-taking being key. However, traits alone do not adequately explain entrepreneurial behaviour. Other elements such as aspirations, experience and cultural background undoubtedly make a contribution. Moreover, responding appropriately to the environment is also a fundamental enabler of new venture formation. The political, economic, social and technological landscape must therefore also be favourable for entrepreneurship to flourish.

Reflective practice

1. Can you think of a famous entrepreneur or someone you know would be recognized as an entrepreneur? To what do you attribute their success, luck, skill, talent, propensity for risk-taking, leadership ability or a combination of them?

Once an opportunity is identified, the potential venture must be assessed by various means at the entrepreneur's disposal. There is no standard way of doing this and the complexity and extent of feasibility studies, business plans, marketing plans and so on will vary depending on the idea and the market. A decision has then to be taken whether to continue with the notion or to abandon it. Typically, decisions to pursue (or not) an entrepreneurial idea are taken within the context of either a 'push' or 'pull' environment. The former is where the individual has been made redundant or is unhappy with their current working conditions. The latter pull factors concern market attractiveness such as opportunity to increase personal wealth, personal development and status. Once all of these variables have been assessed, compared and scrutinized, a final decision to continue with the venture can be made. This is a crucial phase in the process and Figure 1.1 suggests that it is a rational one. However in practice, decisions to exploit an opportunity through venture creation are often a complete mystery! In other words, they appear to be illogical, especially if the rate of small business failures is anything to go by.[1]

Key point 1.2

Typically, entrepreneurial activity is initiated by push or pull factors. Push factors include, being made redundant, low level of income or general unhappiness with current employment. Pull factors include the chance of increasing personal wealth, chance to be own boss and status.

There are a number of reasons for business failure but most fall into the categories of managerial incompetence and lack of experience (Kirby, 2003). Another is that often, budding entrepreneurs become emotionally attached to their business ideas and, despite the odds, will pursue them even though objective evidence suggesting the contrary. This is particularly the case in the hospitality industry where individuals consistently fall in love with the idea of opening their own restaurant or public house or opt to become self-employed for non-economic reasons (see Thomas, Friel, Jameson, and Parsons, 1997). For example, there seems to be a notion that running a restaurant or bar is not really serious work at all. Besides, fraternizing and socializing with customers cannot be that difficult or taxing can it? Well actually, it can. In practice, owners will be working incredibly long hours

---

[1] Although difficult to be accurate, Kirby (2003) estimates small business failures within the first year of trading at 38 per cent and by the end of year two at 57 per cent. Similar estimates are made by others including Zimmerer and Scarborough (1996).

TABLE 1.1 Entrepreneurs: pros and cons	
Pros	**Cons**
Independence and relative freedom from constraints including decision-making	Change, risk, uncertainty of income and the requirement to make many decisions in new 'unknown' areas
Able to use many skills, abilities and talents	Many skills and abilities required, complete responsibility
Accountable to oneself and control over own destiny	Lower quality of life in early stages with notable potential or failure
Status, achievement and chance to reach one's full potential	Long hours and 'hard work'
Potential for greater financial rewards	

Adapted from: Zimmerer and Scarborough (1996) and Coulter (2001).

occupying many different roles ranging from bar tender, bookkeeper, receptionist, room attendant, chef, wait person whilst at all times maintaining an air of 'mein host'. Indeed, several studies have shown that a lengthy working hours contributes to early business failure (for example, see William and Collins, 1995). Therefore before taking the 'plunge', entrepreneurs should always remember not to 'fall in love' with the idea of owning and running their own business.

Reflective practice

1. Give some examples of business entrepreneurs who despite prevailing economic conditions or against advice of others continued with their dream; were they successful or unsuccessful?

There are undoubtedly benefits of being an entrepreneur but there are also a number of challenges; Table 1.1 provides a summary.

HISTORY, GOVERNMENT AND THE ECONOMY

Entrepreneurship is not a modern concept and the term is said to have originated with the 18th century economist Richard Cantillon who used it to describe someone who bore risk, made plans, organized and owned factors of production–land, labour and capital (Coulter, 2001). The term entrepreneur evolved over the next two centuries and with the advent of the industrial revolution it became viewed as something separate from management with similarities to what is currently considered a venture capitalist or 'business angel'. More recently, writers such as Joseph Schumpter and Peter Drucker added other dimensions to the term. For example, Schumpeter considered the entrepreneur as one engaged in 'creative destruction', that is, one who replaces inefficient and ineffective approaches with better and improved ones. For Schumpeter, innovation was a key element of entrepreneurship. A complimentary addition to the term was that of Peter Drucker who introduced the notion of spotting opportunity and acting upon it.

Excerpt from 'Only Fools and Horses' BBCTV, UK, 1983

2. Del Boy is explaining to his grandad what a good week's trading he's enjoyed:

Del: I've had a good week as it goes. I've sold everything including those multicoloured woolen tea cosies I bought.
Grandad: Who on earth want woolen tea cozies in this day and age?
Del: No, no, no. I took them over to Mrs Murphy to stitch up all the holes and then flogged (sold) 'em down at the youth centre as beanie hats.

Until fairly recently international and domestic markets were relatively structured and insular with a legal framework which arguably discouraged entrepreneurial activity. Large companies and corporations with 'traditional' vertical higherarchies and centralized decision-making processes benefited from these turgid conditions. At the same time individuals enjoyed job security and usually had only one career in their working lifetime. In the 21st century this is no longer the case, with the gradual rise in economic importance and employment of the international service sector at the expense of manufacturing (see Sweet, 2001; Economist intelligence Unit, 200). Additionally, there are at least two generations of people (X – born 1965–1976 and Y – born 1977–1994) who know nothing other than employment flexibility, multi-careers and job changes. In the new globalized business environment many large corporations have downsized, 'outsourced' and implemented sweeping changes resulting in massive redundancies and further job insecurities. In part, this has resulted in an increased pool of talented and creative people willing to engage in entrepreneurial activity.

Key point 1.3
Global entrepreneurial activity is now higher than at any other time in recent history.

Government has a key role to play in creating an environment conducive to entrepreneurship. Many have recognized the key contribution of the small business sector to the economy and have liberalized the marketplace aggressively implementing 'entrepreneurship friendly' policies such as removal of barriers to competition and other trade restrictions. The prospect of starting one's own business is therefore not as daunting as it used to be. Literally hundreds of government agencies and non-profit organizations have been established to provide free expertise, research grants and advice to nascent entrepreneurs and small business owners. A small international sample is shown below:

UK Government Department of Trade and Industry – Small Business Service;

Australian Government – AusIndustry – Small Business Incubator Program, Small Business Advisor Service;

US Government – Small Business Administration Agency;

Government of India – Ministry of Small Scale Industries – National Institute for Entrepreneurship and Small Business Development;

The Asia Foundation – Indonesia;

New Zealand Government – National Economic Development Agency – New Zealand Trade and Enterprise;

Jamaican Government – Jamaica Business Development Center; and

Brazilian Government – National Deliberative Council – Brazilian Micro and Small Business Support Service.

Such initiatives have helped a booming small to medium-sized firms sector create more wealth than firms at any time previously (Burns, 2001). The UK's DTI (2006) estimate the number of SMEs in 2005 to number 59 000 (1.4 per cent) more than at the start of 2004. They note, '. . . this is the eighth successive year that companies have increased in number' (p. 3). Furthermore, small and medium-sized enterprises (SMEs) together accounted for more than half of all employment (58.7 per cent or 13 million) and turnover (51.1 per cent or £1300 billion.). Small enterprises alone (0–49 employees) accounted for 46.8 per cent of employment and 36.4 per cent of turnover.

A similar picture emerges elsewhere, for example, SMEs comprise around 90–95 per cent of all firms in the European Community and the USA with an increasing number of new firms emerging year after year (Burns, 2001, p. 3). According to the Global Entrepreneurship Monitor 2005 Executive Report, other countries having notable increasing rates of entrepreneurial activity include Venezuela, Thailand, New Zealand, Jamaica, China, Brazil, Australia and the USA where a range of between 25 (Venezuela) to 11 (USA) per cent of the adult population is either a new business owner or in an early stage of entrepreneurial activity (Minniti et al., 2006, p. 18). In short, there has been a significant global movement toward self-employment through individual choice and (probable) government-driven entrepreneurship-friendly macro–conditions.

Reflective practice

Identify any local government (and other agency) support structures and systems available to entrepreneurs in your region. How easy are they to access.

What are Small Firms?

Generally small or small to medium-sized (SME) firms are used as a proxy for entrepreneurial activity but what exactly are they? Many definitions exist because of their global diversity and characteristics. One UK-based definition supplied by the Bolton Committee Report (Bolton, 1971) considers them to be independent, managed by owners or part-owners and having a small market share. The report also recognizes size in terms of relativity. For example, a firm could be small in one sector where the market is large with many competitors; whereas a business of similar size could be deemed large in another sector with fewer and smaller firms within it. In North America, the Small Business Act states that a small business is independently owned and operated and not dominant in its field of operation but recognizes that the definition will vary from industry to industry to reflect industry differences accurately (http://www.sba.gov/services/contractingopportunities/sizestandardstopics/size/index.html, 2007). However, these contributions are not particularly helpful when making comparisons international or otherwise.

More definitive help is provided by the UK Companies Act of 1985. A company is said to be 'small' if it either has a turnover of not more than £5.6 million; a balance sheet total of not more than £2.8 million; and not more than 50 employees. Medium-sized companies similarly must have a turnover of not more than £22.8 million; a balance sheet total of not more than £11.4 million; not more than 250 employees.[2] Similar 'financial' approaches are evident from the USA, Australia and the EU but suffer from a problem of obsolescence due to national and international economic fluctuations of interest rates and inflation for example. Furthermore, despite a European Commission directive for a single definition of SMEs from 2005, annual adjustments still have to be made to financial thresholds; these changes are not necessary for numbers employed (http://www.sbs.gov.uk/sbsgov/action/layer?r.l1=7000000229&topicId=7000000237&r.l2=7000000243&r.s=tl, 2007).

---

[2] Must satisfy at least two of these three criteria to qualify for small or small to medium-sized form status.

TABLE 1.2	A comparison of international definitions of firm size by employees
UK	Micro: up to 9 employees
	Small: up to 49 employees
	Medium: up to 249 employees
European Union	Small: up to 50 employees
	Medium: up to 250 employees
Australia	Micro: fewer than 5 people, including non-employing businesses
	Small: 5 or more employees, but less than 20
	Medium: up to 200 employees
USA	Small: up to 100
	Medium: up to 500

Sources: Department of Trade and Industry, Trewin, D. (2002) and http://encyclopedia.thefreedictionary.com/small+business, retrieved July 2008.

It is also the case that whilst similar, in practice, working definitions of small firms occupy a range driven by the particular aims and objectives of the event, for example, a research study, census, industry sponsored event and so on. Therefore for practical statistical and international comparative purposes, the number of employees working in a firm is probably the most useful measure of size and some examples are shown in Table 1.2.

Size however defined, is not the only thing that distinguishes small firms from their larger counterparts. There are a number of other key characteristics including the personality and behaviour of the owner/entrepreneur. This individual will make most, if not all, business decisions including those directly effecting employees. Indeed, the small firm can easily be understood as an extension of the entrepreneur with all of their decision-making idiosyncrasies rolled into one! The contact between employer and workers is likely to take on more of a personalized tone as there are fewer employees and they spend much of their time working alongside their employer. Furthermore, small organizations have less well-defined guidelines for roles, responsibilities and relationships; they are in effect an extension of the entrepreneur's personality and attitudes.

> **Reflective practice**
> How useful is using number of employees to define firms as small medium or large? Is this a global standard measure of a firm's size?

Other issues that small businesses typically have to contend with include a shortage of funds. Internationally, most small businesses are still financed 'informally' by personal savings and donations from family and friends.

Fewer than 0.01 per cent of nascent entrepreneurs launch new ventures with formal venture capital or business angel investments despite the amount of attention they receive by policy makers (Minniti *et al.*, 2006, p. 55).[3] However, that is not to underplay the emergence of 'microfinancing' and its role amongst the 'working poor'. Essentially, this is where social innovators provide small loans to entrepreneurs without the need for collateral. Since the inception of microfinance in the 1970s, it has become one of the most sustainable ways of fighting global poverty. According to Minniti *et al.* (2006) in 2005, 'The International Year of Microcredit, around 40 per cent of the world's poorest people were being reached by the initiative.

Lack of finance means that entrepreneurs generally operate within a short timeframe and have to make a healthy turnaround (although not always a profit) within a matter of months rather than years. This is particularly so in the seasonal seaside sector of the hospitality industry where operators have to earn a sufficient income in a short period to remain solvent during the fallow non-trading period in any 1 year. This puts an enormous burden on the entrepreneur and most decisions are short-term and directly related to this constraint. Long-term strategies are therefore inappropriate for small firms apart from those with key potential financiers such as banks and other similar institutions. Small firms also tend to operate within a narrow market so diversification to spread risk is not an option. For example, a small seasonal hotel may have a contract with a coach operator for say, weekly senior's holidays; it is likely that all rooms will be taken. If the contract is cancelled at short notice the loss of this one customer would have a significant impact on the business. A larger national hotel chain would not be so vulnerable as it would have alternative markets on which to draw. According to Burns (2001), characteristics which really define small firms can be summarized in Table 1.3.

Entrepreneurs and Owner-managers

So what is the difference between entrepreneurs and owner-managers? This is a much debated issue. In one sense, there may be no difference if the entrepreneur owns and manages the firm as a Sole Trader. On the other hand, managers do not always own the enterprise; it may be a smaller unit of a huge conglomerate. Would this necessarily mean that the manager fails to qualify for entrepreneurship status? The answer is 'possibly', depending on how much control the manager has over the firm and whether they display certain

---

[3] The United States continues to dominate venture capital investment in high-tech companies. For example, six times as much classic venture capital was invested in the USA as in all the European nations combined.

TABLE 1.3	Characteristics of small firms

One or two owners often family
Financed by owners, relatives and friends
Limited and uncertain markets
Low levels of new profit
Inability to influence prices
Uncertain entrepreneurial aspirations and motives (lifestyle firm or growth firm)[a]
Short-run decision making
Short seasonal business cycle (for most sectors of the hospitality industry)
One location

Adapted from: Burns (2001) and Shaper and Volery (2004).

[a] *Lifestyle firms are those set up primarily to provide 'adequate' income with no growth aspirations. Growth firms on the other hand are set up with the aim of prospering and growing.*

entrepreneurial characteristics like innovation and risk (to be discussed and developed in Chapter 3). Indeed, others have addressed this very issue by introducing the term 'intrapreneur' into the nonclemature. This simply means someone behaving as an entrepreneur within a broader framework of a large company at the behest of the employer. However, even this term may not necessarily apply to the manager.

Burns (2001) provides a useful summary of this conundrum indicating that irrespective of ownership, owner managers and managers may both qualify for the title entrepreneur. This, with the additional category of intrapreneur is shown in Figure 1.2.

TABLE 1.4	Differences between entrepreneurship and owner-managers	
	Entrepreneurship	**Owner–management**
Definition of the field	Process where an individual discovers, evaluates and exploits opportunities independently	Administration of a small independent business venture
Firm size	Large, medium or small	Small
Degree of risk	Variable	Lower
Number of people involved in the business	Small to large number	Small
Economic sector	Private, government and not-for-profit	Private sector
Growth focus	High	Variable
Key attributes of individual	High need for: achievement; internal locus of control; creativity and innovation; growth	Moderate need for Achievement; good organizational skills to manage efficiently; little innovation; moderate growth

Adapted from:Holt (1992, p. 11).

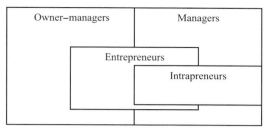

FIGURE 1.2 *Managers, owner–managers and entrepreneurs/intrapreneurs.*
Adapted from: Burns (2001, p. 7).

Holt (1992) is more prescriptive and his position is summarized in Table 1.4.

THE ECONOMY AND ENTREPRENEURSHIP

Whilst governments have long recognized the importance of entrepreneurial activity on the broader economy, the exact relationship between them is not simply cause and effect. For example, different levels of economic development set the environment where entrepreneurs make decisions. These decisions pre-determine the type and quantity and capacity for entrepreneurship in any one country. In other words, the causal link between entrepreneurial activity and economic growth and the role of small firms in determining a country's competitiveness and productivity is equivocal. However, countries having similar per capita GDP often show similar levels of entrepreneurial activity (Acs, Arenius, Hay, and Minniti, 2005). There is little doubt that the entrepreneurial sector provides employment opportunities and scope for the creation of new markets at low levels of per capita income but as this increases, larger and established organizations tend to satisfy the demand of growing markets. As large companies become more active, there is usually a reduction in the number of newer smaller ones. Interestingly, as per capita GDP increases, the level of entrepreneurial activity increases again as individuals have more personal resources on which to set up new businesses and establish a competitive advantage. In short, entrepreneurial activity and economic development have something of an 'ebb and flow' relationship depending on a number of prevailing pre-existing circumstances. Despite this inexact association, Minniti *et al.* (2006) characterize the relationship between entrepreneurship and aggregate economic activity as shown in Figure 1.3.

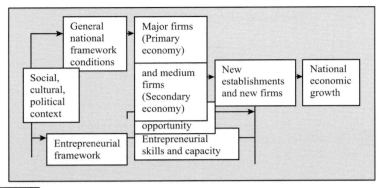

FIGURE 1.3 *The global entrepreneurship monitor conceptual model.*
Source: Minniti et al. (2006).

These authors consider entrepreneurship to be vital for economic growth as small firms innovate, fill market niches, increase competition and promote economic efficiency.

Reflective Practice

Could you be an entrepreneur? Answer the following questions to find out:

1. When you look at an ink blot how many things can you see?

      Just one

      More than just one

The inkblot or Rorschach test targets a tolerance for ambiguity which is thought to be a good indicator of an entrepreneur.

2. You are seated in the front row of a theatre and the performer beckons you on stage to help with the act. Would you:

      Run out crying?

      Accept the invitation with glee?

Entrepreneurs must have an ability to think on their feet and to sell themselves and their business to everyone.

3. You are considering taking a cycling holiday, which would you prefer?

      A mountain bike excursion over rugged terrain

      Riding on a smooth road surface

In business, there is no such thing as a smooth ride. Success is very often littered with hazards, potholes and frustrations.

Can you take no for an answer?

      Yes

      No

Banks, investors, venture capitalists and other financiers may turn your proposals down many times. Rejection should motivate you to try harder.

You are thinking of buying a new home. Do you:

> Purchase one that's already built
>
> Find a vacant plot of land and build a new one?

Entrepreneurs are builders and architects of their own businesses. They have to identify an opportunity, establish a robust and appropriate structure whilst staying within budget. Some may literally opt for property development as their entrepreneurial business!

Your neighbour's cute little kids knock on your front door trying to raise money for their school by selling raffle tickets. Do you:

> Buy some
>
> Buy none

If you can say 'no', so much the better. Running your own business often means saying 'no' as well as 'yes' to family, friends, relatives and others.

Can you watch and absorb a news programme, edit presentation, listen to music:

> Yes
>
> No

Start-up firms do not have the luxury of division of labour. You will have to occupy many different roles including that of CEO, marketing manager, HR manager, technical roles and often at the same time.

You've made plans for taking a holiday. Just prior to leaving, the plumbing springs a leak and the electricity blows a fuse. Do you:

> Get really angry
>
> Take it in your stride, postpone the holiday and fix the problems

Entrepreneurs must be flexible and deal with problems as they arise.

Entrepreneurial aptitude:

If you answered all eight correctly you fall into the category of individuals having an entrepreneurial aptitude. If you answered four correctly, start a part-time entrepreneurial venture or find a 'co-preneur' to help. Fewer than four answered correctly; don't give up your day job

Adapted from:Coulter (2001).

SERVICES AND HOSPITALITY

The service sector of many economies has a high proportion of small to medium-sized entrepreneurial firms. Entrepreneurial and small business 'activity' in Minniti *et al*'s, (2006) 'four business' sector comparison reveals that "consumer-oriented" (p. 31) firms dominate the global economy.[4] In the USA for example, the service sector is responsible for 92 per cent of all jobs and 85 per cent of the gross domestic product (Zimmerer and Scarborough, 2005, p. 12).

---

[4] "Consumer-oriented: where the primary customer is a physical person (e.g. retail, restaurants and bars, lodging. . .and recreation" (Minniti *et al.*, 2006, p. 30).

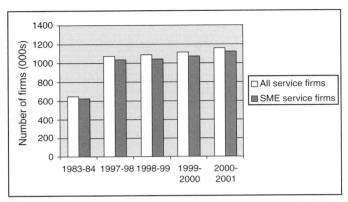

FIGURE 1.4 *All service and small to medium-sized firms in Australia 1983/4–2000/1. Adapted from: Small Business in Australia, 2001, ABS Catalogue No. 1321.0 (2002) number of businesses and persons employed in the private sector by industry division, Chapter 3.*

This is partially explained with recent advances in technology via the laptop computer, printers, faxes, voice mail and so on. However, hi-tec services industries are not the only ones dominated by small firms. More 'traditional' areas such as hospitality and tourism have always been characterized by small firms (Haber, 2005, p. 582). Many commentators suggest that this is due to relatively low barriers to entry including modest start up costs, marginal economies of scale, chance to establish small 'lifestyle' businesses and nature of the hospitality service product. Figure 1.4 shows a comparison between all service and small to medium-sized firms in Australia. Figure 1.5 compares the number of all firms and SMEs in the accommodation, café and restaurant sector.

In Australia, SMEs have consistently dominated the services sector with around 96 per cent of all firms falling into the small to medium-sized category. From 1983–1984 to 1997–1998 SMEs showed significant growth, with more moderate but consistent growth thereafter.

Likewise, the Australian accommodation, cafés and restaurants sector is dominated by SMEs with approximately 89 per cent of all firms falling into this category. Additionally, the number of SMEs increased dramatically between 1983–1984 and 1997–1998 with a more uniform growth from 1997–1998 to 2000–2001.

A similar scenario exists in many other countries, for example, in the UK 98.5 per cent of all hotels and restaurants (category 55) employ less than 50 people (www.sbs.gov.uk/SBS_Gov_files/researchandstats/SMEStatsUKAnd Regions2005.xls 'UK Whole Economy'!A1, 2007). In the USA, the Accommodation and Food Services sector is dominated by small businesses with

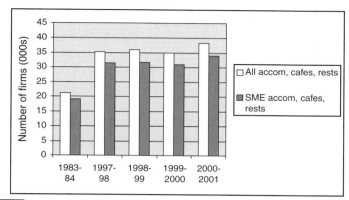

FIGURE 1.5 *Comparison between all firms and SMEs in the accommodation, cafes and restaurants sector in Australia 1984–2000/1.*
Adapted from: Small Business in Australia, 2001, ABS Catalogue No. 1321.0 (2002) number of businesses and persons employed in the private sector by industry division, Chapter 3.

approximately 75 per cent of all firms employing fewer than 50 people (US Census Bureau, 2005).

SUMMARY

After some discussion, entrepreneurs were identified as being 'atypical' that is not easily defined as they appear in a number of guises having different backgrounds upbringings and so on. After a brief review of key historical developments and definitive insights, it was noted that successful entrepreneurs must be able to spot an opportunity and environmental conditions need to be sympathetic to any innovations advanced. Furthermore, the entrepreneurial process was outlined from an initial 'opportunity spotting' to the eventual decision to either pursue the idea or to let it be. The final stage of the process was advanced as logical 'decision-making' Unfortunately, this stage of the model is arguably the most difficult to understand as many decisions to proceed with an entrepreneurial idea have little relevance with prevailing economic or market conditions. This is particularly the case in the hospitality industry where there is a perennial preconceived notion that running a small restaurant or hotel is at best risk-free and at worst physically undemanding.

Whilst there is general agreement that entrepreneurs play a pivotal role in broader economic development, the exact relationship between them was described as a complex 'ebb and flow', with one not always being able to predict the other. An overview of economic enablers revealed the pivotal role of contemporary business practice in setting appropriate conditions for entrepreneurial activity with registered small businesses more prevalent globally now than at any other time. Government agencies and not for profit organizations now provide a myriad of initiatives, support and advice for nascent entrepreneurs including information and access to venture capitalists; although this is form of finance is six times more prevalent in the USA than the rest of the world combined.

Small firms were described and defined in statistical terms and through characteristics specific to small organizations including, limited capital raising capacity, frenetic activity during busy trading periods (typically seasonal in the hospitality industry), and a lack of formal rules, regulations and procedures. Entrepreneurs and small business owner–managers were also discussed with these terms not always being mutually exclusive.

Finally, the service sectors of several developed countries were overviewed showing the clear dominance of small and SMEs. A similar picture was also revealed for the hospitality and restaurant industry where around 75–99 per cent of all firms were identified as small or small to medium sized.

Reflective practice

- Define entrepreneurship.
- Discuss the notion that entrepreneurs are neither made nor born.
- What role does the government play in enabling entrepreneurial activity?
- What is the relationship between economic development and entrepreneurial activity?
- What are the similarities and differences between entrepreneurs and owner managers?
- How important are entrepreneurs in the tourism and hospitality sectors of economies?

CASE: The Windsor Hotel Ltd.

In the late 1950s, a young couple worked and met at the Queen's hotel in Birmingham, UK. The Queen's was only one of many British Transport hotels dotted around the country at that time built originally to accommodate rail passengers using the network. In the early 1960s, this along with many other sister hotels was sold or demolished. Regrettably, David and Greta were forced to look elsewhere for work. In those days, job opportunities were in abundance especially in industrial Birmingham and so both found jobs soon after being made redundant from the Queen's hotel. Ideally, they would both have liked to remain in the hospitality industry but they now had a young son and so opted for factory work as it was much better paid.

Over the next couple of years, Greta's family decided they would like to move to Great Yarmouth where they had enjoyed many happy holidays. Greta's parents were coming up to retirement age and thought the change of surroundings would be appropriate at their time of life. After much family discussion, David and Greta decided to follow them but for reasons quite different to her parents. Great Yarmouth in the 1950s was booming seaside resort much like others including Blackpool, Margate and Bournemouth. These were the days when hospitality firms needed very little (if any) promotion due to the excessive demand from the domestic mass-tourist market. Having a hospitality industry background and experience both David and Greta had an inkling that setting up their own small guest house business might just be viable. On the basis of this hunch, and that Greta wanted to be near to her parents in their declining years, they sold their property in Birmingham and bought an eight-bedroom guest house a couple of streets back from the sea front esplanade.

To their delight, the guest house was enormously successful although David and Greta had to do most of the work themselves. Recognising the 'healthy' state of the market a couple of years later in 1966, they bought the house next door and converted both into one 16 bedroom guest house. Over the next 10 years David and Greta became well-known in the town as they joined their local Rotary and Lions clubs, attended many employer association meetings and networking events. Whilst their business continued building on its initial success there was one increasing threat on their business horizon, that of the cheap Spanish continental package holiday. Recognising this, they set about undertaking some elementary business research to see what could be done to counter this challenge. In short, David and Greta identified a market that they were not currently satisfying, that of a higher spending quality conscious segment; not at all like what the traders in great Yarmouth referred to as 'the bucket and spade brigade'. Worryingly, the image of their existing guest house appealed only to the extant lower income tourists. They decided that the purchase of a new upmarket hotel was probably the only answer for continued success into the future. However, even the sale of their business, accrued savings and a bank loan would not be enough to secure a business property of the type they had envisaged. For the next few years, they thought long and hard about the issue but resolved that they would never be able to realize their dreams. Instead they, together with other small guest house owners, debated and discussed what Great Yarmouth as a town could do to address the falling tourism demand.

At one particular Lion's club meeting, David was approached by one of the town's leading hotel owners. In fact, Jeremy Ingold owned his own 60 bedroom four star hotel and was a partner in the Windsor hotel, the largest privately owned hotel in Great Yarmouth. In brief, he and the other partners had seen the Windsor's performance decline uniformly since they had bought it from Trust House Forte some five years earlier. Their strategy was to take a 'hands off' approach to running the Windsor by employing a manger to take care of operations. After a five year period and a succession of unsuccessful managers, the Windsor was in danger of failing. Jeremy explained the situation to David and, based on the reputation of the guest house, invited him and Greta to become full salaried managers of the hotel.

The Windsor was just like the hotel that David and Greta had identified a whilst earlier. It had three stars (Royal Automobile Club), 80 bedrooms, four bars, a huge ballroom and several function suites. Excitedly, David discussed the proposal with his wife. Despite the misgivings of their current situation, Greta was far more cautious about the idea, pointing out that they would no longer be their own boss nor have the security of their own small firm. ''Why would you want to go back to earning a wage?'' she said. David had to agree and admitted that his emotions had got the better of him but the proposition started a long process of deliberation and extended discussion with Jeremy Ingold and the other partners to see whether their idea could be amended to David and Greta's advantage. One potentially key point strategically was that all partners were in their mid fifties and upwards. Greta pointed out that they would soon be retiring and would need to make some significant decisions about the Windsor and their role as partners. In other words, they would soon be considering appropriate exit strategy. "If they are taking this hotel seriously, they must also recognize that any manager must be fully committed to the business. I think we should negotiate first an equal partnership deal and second speak about their impending retirements, after all it cannot be more than 10 years away at most." said Greta. David and Greta agreed and decided to propose a clause whereby they would have an option to buy out the other partners in due course. Over the next couple of months a deal was struck including the equal partnership and buy out options. During their first summer season at the Windsor, they befriended a bank manager who stayed at the hotel for three months during the first year of trading. He was to manage the local branch and stay at the hotel whilst searching for a house and moving his family to Great Yarmouth. David and Greta spoke to their new friend about their plans and that they intended to buy out their partners the following year. In short, the bank manager arranged for an 'unsecured loan'[5] of a specific amount for David and Greta to buy the hotel. Fortunately, their partners were not unreasonable and were happy to take a modest sum each for their portion of the Windsor.

David and Greta owned and operated the Windsor successfully for just over 25 years. By 2000, the domestic tourism market in great Yarmouth had declined to such an extent that even the larger three and four star hotels had become effected. They had little option but to sell the business but to whom? Clearly it would not be to anyone or any company that relied on domestic tourism income alone. David and Greta decided to advertise the sale of their business via a few selective media ensuring a wide range of potential buyers. After 2 years and a number of unsatisfactory offers, they accepted a modest proposal from a Chinese company already owning a number of other tourism-related businesses including travel agents and tour operations. For David and Greta this was a stroke of fortune as the purchase represented a form of vertical integration for the Chinese buyers. Thus they would not be relying on the ever dwindling domestic tourist. Currently, the Windor hotel remains successful but the focus has moved toward the international market, specifically Chinese.

1. Discuss David and Greta's ability to spot an opportunity
2. How ambitious are this couple?
3. Can you identify some key entrepreneurial characteristics for David and Greta? Are they the same for each person?
4. How important was 'fate' in David and Greta's entrepreneurial career?
5. How important are exit strategies in entrepreneurship?
6. Comment on whether David and Greta's businesses were 'lifestyle' or 'growth'.

---

[5] A loan where investors (in this case the bank) do not require the security of an existing asset; usually only for small amounts.

CHAPTER 2

Indigenous and Ethnic Entrepreneurship: A Cultural Perspective

After working through this chapter you should be able to:

- Define indigenous entrepreneurship
- Discuss the role of culture upon indigenous and ethnic entrepreneurship
- Recognize the crucial developmental role of entrepreneurship amongst indigenous societies
- Appreciate the key differences between indigenous and ethnic entrepreneurship

INTRODUCTION

According to Legge and Hindle (2004) the received wisdom that all entrepreneurs are purely profit motivated is only partially true. Indeed, it may be argued that engagement in entrepreneurial activity linked exclusively with financial profit (see Chapter 1) is fleeting depending on what drives the entrepreneur, the developmental stage of the venture and the environment in which the business is operating. This is especially the case in the hospitality industry where a majority of firms are small and of the 'lifestyle' nature (see Chapter 5). Evidence also suggests that this may be true for entrepreneurs in indigenous societies albeit a function of their culture rather than simply opting to focus attention elsewhere (Hindle and Lansdowne, 2005). Culture is important in a general business communication sense as differences in language, philosophies and traditions between nations have the potential to create barriers to international trade. However under closer scrutiny, several studies have shown that culture has a powerful influence on entrepreneurship (for example, see Shane, 1995).

The aim of the current chapter is to illustrate and discuss the role of culture upon indigenous and ethnic entrepreneurship. It does this by defining culture and:

- comparing global geographical regions to give a generic perspective on entrepreneurial activity;
- introducing Hofstede's (1994) construct of cultural dimensions as a framework for identifying specific cultural variables amongst indigenous entrepreneurs;
- identifying some cultural differences between indigenous and non-indigenous entrepreneurship;
- outlining recent studies of entrepreneurship amongst indigenous Australians including Torres Strait islanders linking Hofstede's cultural dimensions with key entrepreneurial characteristics;
- introducing ethnic entrepreneurship and identifying the differences between it and its indigenous counterpart.

Key point 2.1

Profit maximization is not usually the aim of lifestyle firms in the hospitality industry, nor is it that of indigenous entrepreneurial firms. However, culture has a key role to play in this respect for the latter.

DEFINITIONS AND CONDITIONS

Many definitions of culture exist, for example:

'The beliefs, values and mores that the inhabitants of a nation share' Zimmerer and Scarborough (2005, p. 479).

'. . . the collective programming of the mind that distinguishes the members of one category of people from another' (Hofstede, 1980, p. 5)

Tayeb (1994) considers culture to be shared feelings, thinking, norms and values that guide people's behaviour. We may also consider culture as a complex mix of common enduring values, norms, ideas and symbols handed down generationally which shape current attitudes and behaviour. However, this does not mean that a single 'national culture' is common to all inhabitants of a country. Nations or peoples are seldom homogenous and many cultural 'pockets' exist for a variety of historical reasons. For example, former British colonies including Australia, Canada and the USA will almost certainly have had their indigenous culture usurped by invading nations to a greater or lesser extent.

The Changing Entrepreneurial Environment

Prior to the abolition of slavery in 1838 many unscrupulous Non-indigenous entrepreneurs thrived all over the former British Empire (particularly in the Caribbean) ranging from plantation owners to slave captains. Once the practice was abolished the outcome was significant (although well deserved!) for these business owners as the following extract from *Pax Britannica: Heaven's Command* attests:

'The greatest triumph of the evangelicals was the abolition of slavery. Economically its results had been devastating. Planters were ruined from Antigua to Mauritius. Middlemen of Ashanti, slave captains of Merseyside, overseers of Nassau, found themselves without an occupation' (Morris, J. 1993, p. 19).

The immediate and frantic emigration of entrepreneurs, wholesale mismanagement and abdication of duty by the British government brought about rampant poverty and dependency to the region. However, in the 21st century regions of the Caribbean are thriving. For example, Jamaica is ranked fourth globally for its entrepreneurial activity (see Minniti, Bygrave, and Autio, 2006), much of which is provided by tourism. http://www.islandhideaways.com/islands.php?island_id=11. Nonetheless, indigenous entrepreneurs in other Caribbean nations including Barbados have experienced more difficulty. This is due to the legacy of business domination by the minority white community and a deliberate move to undermine the efforts of the indigenous population through restrictive legislation and other discriminatory policies (Neblett and Green, 2005).
Source: the present authors

Commentators consider most indigenous societies to be a collective valuing community and heritage. However, these findings are necessarily moderated by the impact of the colonization process and some challenge these commonly held notions. After reviewing the evidence, Peredo, Anderson, Galbraith, Honig, and Dana (2004) reveal that prior to European influence many Native American communities paralleled the former showing individualism, personal property ownership, use of individual capital and exploitation of natural resources. Galbraith and Stiles (2003) argue that the artificial community-based land tenure and ownership system of modern reservations forces a more collective orientation on entrepreneurial behaviours than would otherwise have existed. Indigenous communities in Australia may also have shared a more individualistic cultural orientation for the same reasons. Whilst this is a difficult point to argue, it is clear that shifting forces of economics, colonialism and enforced regional migration is a pattern all indigenous communities have endured giving rise to poverty, poor education and health (Peredo *et al.*, 2004). Indigenous Australians have certainly borne the brunt of many unfortunate but well intended governmental policies. Aboriginals and Torres Strait Islanders are the most socially, economically and culturally disadvantaged group in Australian society (Commonwealth of Australia, 1992). As a result they rely on welfare systems which Pearson (1999) refers to as flawed as they do not demand economic and social reciprocity which is a fundamental feature of indigenous culture. Mead (2000, p. 44) agrees commenting that long-term dependence of welfare payments results in a 'culture of defeat'. According to Anderson (2002) these extreme conditions underscore the need to encourage entrepreneurship in indigenous societies to rebuild their communities and improve their socio economic conditions based on a solid foundation of tradition and culture. Furthermore, research into indigenous entrepreneurship would permit culturally appropriate education for nascent entrepreneurs with a particular focus on generic economic development of indigenous society for the benefit of whole communities.

To remedy this situation, many including indigenous leaders, have advocated a coordinated governmental approach in facilitating indigenous entrepreneurial activity, particularly in the tourism and hospitality industry (see Foley, 2003). Among indigenous peoples, leaders such as Noel Pearson holds entrepreneurship as an important way to construct a vibrant economy leading to nation-rebuilding and self-determination (Anderson and Gilbertson, 2004). These initiatives for economic development are known as 'second wave' and attempt to wean many in indigenous society off welfare dependency resulting from early public sector 'first wave' interventions (Peredo *et al.*, 2004). The New Zealand government has been particularly proactive in this respect resulting in an increasing number of Maori self-employed (Sullivan and Margaritis, 2000). However, this is no easy accomplishment as many indigenous individuals lack required business skills and have relatively low level of education. In the case of Maori, the problem has been overcome by the Tainui and Ngai Tahu seeking professional help outside their community (*New Zealand Herald*, 15 July 1999). The casino gaming initiative amongst the Kumeyaay peoples in California has also been similarly successful (Galbraith and Stiles, 2003).

Reflective practice

1. How would you help overcome the challenge of low education levels amongst indigenous entrepreneurs?

MODELS OF ECONOMIC DEVELOPMENT

Whilst there is an obvious case for encouraging entrepreneurship in indigenous societies, authorities need to proceed with caution and scrutinize their underlying assumptions. For example, from the 1950s onwards 'Modernization' models of economic development were held as the primary form of transforming traditional societies into contemporary ones (see Inkeles and Smith 1974; and Kuznets, 1971). These are based on the Taylorian notion of 'economic rational man', where humans are self-interested, clear thinking and logical being motivated by money. More subtly, traditions, heritage and language are all considered obstacles in the modernization process. Understandably, applications of this philosophy have been largely unsuccessful with initial levels of poverty and other uniquely contextual issues being ignored but ultimately undermining such developmental efforts (Peredo *et al.*, 2004).

Another major development in this context is that of the 'Dependency' model of modernization. Here, multinational corporations, International Monetary Fund, developed industrial nations and others are viewed by some as colonists (Klitgaard, 1990). Peredo *et al.* (2004) note that rather than leading developing nations, they are held in a constant state of dependency through economic exploitation by the very agencies designed to do the opposite. In sum, they consider both Modernization and Dependency models to be fundamentally flawed in their pursuit of equity, economic development and self-determination for developing countries. However, there is now interest in the 'Contingency' construct which is quite different to the above in that it considers:

- development need not be defined by the developed world; and
- interaction between peoples and the global economy may be different to that advocated by the modernization and dependency perspectives.

Indeed with Contingency, it is important to understand and respect the definitions offered by those who require development. The main advantage here is flexibility and inclusiveness, that is, it allows the input of experience from other societies, perspectives and cultures (Tucker, 1999) and promotes:

■ sustainable coalitions
■ partnerships;
■ trust;
■ reciprocity; and
■ due diligence.

The contingency approach would appear to potentially accommodate the moderating impact of many variables including that of culture upon business activity and entrepreneurship. The big questions are does culture have an impact on entrepreneurial activity and does indigenous entrepreneurship involves values, motives and performance evaluations that differ from non-indigenous entrepreneurship. If national cultures are being used as the cornerstone of the current argument, the answer is most certainly 'yes' depending on the recency and regularity of contact between both parties and the extent to which the indigenous community values it traditions and heritage. Foley (2003) believes that culture is a powerful driver of attitudes. Lindsay (2005) goes further and considers culture to be a key enabler of entrepreneurship amongst indigenous society. He suggests that no significant differences exist between indigenous cultural values and those of the entrepreneur, that is, they are one and the same. Others making this connection include Shane (1995); McGrath, MacMillan and Scheinberg (1992); Mueller and Thomas (2001); and Lindsay (2005).

Thus, attempts to better understand indigenous entrepreneurship should avoid using non-indigenous entrepreneurship constructs as they:

■ Fail to adequately consider some key cultural characteristics likely to impact on associated traits, characteristics and behaviour;
■ do not value preservation of heritage, self-determination and the community (Hindle and Lansdowne, 2005); and
■ do not embrace a whole economic development perspective nor consider the position of indigenous self-determination.

Reflective practice

1. Do you believe this to be a fair critique of the modernization and dependency models of economic development? What other constructs could be used in the context of indigenous tourism and hospitality services?

> **Key point 2.2**
> Among indigenous peoples entrepreneurship is an important way to construct a vibrant economy leading to nation-rebuilding and self-determination.

THE BIG PICTURE

Geographical location linked with culture would appear to have an impact on entrepreneurship. Figure 2.1 shows averaged data from the *Global Entrepreneurship Monitor* (Minniti *et al.*, 2006) and reveals some acute differences between regions in terms of entrepreneurial activity.

With the exceptions of Eastern Europe and Latin America, all global locations show an increase in entrepreneurial activity between 2002 and 2005. However, there are notable differences between some regions with a 'low' activity cluster of developed Asia, Eastern Europe and the European Union and a 'high' clustering of the Commonwealth including the USA, Latin Americas and developing Asia[1]. In short, there has been a significant global movement toward self-employment through individual choice and government-driven entrepreneurship-friendly macro conditions. However within this complex set of drivers, culture has a key role to play, particularly amongst indigenous societies. For example, the Total entrepreneurial activity index (TEA) of indigenous Torres Strait islanders by far outstrips that of other states with a comparable gross domestic product (GDP) and is actually similar to those with a higher GDP[2]; Table 2.1 shows these comparisons.

The TEA index for the Torres Strait Islands is almost double that of Argentina and around five times higher than that of South Africa. This is consistent with the notion that where waged employment is scarce and economic conditions poor, individuals are motivated toward self-employment. However, Noorderhaven, Thurik, Wennekers, and van Stel (2004) point out that economic 'pull' and 'push' (see Chapter 1) variables have a 'low explanatory

---

[1] Between 2002 and 2005 some countries shifted categories and others took no part in the 2005 GEM survey whilst others were added.

[2] To obtain a relative impression of entrepreneurism in the Torres Straits, two techniques were used. The first was based on the Global Entrepreneurial Monitor Research Program (GEM) construct which calculates a total entrepreneurial activity score (TEA). This is obtained by dividing an estimated 500 entrepreneurs (**TSPZA, 2005**) by the total workforce (2116) and provides a standardized picture of entrepreneurial activity by country. The second technique examines the gross domestic product (GDP) *per capita* index internationally as advocated by Sullivan, Buckingham, Maley, and Hughes (1999) and Sloman and Norris (2002).

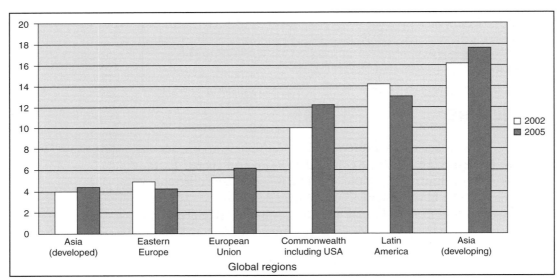

FIGURE 2.1   *Total entrepreneurial activity by region 2002–2005*
Source: Adapted from: Legge and Hindle (2004) and Minniti et al. (2006).

power' (p. 460) and that culture is key in predicting a nation's rate of entrepreneurial activity. Carree, van Stel, Thurik and Wennekers (2002) also challenge the notion that the state of industrial development fully explains a nation's entrepreneurial activity. Wennekers, Noorderhaven, Hofstede and Thurik (2001) argue similarly noting that culture is an important explanatory supply-side factor along with demographics and a person's economic situation. Similarly, they hold that entrepreneurial activity is culturally bound stemming from differences between countries which are risk averse and risk-seeking for example. In other words one would expect greater entrepreneurial activity

TABLE 2.1   A comparison of TEA and GDP between the Torres Strait and other nations

Country	Total entrepreneurial activity (TEA) Index[a]	Gross domestic product *per* capita ($)
Torres Strait Islands	23.6	3 590
Argentina	14.1	3 865
South Africa	6	3 746
Australia	20.4	30 695
New Zealand	28.2	23 460
Japan	7.4	36 105
Singapore	11.9	23 041

Adapted from: Lee-Ross and Mitchell, (2007) andMinniti et al. (2006).
[a] *Nascent, new and established businesses.*

where individuals have a high propensity for risk-taking. Conversely, societies which are culturally predisposed to avoid risk are likely to prefer waged employment rather than owning their own business. Risk-tolerance is a key characteristic of some emerging economies and certainly of many indigenous societies (Lee-Ross and Mitchell, 2007, p. 15). Therefore, in order to empower indigenous communities through entrepreneurship successfully there must first be an understanding of the role culture plays in this regard.

HOFSTEDE'S CULTURAL DIMENSIONS

Probably the most often cited researchers in the field of national culture linked to entrepreneurship and business activity are Trompenaars and Hofstede. In particular, Hofstede (2001) seeks to explain organizational behaviour by framing it in a broader cultural framework. His model of cultural dimensions was developed from studying values in the workplace and how they are influenced by culture. Hofstede's original model identifies four primary dimensions:

- Power distance (PDI) – 'the extent to which the less powerful members of institutions and organizations within a country expect and accept that power is distributed unequally' (Hofstede, 1994, p. 28). A 'low' score indicates a non-acceptance of unequal power distribution;
- Individualism/collectivism (IDV) – 'everyone is expected to look after himself or herself and his or her immediate family [with] collectivism as its opposite . . . [from] birth onwards [societies] are integrated into strong, cohesive in-groups, which throughout people's lifetime continue to protect them in exchange for unquestioning loyalty' (Hofstede, 1994, p. 51). A low score indicates a strong cultural predisposition for collectivism;
- Masculinity/femininity (MAS) – 'gender roles are clearly distinct, men are . . . assertive, tough, and focused on material success whereas women are . . . modest, tender, and concerned with the quality of life; femininity pertains to . . . gender roles overlap[ing]' (Hofstede, 1994, p. 82–3). A low score indicates a cultural predisposition towards femininity; and
- Uncertainty avoidance (UAI) – 'the extent to which the members of a culture feel threatened by uncertain or unknown situations' (Hofstede, 1994, p. 113). A low score suggests a society that is comfortable with uncertainty.

Consistent with its popularity elsewhere, Hofstede's construct has also been used to examine the culture of indigenous societies relative to entrepreneurship. Specifically, researchers have made correlations between cultural dimensions and various entrepreneurial traits (for example, see Wennekers *et al.*, 2001; and Lindsay, 2005).

Reflective practice

1. Think of a tourism or hospitality owner known to you. Intuitively, can you identify any of Hofstede's cultural dimensions for this person?

TOWARDS A DEFINITION

Definitions of indigenous peoples vary considerably as they tend to focus on different aspects. However following the work of Peredo *et al.* (2004, p. 5), this chapter considers that they may be defined operationally via three main elements with the last playing a key role in an understanding of indigenous entrepreneurship:

- descent from populations inhabiting a region prior to later inhabitants;
- geographical, political, and/or economic domination by later inhabitants of immigrants; and
- maintenance of some distinctive social cultural norms and institutions.

The final element is important because indigenous communities regard the activity of entrepreneurship as more than a means of providing economic benefits. It is regarded as a key way of rebuilding their communities and re-establishing control over their traditional lands and heritage. Some examples of indigenous societies currently engaged in entrepreneurial activity include:

- First Nations – Canada
- Metis and Inuits – Canada
- Quechuas – Peru
- Aymaras – Peru
- Maoris – New Zealand
- Kumeyaay – USA
- Australian Aboriginals – Australia
- Torres Straits – Australia.

An additional but complimentary definition, considers indigenous entrepreneurs as those who create, manage and develop new ventures by and for indigenous people underpinned by strong desires for self-determination and heritage preservation (Lindsay, 2005).

TABLE 2.2 A comparison of cultural entrepreneurial values using Hofstede's cultural construct

Hofstede's cultural value dimension	Indigenous entrepreneurial values Redpath and Nielsen (1997)	Non-indigenous entrepreneurial values (McGrath *et al.*, 1992)
Individualism/collectivism	High collectivism/low individualism	Low collectivism/high individualism
Power distance	Low power distance	High power distance
Uncertainty avoidance	Low uncertainty avoidance	Low uncertainty avoidance
Masculinity/femininity	High femininity/low masculinity	Low femininity/high masculinity

Source:Lindsay (2005).

Entrepreneurship therefore becomes a more holistic culturally-bound construct than its non-indigenous counterpart. According to Lindsay (2005), this helps explain why there are relatively less 'recognizable' indigenous entrepreneurial firms as the objectives are different. For example, indigenous culture requires that the entrepreneur's family, extended family and community become involved in the development of new venture[3] as opposed to a focus on individual autonomy in entrepreneurship. There is therefore more complexity than in non-indigenous firms. In short, economic objectives including rapid growth, increasing assets and share prices are at best only equally important as non-economic ones. Issues including self-determination, heritage orientation and other indigenous values must also be considered. Encompassed in this definition are a number of cultural factors which impact on the attitudes of indigenous peoples in particular ways. Lindsay's (2005) comparison of 'common' indigenous entrepreneurial cultural values with those of non-indigenous entrepreneurship (using Hofstede's construct) serves as a useful starting point in this respect and is shown in Table 2.2.

DIMENSIONS, ATTITUDES AND INDIGENOUS ENTREPRENEURSHIP

Conceptually, it is evident that cultural values between indigenous and non-indigenous entrepreneurs are quite different with the exception of low uncertainty avoidance. Several researchers have attempted to link cultural dimensions with entrepreneurial attitudes. Risk-taking and innovation are two such traits with the latter being understood as the generation of new ideas. Redpath and Nielsen (1997) note that tolerance of ideas (risk-taking) is an

---

[3] In terms of population, indigenous Australians represent only 2.2 per cent making them a minority, alienated from mainstream society with little recognition for their business activities (Foley, 2003).

indigenous cultural value so long as these notions resonate with the community's collective norms. After reviewing the evidence Lindsay argues that innovation is one composite part of an overall 'Entrepreneurial attitude'. Other components are:

- Achievement – associated with business start up and growth results; and
- self-esteem – amalgam of self-confidence and perceived business competency.

From the earlier definition of indigenous entrepreneurship, attitude is influenced uniquely by indigenous culture as it is driven by self-determination and preservation of heritage. Furthermore, success is measured by both economic and non-economic dimensions. Individual autonomy is also redundant as it is replaced by the whole community to whom the entrepreneur must be accountable. This limits the effect of individual personal control as it is subordinate to collective influences, that is, personal control over business becomes supplanted by a preoccupation with family and community influence over business.

Taking each of the above attitudes in order, Lindsay (2005) argues that:

- Achievement is at odds with the non-indigenous preoccupation of economic growth due to differences in time orientation and a disinclination to compete. Consensual decision-making and prioritising family issues also detract from non-indigenous entrepreneurship. In Hofstede's terms, decision-making is influenced by a cultural orientation of femininity (Redpath and Nielsen, 1997). This is quite different to masculine cultures where work is prioritised. Measurements of success (achievements) are directly related to quality (of life) rather than quantity (of work). This is a key factor in starting and running a business as evidence suggests that hours of work have a direct and positive correlation with business success (measured in non-indigenous terms of course!).
- Access to sufficient start-up funding is also important for future success. Although indigenous society is a collective, the typical sharing of financial resources from family and friends in a start-up business phase is non-existent because of societal poverty (Fuller, Dansie, Jones and Holmes, 1999). Having no resources and lack of business education is likely to cause feelings of low self-esteem in indigenous communities.

Additionally, Shane and Venkataraman (2000) consider opportunity recognition another important entrepreneurial attitude. This is the ability to identify gaps in the market and to take advantage of them economically. Indigenous society (which has already been identified as collective, consensual and feminine) bases these on the likely benefits accruing to the community in non-economic and economic terms rather than a non-indigenous focus on the latter. Lindsay (2005) notes that indigenous entrepreneurs do not lack this ability but appropriate opportunities in their society are different to those of others. Moreover, if they adopt a non-indigenous approach they may become ostracized from their community given the sharp differences between the two value and culture systems. Indigenous society is pluralist based on resource-sharing where individualism is seen as exploitation as one over another. Success then concerns what you do and how you do it rather than increasing personal wealth which is in conflict with the cultural value of sharing.

Key point 2.3

Indigenous entrepreneurs as those who create, manage and develop new ventures by and for indigenous people underpinned by strong desires for self-determination and heritage preservation.

Other studies have also identified culture-specific characteristics of indigenous entrepreneurship. For example in Foley's (2003) study of urban indigenous Australians, entrepreneurial success was not linked with acquisition of tangible personal assets. Instead it was measured by increased levels of inventory or that a business had been established and not failed. Mapunda's (2005, pp. 10–11) study of indigenous Australian and Tanzanian enterprises reveals a similar finding and cites 'maintaining the soul and spirit through relationships' and 'providing employment for indigenous people' above profit maximization. However, in Foley's study, some 'successful' entrepreneurs appeared to be moving away from traditional cultural norms and values. As a result they felt somewhat distanced from their indigenous community experiencing discrimination resulting in temporary ostracism. This is quite unlike non-indigenous entrepreneurial culture (particularly amongst ethnic groups) where the community tends to embrace and value their success and the entrepreneur is drawn closer to the community as a result (Holt and Keats, 1992). An acute sense of dissonance becomes clear amongst Foley's interviewees where even investment in their own business creates feelings of guilt about not sharing with family/community. For example, one particular indigenous entrepreneur purchased a used sedan for business use. The community felt that he had come into money and not shared it. Another example Foley cites is the family's expectation of credit or goods for free is when 'borrowing' from successful indigenous retailers.

In an almost contradictory cultural sense these individuals had a notion of 'face' where establishing oneself as a 'legitimate' business role model for the community became important through networking with others including 'white fellas' committees and panels (Rotary, Lions, golf club and so on). Interviewees felt that they were creating a positive role model to counteract racial stereotyping. Additionally, business 'accountability' was established through employing non-indigenous accountants. Community communication based on kinship and community obligations was replaced by 'networking' due to increased time constraints linked to the business enterprise. Thus, a positive face was established by actions geared for wider social acceptance and increased business connections to improve social acceptability for themselves and their children. The benchmark of success became social acceptance in the broader business environment. Foley (2003) concludes that the shift away from long held cultural values and norms to that of business enterprise and social networking effectively changes the traditional pattern of indigenous behaviour.

Reflective practice

1. Consider the long-term impact of entrepreneurial success amongst indigenous societies. What cultural changes are likely to be created and how will they impact in practice?

Similar patterns have been found elsewhere amongst other indigenous communities.

Indigenous Canadians recognize that alliances and joint ventures among themselves *and* non-aboriginal partners are important to build capacity for sustainable economic development and self-sufficiency through education and *training* (Anderson, 1999). Peredo's (2001) research amongst indigenous Andean countries confirms similar objectives and business arrangements.

Another more recent study of indigenous entrepreneurship and culture focused on the Torres Strait region of Australia (Lee-Ross and Mitchell, 2007) using the first four of Hofstede's cultural dimensions. Here, the relationships between culture and entrepreneurial attitudes were[4] assessed. The first objective of this study was to calculate cultural dimension scores and position them relative to those of other nations following the predictions of Redpath and Nielsen (1997) shown in Table 2.2. All scores for the

---

[4] Power distance (PDI); individualism (IDV); masculinity (MAS; and uncertainty avoidance (UAI).

Torres Strait Islands were ranked consistently below those of other non-indigenous nations. These outcomes broadly corresponded with those shown in Table 2.2 as:

- Relatively low power distance;
- high collectivism;
- high femininity; and
- low uncertainty.

Following Foley's (2003) earlier proposal that cultural orientations are likely to impact on entrepreneurial attitudes; the results confirmed the notion that this particular model of indigenous entrepreneurship differed from the non-indigenous construct by virtue of culture. Table 2.3 outlines the propositions tested in the study.

Table 2.4 shows how entrepreneurial traits were ranked by a comparison of mean scores calculated from five-point Likert-type questions where 1 = 'Utmost Importance' and 5 = 'Very Little Importance'. All attitudes were scored above 4 on the original Likert scale which suggests that even the lowest ranked attitudes were considered as moderately important. Rankings shown below must therefore be interpreted relative to each other rather than in an absolute sense.

'Persistence', 'vision', 'respond quickly to problems', and 'desire to succeed' were highest of all attitudes. 'Being curious, 'being alone', 'experimenting', 'gamble on a good idea', and 'take chances' were ranked the lowest.

According to Table 2.3 the Torres Strait community is culturally feminine and more concerned with quality than quantity when linking with the collective of achievement. One would therefore expect collectivity and consensus rather than a narrow focus on turning a profit or economic development, hence the expectation of low achievement in financial terms. However, it is quite difficult to confirm this as persistence, vision, responding to problems and desire to succeed do not preclude non-economic aspects, nor are they exclusively masculine attitudes. They are perhaps key attitudes which are held as important in both indigenous and non-indigenous cultures. The difference occurs in how they are interpreted, that is financially or not. On the other hand, working with people, motivating people and working in a team are linked with femininity. Furthermore, doing things own way, total control and being alone are ranked relatively low and are alleged to be masculine attitudes characterizing non-indigenous entrepreneurs. Thus, these attitude rankings appear to support the notion that Torres Strait culture has a female orientation.

TABLE 2.3	Proposed impact summary of indigenous culture on entrepreneurial traits		
Cultural dimension	**Area and brief**	**Associated traits**	**Propositions**
High femininity	Quality of life: attitudes towards achieving 'quantity' of work needed for new venture creation based on quality of life rather than economic development	Working with people, motivating people, working in a team, being creative, desire to succeed, leadership, persistence, vision, feeling sure about yourself, doing things own way, being alone, total control	Low levels of achievement will be demonstrated amongst indigenous Torres Straits' entrepreneurs via associated traits as achievement is linked with economic growth from a non-indigenous perspective
Low uncertainty avoidance	Innovation: generation of new ideas outside cultural norms of collectivity, self-determination and heritage preservation will not hold sway	Being creative, experimenting with new ways, take chances, gamble on a good idea, being curious, clear goals	Low levels of innovation will be demonstrated amongst indigenous Torres Straits' entrepreneurs via associated traits
Low power distance	Self confidence and self esteem: high unemployment and welfare dependencies, poor housing, discrimination undermine social and economic development and little confidence in developing successful business venture and dissatisfaction with the situation	Feeling sure about yourself, leadership, desire to succeed, total control	Low levels of self-confidence and self-esteem will be demonstrated amongst indigenous Torres Straits' entrepreneurs via associated traits
High collectivism	Personal control: emphasis on personal relationships whist maintaining group harmony and how they benefit the community.	Being alone, doing things my own way, working with people, leadership, working in a team.	A low level of personal control will be demonstrated amongst indigenous Torres Straits' entrepreneurs via associated traits
	Opportunity recognition: consensual decision-making and problem-solving, benefits for the community in non-economic and economic terms, pursuing opportunity for individual economic returns is at odds with community and culture	Being curious, vision, respond quickly to problems, desire to succeed	A low level of opportunity recognition will be demonstrated amongst indigenous Torres Straits' entrepreneurs via associated traits

A second cultural predisposition of low uncertainty avoidance suggests that Torres Strait islanders are risk-takers, accept uncertainty and are innovators. The relatively lower rankings of experiment with new ways, gamble on a good idea, take chances and being curious does not seem to support this claim.

TABLE 2.4   Rank order of entrepreneurial attitudes in the Torres Straits

1 Persistence
2 Vision
3 Respond quickly to problems
4 Desire to succeed
5 Working with people
6 Leadership
7 Clear goal
8 Solving problems
9 Motivating people
10 Working in a team
11 Feeling sure about yourself
12 Doing things own way
13 Total control
14 Being creative
15 Being curious
16 Being alone
17 Experiment with new ways
18 Gamble on a good idea
19 Take chances

However, the first caveat is that innovations will only be supported if they resonate with broader cultural norms and second, there is no direct translation of the word 'risk' into any Torres Strait native language. When seeking clarification, an overwhelming majority of respondents simply said 'either you do it [take the risk] or you don't'. The interpretation is that there was no risk associated with their business start-ups due to their cultural predisposition and language structure; hence linked attitudes were deemed as unimportant. However, other low uncertainty avoidance traits of responding quickly to problems, clear goal, leadership and solving problems were ranked relatively highly.

Torres Strait islanders appear to have a low tolerance for unequal power distribution amongst themselves (Hofstede's third dimension). This is in contrast to a non-indigenous notion of entrepreneurship where individuals believe in dominating their social structure (McGrath *et al.*, 1992). This interpretation is supported by the relatively low ranking of total control and feeling sure about yourself but does not explain the relatively high ranking of leadership. One plausible explanation is that many individuals were found to engage in 'temporary' entrepreneurship to raise extra money for one-off cultural events like tombstone openings, weddings, sporting carnivals, concerts and related travel between islands. As such, these entrepreneurial fund-raising activities are often 'unofficial' and may be also considered as acts of individual defiance against perceived inequality (and resultant low self-esteem) wrought by relatively poor wages paid to individuals working on the CDEP scheme and the negative affects of other initiatives beyond the community's control.

Unlike the non-indigenous entrepreneurial value system which emphasizes individualism, the results suggest that Torres Straits islanders are a cultural 'collective'. Hence the first of two propositions that low levels of personal control will be demonstrated via associated attitudes. There are clearly some overlaps with other cultural dimensions (for example masculinity/femininity) as collectivism is an overarching cultural norm. Unsurprisingly, attitudes of working with people, motivating people and working in a team have relatively high rankings. Whereas, doing things my own way, being alone and total control appear towards the latter half of Table 2.4. This is at odds with non-indigenous interpretations of entrepreneurship, for example, Mueller and Thomas (2001) consider collectivism to be the antithesis of entrepreneurship. They note that [non-indigenous] entrepreneurs are '... frequently characterized as exhibiting [a high] locus of control' (p. 59). Simply, this means that entrepreneurs believe in their own abilities to bring about changes and business success rather than relying on anything else. Indeed, in their study of nine countries, locus of control was found to be more prevalent in individualistic cultures than in collectivist cultures.

The second proposition for the cultural dimension of collectivism shown in Table 2.3 relates to opportunity recognition. In short, Torres Strait islanders should demonstrate a low level of this because of the tendency for consensual decision-making and problem-solving. Furthermore, the ability to spot and pursue an opportunity effectively is hindered by lengthy community consultation. Additionally, benefits for the community are valued in both non-economic and economic terms. The relatively low rankings of all attitudes from 12 to 17 appear to support this notion as do the relatively higher rankings of more 'collective' attitudes.

In summary, there would appear to be a number of key attitudinal differences between Torres Strait and non-indigenous entrepreneurs. Moreover, the notion that these disparities are culturally driven seems to be a reasonable conclusion. In a general sense all the foregoing evidence including that of other studies suggests that indigenous entrepreneurship is novel (because until relatively recently, it has been ignored) and different to its non-indigenous counterpart. Nonetheless, there are still several important questions yet to be addressed adequately:

■ What is the process of indigenous entrepreneurship or are there many depending on individual societies and are the aims different?

■ Does indigenous entrepreneurship in different locations show similar and distinctive patterns of entrepreneurial features and goal structures?

■ Does entrepreneurship amongst indigenous society have distinctive combinations of entrepreneurial features and how has the process of colonization impacted on them including the creation of pseudo-societies by virtue of colonists?

■ Do indigenous entrepreneurs have unique cognitive processes and decision-making patterns and if so, how do they impact on key outcomes?

■ How do legal, economic and structural characteristics impact on culturally occurring attitudes and behaviours in indigenous communities?

■ Given that some indigenous societies are less collective than others (e. g. Tohono O'odham and Apache tribes of Arizona) what would be an appropriate mix of collective and individual enterprises for optimum economic development

■ How do language and 'story-telling' affect indigenous perspectives of their world and that of others?

■ Can indigenous societies become self-determining and economically sustainable whilst maintaining their cultural heritage and how useful will the Contingency model of development become in this context? In short, how is indigenous tradition reconcilable with innovation.

Reflective practice

1. How much is really known about indigenous entrepreneurship? Can you think of other questions that might be added to the above list?

Key point 2.4

Unlike the non-indigenous entrepreneurial value system which emphasizes individualism, Torres Straits islanders are a cultural 'collective'.

Whilst the above are key questions in the search for a better theoretical understanding of indigenous entrepreneurship, in a practical sense, many new indigenous owned and operated hospitality/tourism firms currently exist. Approximately 200 indigenous tourism businesses exist in Australia generating $5 million per year with an additional contribution of $200 million per

TABLE 2.5	Positive and negative impacts of indigenous entrepreneurship
Positive impacts	**Negative impacts**
Economic base to revive indigenous communities	Increased cost of living for locals
Maintenance and growth of income generating arts and crafts	Decline in artistic quality and authenticity
Job and wealth creation amongst indigenous community by own entrepreneurs	Domination of external interests and control of management decision-making process by outsiders
Cultural revival and preservation	Exploitation of human cultural resources
Investment in environmental conservation	Desecration of sacred sites and natural resources
Development of remote communities	Exploitation of remote communities and loss of cultural identity

Source: Adapted from:Mapunda (2005, p. 7).

year from the sales of indigenous arts and crafts (Zeppel, 1998). In the tropical north of Queensland Australia there are several new and thriving businesses including:

- Aurukun Fishing and Wetland Charters;
- Cape York Turtle Rescue Camp;
- Djabugay Country Tours;
- Echo Adventure and Cultural Experience; and
- Kuku Yalanji Dreamtine Walks

Whilst the above are examples of indigenous-owned tours and attractions, indigenous entrepreneurs are involved in other less culturally-defined businesses including accommodation, visitor service facilities and restaurants (Mapunda, 2005). However, the long-term success of cultural and 'extended' operations depends on careful and appropriate management as a number of potentially negative outcomes are possible; some are shown in Table 2.5.

In order to minimize the potential negative impacts of indigenous entrepreneurship it is essential that guidelines should be followed including:

- Emphasize hard work based on structured understanding between indigenous and non-indigenous peoples;
- Establish empathy between mainstream and indigenous cultures based on sensitivity to issues of heritage;
- not turn indigenous peoples into museum curious; and
- not expect indigenous peoples to act in a manner counter to their traditions; and
- welcome diversity and respect right of indigenous decision-making within broad public policy guidelines.

TABLE 2.6 Some key differences between indigenous and ethnic entrepreneurs	
Indigenous entrepreneurs	**Ethnic entrepreneurs**
Exclusively concerned with individuals having a close bond with ancestral territories and the natural resources in them. A prominent goal of is recovery of access to and use of their traditional lands	Ethnic entrepreneurship usually concerns immigrant populations and the situation of relative newcomers to a region or nation
Lands and resources often represent a basis for the capacity to engage in entrepreneurial development	Ethnic entrepreneurship looks at the economic interactions with a particular area of new settlement
Ostracism from community of personal wealth is perceived to exist	Personal wealth and success valued and embraced by community
Usually connected with community-based economic development	Typically involves enterprise development at the individual or family level
In many countries indigenous people have obtained quasi-governmental or nation status	Assimilated into host nation

ETHNIC ENTREPRENEURSHIP

There is a temptation to consider indigenous and ethnic entrepreneurship as one and the same. This is probably because the impact of 'culture' features significantly in both categories. The fact of the matter is both are quite distinct and separate. Peredo *et al.* (2004) provide some useful guidelines to help differentiate the two shown in Table 2.6.

It would also be similarly imprudent to minimize the economic importance of ethnic entrepreneurship. This is because ethnic firms have an enormous wealth-generating potential. In the USA small ethnic firms account for over 15 per cent of all businesses generating over $591 billion (US) annually and employ over 5 million workers (Zimmerer and Scarborough, 2005). In the UK the percentage of ethnic entrepreneurial firms is smaller but still substantial at 7 per cent (220 000 businesses) http://www.bytestart.co.uk/content/19/19_1/small-businesses-in-the-u.shtml, August, 2007. South Asian entrepreneurs alone own approximately half of all independent shops in Great Britain and spend around 5 billion Sterling per annum (*Management Today*, September 1990, p. 57). Furthermore South Asians account for just over 2 per cent of Britain's working population with a higher contribution towards employment and wealth generation since they represent 4 per cent of all employers (Basu and Goswami, 1999). A similar picture emerges in Australia with a total ethnic presence of nearly 23 per cent which is higher than the USA, Canada, UK, Switzerland, France or Germany. Approximately 30 per cent of all small businesses are owned by ethnic entrepreneurs (ABS 2004).

Successful Australian Ethnic entrepreneurs

Ethnic Business Awards 2006 Winners Announced at the Sydney Opera House

The Ethnic Business Awards were created 18 years ago by Mr Joseph Assaf, to recognise the contribution of migrants to Australian Business. They have since become one of the longest running awards in Australia, which is a testament to their success and prestige. This year's winners were migrants from Italy, Sweden, South Africa and Macedonia, who all now proudly call Australia home.

The Sydney Opera House set the stage last night for the 18th Ethnic Business Awards (EBA). His Excellency Major General Michael Jeffery AC CVO MC joined other distinguished guests at the annual Gala presentation, where immigrant business owners were recognized for their outstanding contribution to the Australian economy.

Accepting the Medium/Large Business Award, Mr Silvio Pitruzzello of Pantalica Cheese Company attributed the win to his father Sebastiano. 'The success of our business comes from the hard work and passion of my father. He came to Australia from Sicily in the 1960s with a suitcase and a dream, and now 33 years on, the Pantalica Cheese Company is a thriving business.' Mr Pitruzzello said. Representing an assortment of cultural backgrounds and covering a broad range of industry sectors the EBAs has welcomed over 6000 entries since its inception. The following businesses were presented with an award: Large Business Award: Pantalica Cheese Company – received by Mr Silvio Pitruzzello from Italy. Small Business Award: kikki.K Pty Ltd – received by Ms Kristina Karlsson, Managing Director, from Sweden. Initiative Award: Skybury Coffee Pty.Ltd – received by Mr Ian MacLaughlin, Company Director, from South Africa. Women in Business Award: The Education Group – received by Ms Neda Morris, Director, from Macedonia.

Accepting the Special Initiative Award, presented by Fran Bailey MP, Minister for Small Business and Tourism, Mr Ian MacLaughlin, who set up Skybury Coffee with his wife Marion said, 'Australia was a place where we thought that we could bring up our family in freedom and prosperity . . . but when we arrived in 1987 we were told that this used to be the lucky country. My first thought was 'goodness we have missed the boat', but I am here to tell you that this is still the lucky country'. The Hon Fran Bailey MP later commented, 'The Australian Government is proud to be associated with the Ethnic Business Awards. These Awards recognise achievements of people born outside of this country and who have come here and made a significant contribution to our country. As Small Business Minister, I congratulate all of tonight's winners and finalists on their vision and initiative at achieving this success.'

Group Managing Director of Telstra Business, Deena Shiff, said Telstra's ongoing support of the Awards recognized the contribution that migrants had made to the success of many Australian businesses. 'The courage and determination needed to move to another country are also essential to build and run a successful business – our winners have clearly demonstrated the characteristics needed to compete and win in a highly competitive marketplace and Telstra congratulates them on their efforts.' In a country where approximately 20 per cent of the population speak a language other than English at home the Ethnic Business Awards has grown to become a most anticipated annual event. In his speech last night founder of the Awards and Chairman of Etcom, Mr Joseph Assaf commented on the positive impact of multiculturalism to Australian society, a strength reflected in the Ethnic

Business Awards. 'In Australia, diversity is a fact of life and because of that, multiculturalism is a way of life. It is a way of life that enables Australia to harness and promote the ingenuity, vision and enterprise that characterises many of its new citizens.' George Frazis, Executive General Manager of Business and Private Banking at the National Australia Bank (NAB), said: 'NAB is as extensive as the community it serves. The myriad of services available to our clients are as broad as the backgrounds from which they come. We pride ourselves in taking the time to understand and connect with our clients. That's one reason why we sponsor these awards, to help recognise great business.' The Awards will be televised on SBS at 1pm on Thursday, November 30 and repeated at 1pm on Saturday, December 2, 2006. They will be aired twice on Australia Network to an estimated 10.1 million homes across 41 countries, and replayed by 155 broadcasters throughout the region, seen in 200 000 hotel rooms. *Source*: http://www.clickpress.com/releases/Detailed/21997005cp.shtml, 2007.

On the whole, ethnic entrepreneurs have enjoyed much success globally and many commentators are quick to provide the answers; culture often forms the basis of their arguments. That is, one that encourages thrift, hard work and reliance on cheap family labour (Werbner, 1990). According to Deakins (1996), entrepreneurship is popular amongst ethnic communities as it is a way out of poverty (in the UK these include Afro-Caribbean, Indian, Pakistani, Bangladeshi and Greek-Cypriot communities). However, it may be argued that both cultural characteristics and overcoming poverty are common to entrepreneurs generally. Morrison, Rimmington and Williams (1999) insist that ethnic entrepreneurs succeed where others fail because they are able to create market niches which are 'ethnically protected' (p. 12), where restaurateurs for example, are given preferential treatment by ethnic suppliers of raw materials to satisfy own community demands. In a sense this is similar to backward vertical growth whereby one company seeks to secure supplies by buying the supplying firm. This can certainly be seen in the wealth of ethnic restaurants in capital cities and resorts in most first world countries globally. Mars and Ward (1984) offer similar advice in the form of 'immigrant entrepreneurship' theory in the context of ethnic resources and opportunities created by an enclave economy. Whilst this theory has found support (Werbner, 1990), others find that cultural factors may actually restrict development by creating excessive reliance on the local ethnic community market, informal sources of finance and family controlled businesses (Ram, 1994). Waldinger, Aldrich, and Ward (1990) note that long-term business success lies in ability to branch out from the ethnic enclave economy which in turn is influenced by changes occurring within the community.

Reflective practice

1. Are there any specific cultural differences between ethnic and indigenous entrepreneurs? What facets are common to each group.

Key point 2.5

Ethnic entrepreneurship usually concerns immigrant populations and the situation of relative newcomers to a region or nation

---

Ethnic Restaurateurs

Immigrant entrepreneurs in Australia are distributed across all the industries with a particular presence in retail. These niches derive from specific culinary traditions or by chance. In New South Wales, half the entrepreneurs in the 'fish shop, take away food' and associated outlets are first generation immigrants (Collins, Gibson, Alcorso, Tait and Castles, 1995).

Many immigrant entrepreneurs have restaurants in Australian cities and towns (Collins and Castillo, 1998). Chinese restaurants and cafes were a feature of the Australian suburban and country town landscape (Chin, 1988) and most suburbs and towns had a Greek milk bar to sell sweets, drinks and meals Collins *et al.* (1995). Today most Australian regions have 'ethnic' restaurants, it is a very feature of their cosmopolitanism. Most immigrant groups have a presence in the restaurant sector with Italian, Chinese, Thai, Vietnamese and Japanese being very popular.

Source: Reproduced with permission: Collins (2007).

Legge and Hindle (2004) offer another explanation citing trust as the key enabler of success. They consider that people of similar ethnicity share a common denominator in the form of culture. This is different to that of the host nation or society and will give rise to a feeling of marginalization amongst the ethnic group. The perceived 'distance' from broader society may heighten trust between individuals leading to high levels of entrepreneurship. Ward and Jenkins (1984) also consider that ethnic minority entrepreneurs have a unique competitive advantage over others because of an access to informal sources of finance in the extended family network particularly within the Asian community. They state, 'It is common for

TABLE 2.7 Factors for long-term success of ethnic enterprises	
Socio-cultural factors	**Ability to implement an appropriate expansion strategy**
■ Hours worked at start-up, entrepreneur's country of origin and religion	■ Delegation of responsibilities which may include declining reliance on family and ethnic labour
■ Educational qualifications, previous business experience gained from within or outside family	■ Cost reduction through diversification and technological improvements
■ Access to sources of capital and to information by virtue of other family or community members being in the same line of business.	■ Market development involving a move away from ethnic customers towards competing in the wider domestic market and gradually internationally.

members of Asian communities to club together to set up a member in business.' (p. 119).

An important aspect not considered by these culturally oriented explanations is the role of more obvious resources including:

■ education and class background of migrants;
■ entrepreneurs access to and use of market information;
■ decision-making and managerial ability; and
■ strategies used to expand business.

These are important features of generic theories yet are absent from South Asian or ethnic minority entrepreneurship research (Storey, 1994; and Basu and Goswami, 1999).

In their study of 118 ethnic business owners in Britain, Basu and Goswami (1999) found that whilst working long hours, exploiting family labour and serving an ethnic population had a bearing on success, over reliance on these factors limited business growth. They concluded that long run success depends on the origins of enterprise or the initial conditions at start up shown in Table 2.7.

In a practical sense then, education plays a critical role in lowering barriers to business entry and growth. Entrepreneurs must invest in skilling employees and having an ability to delegate to non-family members. Finally, if entrepreneurs wish to operate internationally, they should move out of local ethnic markets and internationalise with appropriate knowledge of home and host countries.

Whilst acknowledging the impact of cooperative family and community networks, niche markets and so forth on ethnic entrepreneurial success in Australia, Collins, Sim, Dhungel, Zabbal and Nole (1997) consider this to be similarly common to non-ethnic entrepreneurs. After reviewing the limited amount of research in the field they criticize many studies for failing to compare ethnic with non-ethnic business strategies before proclaiming certain aspects as typically ethnic. Indeed, Collins (1991) acknowledges the various cultural explanations for ethnic success but also the more banal but eminently sensible ideas including:

- the combined policies of the Whitlam (1972–1975), Fraser (1975–1983), Hawke (1983–1993) and Keating (1993–1996) governments; and
- Racialized blocked mobility theory (Lever-Tracy, Ip, Kitay, Phillips and Tracy, 1991) whereby immigrants experience prejudice, discrimination and a never-ending round of other obstacles including non-recognition of overseas qualifications and problems gaining access to professional bodies; and
- Education and class resource theory (Lever-Tracy *et al.*, 1991) where level of education and resources have a key impact on the rise and success of ethnic entrepreneurship.

Thus many immigrants have little option but to start their own businesses (Stromback and Malhotra, 1994).

SUMMARY

The notion of profit maximization amongst entrepreneurs was challenged depending on a number of factors. Culture was introduced a having a potentially significant impact on this position especially amongst societies holding a strong sense of cultural values. Culture was then defined and applied to indigenous societies together with an outline of some key developmental issues to garner nation-building and self-determination. Some generic models of economic development were critiqued with a recommendation of the most appropriate for indigenous society.

Several global regions were compared to identify the role of culture upon entrepreneurial activity. Culture was then reconceptualized according to Hofstede's (2001) model and applied to indigenous Australians through some recent research in the area. Some key findings were discussed including the cultural impact of high femininity, low uncertainty avoidance, low power distance and high collectivism upon entrepreneurial attitudes. Specific attention was then focused on the indigenous peoples of the Torres Strait region of Australia where entrepreneurial characteristics were explained through analysis of cultural predispositions. It was concluded that culture has a significant impact upon indigenous entrepreneurship and that non-indigenous models should be treated with caution when seeking to explain the phenomenon. A number of questions were also posed in order to gain a fuller understanding of indigenous entrepreneurship together with the likely negative impact of business development if undertaken from a non-indigenous perspective.

The chapter proceeded by highlighting the main differences between indigenous and ethnic entrepreneurs and outlining the economic importance of international ethnic entrepreneurial activity. A number of business enablers were discussed with an emphasis on those being culturally-bound, stereotypical, and generic. In short, racism and discrimination were found to be important barriers for ethnic entrepreneurs together with access to capital, low levels of education and prior experience.

Key point 2.6

Creativity and innovation are linked but different. Innovation is a systematic and logical process with the aim of developing a creative idea into a commercially robust product or service.

The Singapore Gourmet

Jenny and Henry Chin emigrated from South-East Asia to Australia in the 1960s. After going back home for a whilst they returned to Australia in 1973, encouraged by the changing political climate that accompanied the election of the Whitlam Labor Government. In Sydney, Jenny worked as a chief accountant at Express Freight, helping to set up their first computing system using punch cards. Pregnancy interrupted her career, but two months after the birth of her first child Jenny returned to work as an accountant, hiring a full-time nanny to look after her son. After the birth of a second child, Jenny and Henry moved into their first small business, a fish and chip shop, previously owned by Turkish migrants, in Hay Street near Sydney's Chinatown.

Gradually, they began to introduce Singaporean food. Business doubled as the fish and chip shop was transformed into a Singaporean restaurant. 'Australian cuisine' was undergoing a gradual ethnic revolution. Fortunes for the Chins took a rosy turn as business prospered, but their ambitions were not fulfilled. They decided to use business profits to expand, opening a tea house across the road and another restaurant, the Bottomless Pit, in nearby George Street, where they employed eight people. Only then did Jenny give up her other job and manage the business full-time. Expansion continued as they opened restaurants on Pier 1 and Pier 2 in the Rocks area under the Sydney Harbour Bridge, and a restaurant in the western suburb of Bankstown. By 1981–1982 the Chin restaurant empire was worth millions of dollars a year. However like Jenny's family in Singapore, the Chins experienced the fickle fortunes of business as a combination of factors destroyed their burgeoning restaurant empire.

Impatient creditors and landlords finally resorted to cutting off the electricity just before big functions. Jenny Chin was forced to sell everything. Shattered and weary, Jenny and Henry decided to start all over again. They moved to a site about 15 kilometres from the centre of Sydney, which became their new shop and living premises in one. They were heavily indebted. Henry worked even when he was ill because, as he put it, 'the whole family and everyone depended on me'. Jenny's professional skills were by then becoming outdated, but in 1985 she was able to find a job with a car provided. With two incomes, after a whilst they were able to take up a lease on a shop in the inner-city suburb of St Peters for $250 per week. This became the new Singapore Gourmet, the site of Jenny and Henry Chin's current business.

Jenny and Henry Chin still work in other jobs and run the Singapore Gourmet restaurant. After work each evening Jenny goes shopping before arriving at the restaurant between 5.30 and 6.00 p.m. to cook. She has the help of three assistants, with her son helping out – 'for tips only' – when they need him. The new Singapore Gourmet has now established a secure clientele and Jenny and Henry are planning to extend the premises and lengthen the opening hours.

Comment

This story of ethnic small business illustrates some of the diversity of experiences in this sector of the economy. For the Chins, restaurants offered a risky business at the luxury end of the food services market. Hard work overlain by their speculative orientation was to lead them onto the roller-coaster of rapid business success and failure.

What characterises this story – as with most of the stories of ethnic small business – is the dreams that these enterprises encapsulate. The post-war immigration net drew in immigrants from eastern, southern and northern Europe, the Middle East, Asia and both Americas. Immigration changed the face of Australian society. In major cities, such as Sydney, Melbourne, Adelaide and Perth, one-half of the population are first or second generation immigrants. However, the migrant entrepreneur's freedom may be no more than the freedom to work at night to finish rush orders. The better opportunities for the children may become the compulsion to work in the family business after school every day, to help make ends meet. The free market may be just a veil for control and exploitation by powerful suppliers or customers. The solution to unemployment may be a costly and temporary one, as ill-prepared and under-capitalised entrepreneurs go bankrupt and lose everything – even the family home.

Questions

1. To what do you mainly attribute the Chins entrepreneurial successes?
2. How important was their cultural predisposition in this case?

Source: Reproduced with permission: Collins *et al.* (1995).

CHAPTER 3

Entrepreneurs and Small Firm Ownership

After working through the chapter you should be able to:

- Critically evaluate the meanings of the term entrepreneur;
- Identify the characteristics of growth style entrepreneurs;
- Identify the origins and motives of lifestyle entrepreneurs;
- Analyse the implications of patterns of entrepreneurship in small firm ownership in hospitality and tourism

INTRODUCTION

The Collins dictionary describes 'entrepreneur' as the 'owner of manger of a business enterprise who, by risk and initiative, attempt to make profits.' (1992: 507). In fact the word entrepreneur covers a range of different meanings and usages in everyday language. The boss of Microsoft, Bill Gates, is described as an entrepreneur, as is the person owning a small hotel, restaurant or bar. Similarly, as the Collins definition highlights, entrepreneur may be used to describe both those who own businesses and also those who manage them. Yet owners benefit directly from making profits, where managers are more likely to be paid a salary and benefit only through bonuses or profit sharing schemes. Furthermore, it is possible to identify 'entrepreneurial' activities even in organizations which are non-profit making, say university lecturers or health services managers may be 'entrepreneurial' in contexts where there are no profits, only services.

This chapter will discuss the notion of entrepreneurs and entrepreneurialism from a range of perspective. Life style entrepreneurs, in particular will be a major focus of the chapter, because small firms represent a major source of supply of hospitality and tourism services across the world. A high percentage of businesses in the tourism and hospitality sector (95 per cent) are small firms, often family operated businesses, this is a common feature to be found across the globe. In the UK, for example, 95 per cent of firms in the sector employ fewer than 50 employees (the generic definition of a small firm) and 75 per cent employ 10 or fewer employees (by definition they are micro-firms) (Lashley and Rowson 2006). Indeed many small hotels, guest houses, cafes, and pubs are not employers, and are run by owner–mangers with family and friends helping out. Getz, Carlsen, and Marrison (2004) describe these as predominantly 'family businesses'. Many held a lifelong ambition to own a hotel, or some business that gives them greater control of their lives, or because they think they will enjoy the life of hotel ownership. Few have any hotel management or business experience and had not worked in a hotel or the hospitality sector before. Research quoted later confirms that in effect many of these businesses are 'commercial homes' (Lynch, 2005), where the division between home and the commercial become blurred.

Whilst the largest number of firms are small firm, micro businesses or merely commercial homes, a small number of large firms dominate large proportions of the total market. In the UK for example, six firms control almost 27 000 (45.8 per cent) of the countries 59 000 pubs, multiple hotel chains control large parts of the total accommodation market. Entrepreneurship is also a concern to these firms. Business growth and sales building require managers, in charge of individual hotels, to behave in an entrepreneurial manner but within the framework of the hotel brand. They have to be entrepreneurial within limits set by the organization. Some might call these *intrapreneurs* (Getz *et al.*, 2004).

Key point 3.1

Entrepreneur is a word that is used to describe a range of different types of individual covering quite different motives and drives in business organizations.

ENTREPRENEURS

There are several different perceptions of entrepreneurs and the role in business growth and development. At the more high profile level, key industry leaders such as Tim Martin at J D Wetherspoon, or Conrad Hilton, are individuals who build a business empire from humble beginnings. In other words, they start with one pub, hotel or restaurant and build up a chain of pubs, hotels or restaurants. They are substantial shareholders in the enterprise and continue to personally lead the business. On another level, managers running a corporate business which owns hundreds, or in some cases thousands of units, are entrepreneurial because they generate growth and profitable businesses as salaried managers with bonuses, though some describe these as *intrapreneurs*, because of their somewhat tangential relationship with the ownership of the business.

The classical view of entrepreneurs assumes that personal reward, through profits and capital growth are what drive these individuals and ultimately successful economic activity. In fact classical economic theory and some neo-conservative commentators set the entrepreneur at the heart of regenerative economic activity. If only restrictions and disincentives were removed entrepreneurs would be free to generate more economic activity, jobs and national wealth, they say. The problem with this view is that people who meet the classic descriptions of entrepreneurs are limited in number. As we shall see later, many of the people who operate small firms as bars, hotels or restaurants are in the main 'lifestyle' entrepreneurs. The numbers of business operators in the hospitality sector who are chiefly economically driven, who have ambitions to make a lot of money, and grow the business to become a multi-sited empire, are few and far between. A survey of around 1300 operators of micro businesses in hospitality and tourism (Thomas, Lashley, Rowson, Xie, Jameson, Eaglen, and Parsons, 2000) put this at somewhere in the region of 10–15 per cent of micro-business operators being strongly motivated by economic incentives.

Getz *et al.* (2004) describe entrepreneurs as individuals who work to increase personal benefits in the form of economic gains or in social standing but who create benefits in the wider social and economic setting through increased economic activity, job creation and wealth generation. 'Walt Disney, Conrad Hilton and Thomas Cook have radically innovated in their respective sectors, significantly redefining the nature of products, services and markets that have contributed to the growth of hospitality and tourism industry over the decades' (Getz *et al.*, 2004: 24).

There are some debates as to whether entrepreneurs are people with particular personality profiles or are merely reacting to the circumstances in which they find themselves. Kuratko and Hodgetts (1998) suggest that all individuals have the potential be entrepreneurs, but this fails to acknowledge that many individuals are not motivated to this economic growth model. Indeed there may even be a more creatively linked set of motives. That these growth orientated entrepreneurs enjoy the act of creation and building the business as much as the economic benefit. Getz *et al.* suggest that entrepreneurial behaviour is embedded in the individual, society and the economy in contemporary settings. Table 3.1 provides a list of behavioural cues for entrepreneurs.

Collins (2002) and O'Mahony (2007) both cite examples of the pressure of being recent migrants into Australia and being excluded form many economic

TABLE 3.1	Entrepreneurial behaviour cues	
	Positive	**Negative**
Social	■ Role of family and intergenerational role models	■ Political/religious displacement
		■ Political unrest
	■ Conducive culture	■ Discrimination
	■ Supportive networks	■ Unhappy with position in society
		■ Dissatisfied with blocked employment opportunities
Economic	■ Move towards services	
	■ Reversal of highly vertically integrated company structures	■ Discriminatory legislation
	■ Phenomenon of 'dot.com' businesses	■ No other way to make money
Psychological	Entrepreneurial aspirations of independence, wealth, need to achieve, social mobility.	

Source: Getz *et al.* (2004: 25).

and business contexts by the discriminatory legislation and practices. O'Mahony shows that many Irish migrants ended up owning bars and breweries because little else was open to them. Collins (2002) suggests that many Italian, Greek, and Lebanese opened restaurants as a response to being in effect, shut out from main stream business activity. Similarly Chinese cafes opened in many towns and cities brought a cultural diversity to the food and drink scene in Australia. In contemporary societies, these processes are still at work. Often migrants use entrepreneurship to break through negative impacts of social class and ethnic barriers in the wider economic world. Morrison (2001: 78) suggests the following model as a way of considering entrepreneurial cues (Figure 3.1).

The advantage of this model is that it does recognise that the entrepreneur is likely to have to work through a multiplicity of influences. The classic growth orientated entrepreneur is likely to display certain personality traits, and characteristics, and be supported by a personal environment and personal goals which enable and drive entrepreneurship. At the same time the business idea needs to be robust and sustainable in a social and economic environment which is both ready for the idea, and which will encourage **entrepreneurship** (Getz *et al.*, 2004).

Key point 3.2

Most growth-orientated entrepreneurs are likely to be influenced through a number internal, such as personality type, and external factors, such as culture and immediate opportunities.

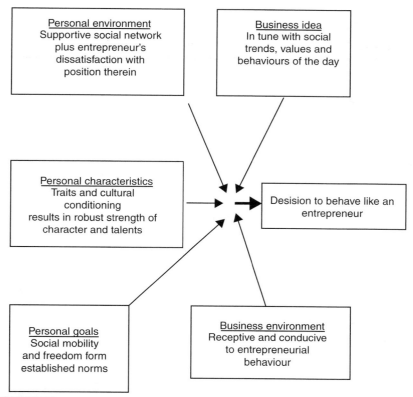

FIGURE 3.1 *Model of entrepreneurial cues.*

LIFE STYLE ENTREPRENEURS

In the UK pub sector, recent changes in the management and operation of pubs and bars reveals much about the perceptions of small firm entrepreneurs. The majority of pubs in Britain are owned by big corporate pub companies, such as the Punch Pub company and Enterprise Inns. In fact these two companies alone own around 19 000 of the nation's 59 000 pubs. Although they physically own the pub properties, individually pubs are operated by small firms in a loose form of franchising (Lashley and Rowson, 2005) through tenancy or leasehold agreements. Tenancies tend to be looser, more short-term arrangements, whilst leaseholds are more formal and give more economic benefits to the leaseholder than the tenant enjoys. The leaseholder can, for example, sell on the lease to another person and the terms of the agreement tend to be over a longer period than for a tenant. The assumption at the root of the recent decision of many licensed retail operators to change from tenanted to leased arrangement is that the short-run relationship implicit in the typical tenancy acted as a barrier to more entrepreneurial drives by the pub tenant. Many firms hoped that a longer-term relationship, more economic rents, and more entrepreneurial motivations would provide the licensees with growth inspired incentives for licensees.

Whilst these factors might be important barriers to the entrepreneurial motives of some, the assumption that all small firms are driven by growth and profit maximization objectives is questionable. The Leeds Metropolitan University (Thomas *et al.*, 2000) survey of 1396 small tourism and hospitality firms showed that only 9 per cent of respondents listed 'to make a lot of money' as a key motivation for owning a small business. Sixty-six per cent identified to 'make a reasonable living', 58 per cent said they 'wanted to be my own boss', and 41 per cent stated that a major reason for owning a small business was 'I enjoy this life style'. These findings are consistent with earlier work on the motives of small firm owners (Beaver and Lashley, 1998). Owners of these 'micro firms' with 10 or fewer employees, are mostly concerned with a cluster of 'lifestyle' motives for their entrepreneurial activities Lockyer and Morrison (1999). Table 3.2 reproduces the responses from the Leeds study. The question asked respondents to identify one or more reasons why they were running their own business.

The values expressed in Table 3.2 lists the total number of respondents who indicated that the statement reflected one of their top three objectives for owning the business. These responses give an interesting insight into the motives of people running small firms. In many ways, those operating tenanted, leasehold and the occasional franchised business are in a similar position. Price *et al.* (2000) have argued that often these businesses are being run at sub-optimal levels partly because the resources used are not charged at a fully economic rate due to family members working in the unit at less than

TABLE 3.2 Motivations for owning a small business	
Motivation	**Value (per cent of respondents)**
To make a reasonable living	926 (66)
To make a lot of money	125 (9)
To be my own boss	813 (58)
I enjoy this lifestyle	576 (41)
To avoid unemployment	197 (14)
To live in this location	287 (21)
It is a form of semi-retirement	125 (9)
I spotted a market opportunity	246 (18)

Source: Thomas *et al.* (2000).

market rates. Often the pub represents a 'free house' to the family. Hence business costs and motives are meliorated by these more domestic considerations. In effect, pub tenancy or lease provides both a commercial and a domestic setting for the tenant/lessee and there is a need to understand 'life style economics' (Andrews *et al.*, 2000) so as to better match potential tenants with properties.

The definitions and categories used by Morrison, Rimmington, and Williams (1999) are helpful because they suggest a number of categories that might apply to the core objectives of those engaged in tenanted or leasehold relationships. In essence they suggest that lifestyle proprietor defines an individual who has a multiple set of goals associated with the business. Profitability in the business will only be one of these goals. In addition to the entrepreneurial venture, Beaver, Lashley, and Stewart (1998) suggest that there a number of other categories of small firm that may well differ in the nature of their business motives. They suggest that the lifestyle enterprise, the family enterprise, the female enterprise, the ethnic minority enterprise and enterprises where the dominant motives are for self employment and control are likely to give different priorities to both profitability and their own developmental needs. They say,

> 'Whilst that this is not an exhaustive list of entrepreneurial types, it is sufficient to show that the motives of those setting up and maintaining small hospitality firms are not always compatible with 'rationale economic' considerations. Motives associated with personal preferences or which relate to self-image do not automatically lead to levels of self-analysis which suggest that a lack of business skills presents a major threat to their business goals' (Beaver et al., 1998: 166).

Reflective practice 3.1

Interview the owner of a small hotel in your area and establish his/her origins and motives for setting up the hotel.

Sweeney (2008) suggests that a number of push and pull factors are at work in the decision to start a business in this micro-business manner. Push factors create a situation where individual feel compelled to start the business, where the pull factors suggest benefits to the individual(s) (Figure 3.2).

Beaver and Lashley (1998) suggest that lifestyle business objectives represent barriers to the perception of the need for personal development and growth. Often these firms are economically satisficing. So long as the owner

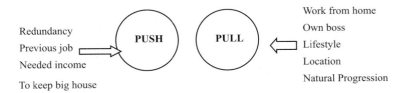

FIGURE 3.2   *Push and Pull factors motivating business start up.*
Source: Sweeney (2008).

is able to meet the requirements of a reasonable standard of living they will not recognise the need to undertake courses that develop their managerial or entrepreneurial skills (Morrison, 2000). That said, those running small firms do learn from their actions (Kolb, 1984) and Morrison suggests that personal networks perform a valuable if informal source of education and training (2000b).

Key point 3.3

Many micro business in hospitality and tourism are run by individuals who are primarily motivated by a cluster of factors which tend be more important than the desire for business growth and profit maximization. They may be referred to as 'lifestyle' firms because their key reasons for running the business are to improve their lifestyle in some way or other.

The relationship between the pub operating company and the tenants/lessees has many similarities with relationships found between franchisors and franchisees. The larger organization is attempting to gain benefits of scale by using the financial and managerial resources provided by the smaller firm. At the same time they aim to gain from the entrepreneurial drives of the tenant/lessee under the assumption that entrepreneurship and personal gain will stimulate extra effort when compared to the performance of salaried managers. From the small firm's perspective, the relationship with the larger firm allows access to the resources and expertise of the larger organization that might be denied a truly independent enterprise. That said, research into the motives of those running small firms in the sector shows that frequently classically entrepreneurial motives are secondary to other more 'lifestyle' motives for operating the business. As a consequence many tenants and lessees are not likely to give the highest priority to business growth and profit maximization. When compared with the formal business format franchising arrangements the support given to tenants and leaseholds by the operating companies is minimal and may prove to be another factor preventing growth in the small firm.

Using a different metaphor to describe many small hospitality and tourism firms Getz *et al.* (2004) describe them as 'family firms', whilst Lynch and MacWhannell (2000) refers to them as 'commercial homes'. This latter term has particular resonance in the accommodation sector internationally and pub sector, in the UK. Typically the domestic accommodation is part of the same premises as the commercial activity. In fact, both Lynch (2005) and Sweeney (2008) in different ways explore the relationship between the private and commercial domains of the same property. The same term can be closely used to describe the restaurant sector, when, the restaurant and kitchens etc., share the same premises as the owners' private domestic living quarters. All these terms used to describe the vast majority of small firms in the sector have merit, and tend to reflect different facets of many small firms operating in hospitality and tourism.

Key point 3.4

Individuals running tenanted and leased pubs and franchisees, as well as, independent firms, frequently reflect lifestyle firm characteristics. That is, motives which are not always primarily concerned with profit maximization and growth.

Clearly, micro-firm reflects a concern with the relative size of the firm when compared with other firms in the sector. Research quoted later (Lashley and Rowson, 2007) shows that many hotels, for example, are run by individuals supported by family and friends, Large numbers of hotels in Blackpool are operated by an owner manager with few, if any employees. Most, though not all, are run by families, or at least by individuals who call on children and other relatives to work in the business as demand and the 'season' require. They are as Getz *et al.* (2004) suggest family businesses with varying degrees of engagement with family. In larger firms, family members have formal jobs and roles which contribute to the services being offered by the firm, and in smaller ones they may help out as and when needed. In many cases, they are 'commercial' homes where customers and family members live under the same roof, though with variations in the degree they share the same rooms. In some cases, 'Private' notices keep commercial guest away from rooms being used by family members. In other cases, commercial guests and family members share common sitting rooms, dining facilities and bathrooms. To varying degrees they will not be economically entrepreneurial firms.

In many cases, economic motives for business ownership are secondary to motives based primarily in a desire to live in a particular location, or to enjoy more personal control over work, or to avoid labour market problems. In this latter case, gender based, ethnic based or age based prejudices practiced by some employers can be avoided through self employment through the lifestyle firm. A point being developed later, is that hospitality services in the form of accommodation, pub restaurant settings provide business opportunities which appear to enjoy low barriers to entry and which appear to require skill sets shared by all those who have offered hospitality to family and friends. These links between private domains of hospitality and decisions to start up businesses in commercial hospitality can be further understood through research into owners of small hotels in Blackpool (Lashley and Rowson, 2007).

Blackpool's hotel sector is dominated by micro-firms usually managed by owner managers operating just one hotel and employing few staff, typically family members often for a few hours per week. Sometimes the owner/manager and partner employ no one and they undertake all the operational tasks themselves. As suggested earlier many of these micro-firms are, to varying degrees, 'lifestyle' business in which personal and lifestyle reasons dominate motives for operating the hotel. In circumstances where motives are clearly not classically entrepreneurial, hotel operators often do not recognise the business skills needed for effective performance (Morrison, 2002). Hence, service quality management; investment, financial and cost management; marketing, people management, and general business strategy, for example, are at best reliant on informal processes, and frequently non-existent (Lashley and Rowson, 2006). As a consequence, there can be a high 'failure' rate of these micro-business hotel operators and an earlier study by Lashley and Rowson (2005) estimates that 20–30 per cent of the hotel stock in Blackpool changes hands each year. Furthermore, the low skill base of hotel owners also limits the quality experiences of services provided to visitors.

Following on an earlier pilot study (Lashley and Rowson, 2005) a survey based on responses from 120 small hotel operators (Lashley and Rowson, 2007) found that just 12 hotels had 20 or more rooms and only 43 (35.8 per cent) employed any staff. Most of these hotel owners undertook the cleaning, cooking and other accommodation service task themselves, or with occasional help of children, parents or other relatives, 'Who live with us'. Most had bought the property after selling a domestic property (99/120–82 per cent). Just 13 (13.8 per cent) had moved to the hotel from the ownership of another hotel and 8 from another business (6.7 per cent). BP 050 reported "*I was a truck driver and lived in Somerset we had a 3 bed roomed house, I was fed up with my job because of being away from my wife and family most of the week, my wife's had this thing about owning a hotel for years now, and we looked*

TABLE 3.3 Funding the purchase of the hotel	
Element	**Number (per cent)**
Sale of house	39 (32.5)
Sale of business	16 (13.4)
Sale of house and mortgage	38 (31.7)
Sale of house and unsecured loan	11 (9.1)
Mortgage	8 (6.6)
Loan	5 (4.2)
Other	3 (2.5)
Total	120 (100.0)

into it and got this hotel in Blackpool. We actually got more money for our house than the hotel cost, but we had a big mortgage on the house, and so when we bought the hotel we had to take a small mortgage but we pay a lot less for this hotel with eight letting rooms than we did for our three bed roomed house'' (p 5). Table 3.3 below shows the sources of finances for those buying small hotels in Blackpool. The high proportion involving the sales of a house confirms that for many, the sale represents move into 'entrepreneurship' rather than a change in entrepreneurial activity.

The Blackpool study showed over 30 per cent of the respondents said that they wanted to work for themselves, with 23.4 per cent saying that they were fed up with their job and wanted to be their own boss. For many respondents, starting in the hotel business as been a life long dream with 25.8 per cent saying that they had wanted to do this for years (see Table 3.4).

Key point 3.5

Many owners of small hotels sell a domestic home prior to buying a hotel. Few have experience of the hotel sector or even small business management.

The following quotations from respondents in the study provide some insights into the motives involved. BP 001 ''My husband was getting fed up with his job and there seemed little future in it, I was working in a dead end, part-time job, and we had talked about having a seaside hotel for years. Anyway we went to see some friends who lived in Blackpool, and we had a look around the place, and noticed how reasonably priced the hotels were, and really it all went from there''. BP 004 ''Redundancy really, my husband was made redundant and we used his redundancy money and the sale of our house to buy the hotel. We had talked about this many times before, but it was

TABLE 3.4 Reasons for buying hotels in the Blackpool study	
Element	**Number (per cent)**
Wanted to work for ourselves	36 (30.0)
Fed up with job decided to be our own boss	28 (23.4)
Wanted to do this for years	31 (25.8)
To avoid unemployment or redundancy	15 (12.5)
Semi retirement	4 (3.3)
Working from home/home with income	6 (5.0)
Total	120 (100.0)

redundancy that finally pushed us this way". BP 020 "This was the only way we could find of running a business were we could work together and basically work from home. Before we worked really hard but barely had enough time together or for our children".

The levels of experience of the respondents varied greatly, of those who claimed to have any previous hotel or business experience, this often amounted to little more than working in a retail business, a pub, or a hotel, very few respondents had actually operated a hotel before, of the 49 (40.8) of respondents who claimed some form of prior experience only 13 (10.8) had any 'real experience' of hotel ownership. Fifty-nine percent of respondents had no business or hotel experience at all when they started in their hotels (see Table 3.5).

There was a common perception amongst the respondents that few skills were required to operate a hotel and that most of it was just 'common sense', as the following quotes illustrate, BP 118 "I've no experience myself but my wife's worked in bars and as waitress for years and she's very good at dealing with people". BP 114 "No experience at all, but my son works in catering he's a chef (when asked if he worked in the hotel). No, he doesn't he works in London but he has given us a lot of tips about commercial cooking that have been useful". BP 109 "We had business experience, but no catering or hotel

TABLE 3.5 Prior experience of hotel owner respondents	
Element	**Number (per cent)**
Prior hotel or business experience	49 (40.8)
No hotel or business experience	71 (59.2)
Total	120 (100.0)

TABLE 3.6	Reasons for entering the hotel business in Blackpool
Five elements	**Number (per cent)**
We had wanted to do this for some time/dream of ours	38 (31.7)
This was business where we could work together	16 (13.3)
This is an easy to start business, with no skills needed	33 (27.5)
This is a home with a income	33 (27.5)
Total	120 (100.0)

experience, it came as a bit of shock for a week or too when we started in the hotel. In the end our business experience did come through, but the first few weeks were a tough time".

The significant majority of respondents' explained their decision to buy a Blackpool hotel around *lifestyle* issues such as, a 'our dream for years', wanting to work together, to have an home with an income, and the majority felt that it was easy to start business which required no particular skills (see Table 3.6).

Many of the respondents thought that having a house with a income was a good idea the following illustrates this point, BP 050 *"Because this business is a 'house, home and job rolled into one' that was our motivation, plus I was fed up with driving trucks for a living and being away from home all the time. My wife hated her job, and so this was a way out for us, and meant that we could be our own boss and have a less stressful life. BP 073 "I liked the idea that we would have a home that would pay for itself and provide us with jobs".*

A significant majority of respondents said that Blackpool was their favourite place and often the decision to buy a hotel in Blackpool was driven by good holiday memories from the past, in many cases this was the hoteliers' childhood visits to the seaside. Thirty-five per cent of respondents said that they had chosen Blackpool because of the long season and 24 per cent cited the cheap hotel prices. There was some overlap between the choices with many citing the long season, cheap hotel prices and the busiest seaside resort as reasons. Respondents' first choices are recorded (see Table 3.7).

Eighty-eight percent of the hoteliers said that both they, and their partner, worked in the hotel business and that this was there sole business. Twenty-six per cent did work or have business interests outside of the hotel. This was typically some form of full-time paid employment Table 3.8.

Twenty-nine of 120 respondent hoteliers (24.1 per cent) in this study were considering or planning to sell their hotels, some with mixed feelings. Those planning to sell up and move out of the current hotel often expressed mixed motives for selling their current. Whilst 5/29 declared they were selling their

TABLE 3.7 Reasons for selecting Blackpool

Element	Number (per cent)
Long season	42 (35.0)
Cheap hotel prices	29 (24.2)
Busiest UK seaside resort	15 (12.5)
We like Blackpool	34 (28.3)
Total	120 (100.0)

TABLE 3.8 Work and business interests outside the hotel

Element	Number (per cent)
We both work in the hotel	88 (73.4)
Working or business outside the hotel	32 (26.6)
Total	120 (100.0)

current hotel so as to buy a bigger hotel, and some declared that they planned to retire 8/29 the majority were disposing of the hotel for negative reasons. Table 3.9 shows that 13 respondents mention poor trade as a reason to sell, seven declared the hotel business had not met their expectations and a further six felt that customers were the problem. Responses are shown as percentages of the 29 respondents planning to sell the hotel at the end of the 2006 season. This represents 24.2 per cent of the 120 respondents in the survey.

BP 006''*We are planning to sell up. The customers are getting worse. We used to have really decent people booking but now it is all 'bell ringers' and you never know what you'll get. Recently we had a family group come to the door they looked really respectable, and 'conned me' by saying that they usually*

TABLE 3.9 Declared reasons for selling the hotel

Declare reason	Number (per cent) (n=29)
Poor trade	13 (44.8)
Not meeting expectations	7 (24.1)
Customers	6 (20.1)
Retirement	8 (27.6)
Buying a bigger hotel	5 (17.2)
Other	2 (6.7)

booked but couldn't get in at the hotel were they normally stayed, they were excellent guests, complements about the food and the room, but when they left they took everything that wasn't nailed down with them, sheets, towels, table lamps, pictures off the wall, I called the police but it appears that they give false details when they booked, they even 'nicked some of my ornaments from the lounge. We were thinking about selling up and this really has made up our minds''. **BP 051** *''We both really wanted this so badly when we started it was our dreams come true, but over the last two seasons it has turned into a nightmare, this place is a 'money pit' we always seem to be spending on it. Really we haven't made any money since we moved in and now I have lost interest and we want to sell up, trade is dropping for family hotels in this area because of the 'stags and hens', the centre is almost a 'no go area' at weekends now with the single groups all over the place drunk at lunchtime, peeing in the street, a few weeks back I drove through the centre of Blackpool at 3 pm in the afternoon and it was packed with single sex groups most of them drunk, and I couldn't believe my eyes I saw a group of girls exposing themselves across the road to a gang of lads, and there were families about at the time I couldn't believe what I had just seen''.*

Key point 3.6

There is a significant churn in small business ownership each year in the hospitality and tourism sector as the realities of pub, hotel or restaurant ownership become realized.

The level of churn in hotel ownership identified here appears to be consistent with observations by professionals in Blackpool's Tourism sector (Lashley and Rowson, 2006) who suggested that the level of turnover in ownership ranged between 20 and 30 per cent. In the original study 10 case study hotels were in their first year of trading in 2005. By 2006 seven of these were in the same hotel. One had sold the hotel and moved to another hotel in North Wales, the other two had sold the hotel and decided that the hotel business was not for them. Again this indicates around 30 per cent churn. Given the estimated number of hotels in Blackpool it is possible that something like 160–230 hotels are changing hands in Blackpool each year. Assuming that the average hotel is valued at £250,000 the value of this churn in ownership is in the region of £40–£60 million per annum. This represents a conservative estimate of the property transactions, it takes no account of the commissions paid to estate agents, solicitors and banks or of the losses incurred by some hotel operators who find trade less buoyant than anticipated or that they have bought a 'money pit'. Nor do these figures take account of the potential lost custom generated by the merry go round of hotel ownership with some hotels having a new owner every year (Lashley and Rowson, 2005).

Reflective practice 3.2

Consider the difficulties faced by a destination management team faced with large numbers of the hotel estate in the destination owned by lifestyle entrepreneurs.

Why do hospitality sector businesses hold such appeal for lifestyle entrepreneurs?

A key aspect of research into small firms in the hospitality sector is the link between the small firm, the domestic domain and hospitality as a business activity. The fact that commercial hospitality involves the sale of accommodation, food and drink which are provided in the home and have been supplied to guests in the home suggests to many of these entrepreneurs that the skills sets are low and it is 'just common sense'. This point was confirmed one of the interviewees in the Blackpool study he said, (BP 056) *"We wanted to start in business and this seemed like a way that we could, we had the money to buy the hotel from the sale of our house and you don't need any special skills, really it's just being level headed and using your common sense"* (Lashley and Rowson, 2007). The fact that a large number of operators churn ownership, perhaps suggests that these estimates of their skill base and the skills required to successfully operate a hotel are woefully out of step. Certainly these links between having been guests and hosts in private life do suggest to many individuals that they have the skills for successful commercial operation. This seems to create a constant stream of people keen to run a bar, a hotel or a restaurant as form of retirement or perhaps disengagement with the world of paid employment. The notion that operators can work at home is an attractive one for many of these individuals.

The opportunity to offer hospitality to fellow human beings is also an attraction for some individuals. Sweeney's interviews with small hotel operators in Scotland confirmed the attractiveness of the hospitality business for many would be entrepreneurs. Her study shows that there are a range of degrees of interest in hospitableness. Figure 3.3 presents the continuum of motives for the hoteliers in her study. On one extreme individuals are running hotels for chiefly economic reasons. These are people who have no particular

Economic	**Eco-social**	**Socio-economic**	**Social**

FIGURE 3.3 *Typologies of Commercial Home Ownership.*
Source: Adapted from Sweeney (2008).

attachment to the hotel business other than as a source of income. At the other end there are people who run hotels because they offer the opportunity to be hospitable, and the economics issues deemed to be less important. There are then two other positions where the motives are primarily economic but hospitableness is important to the operators; and others for whom the hospitableness is primarily important though they have concerns about economic dimensions of the operations Figure 3.3.

These links between the entrepreneur, the home and social opportunities is one of key attractions for many who enter the accommodation, bar of restaurant business. Many interviewees in the Blackpool hotel study (Lashley and Rowson, 2007) refer to customers as friends or wishing to attract 'nice people' as customers. In some cases, entrepreneurs complained about the nature and character of the customers. There were examples of customers who were the 'wrong sort' being turned away the business failing as a result.

Key point 3.7

Given the close proximity of the commercial activity and the home, many hospitality small firm owners evaluate the customers from the perspective of friendship. Are they people like us is a frequently asked question?

SUMMARY

This chapter has suggested the enterprise and entrepreneurship is more complex than might be initially thought. Whilst many commentators often imply that entrepreneurs are the key to business development, employment growth and economic success, there are clearly many running hospitality and tourism whose motives are not so focused on economic outcomes. The industry has its examples of classic entrepreneurs creating and managing multi-site bar, hotel and restaurant empires, Ray Croc of McDonald's; Conrad Hilton of the Hilton group; and Richard Branson of Virgin Air and Virgin trains, amongst other things. The scale and magnitude of these corporate enterprises means, that in most national and international markets, a small number of firms dominate large sections of the market.

However, the majority of firms running bars, hotels and restaurants are owned and managed by individual firms operating just one bar, hotel or restaurant. In some cases, these small firm operators, like their corporate counterparts, are primarily driven by economic outcomes and the potential for business growth. That said, many of these bar, hotel and restaurant operators are not primarily concerned with economic outcomes, they are more concerned with a cluster of personal outcomes from entrepreneurship. Personal circumstances which push, or pull, them into entrepreneurial (Sweeney, 2008) activity are more important. In effect these are lifestyle entrepreneurs who become the owners and operators of a bar, hotel or restaurant business because it primarily allows them to meet personal, social goals or escape disadvantageous economic circumstance.

The chapter also suggested that the hospitality sector is attractive to many of the lifestyle entrepreneurs because the linkage between domestic hospitality and commercial hospitality persuades many that they have the skills needed to succeed. In some cases, the physical proximity of the commercial and the home suggests that the business will enable closer relationships because they do not need to 'go out to work'. In other cases, say in migrant communities, the sharing of the traditional skills of home cuisine is seen as easy entry into the commercial world. In other cases, the seeming common sense of the hospitality offer convinces that they know what to do. Often this fails to recognise the commercial and business skills required for successful small firm management, and as a consequence many of those who enter the sector as first time lifestyle entrepreneurs do not survive in the long-run.

CHAPTER 4

Creativity and the Entrepreneur

After working through this chapter you should be able to:

■ Define creativity in an entrepreneurial context
■ Recognize the relationship between creativity and innovation
■ Understand the role creativity plays in the entrepreneurial process
■ Understand why idea generation is important to the hospitality entrepreneur

INTRODUCTION

Creativity exists in a number of forms and contexts; artists, poets, musicians and even architects might be considered as individuals who personify the term. Most people would agree that creativity is an essential attribute of the entrepreneur. It is both an asset and a process and the outcome can never be predicted accurately. In the hospitality industry, evidence of entrepreneurial creativity can be observed virtually everywhere. It is embodied in a myriad of company logos such as the two 'Ms' (MacDonald's) and Australia's 'Big 4 holiday parks' and the architectural design of hospitality and restaurant buildings like Novotel and Pizza Hut. However, large firms do not have a monopoly on creativity. Indeed given the relative lack of resources enjoyed by small firms, entrepreneurial creativity becomes even more important as a competitive tool and may be seen in many small hospitality firms striving to establish a distinctive character or brand. These points of differentiation may not be as easily recognizable as their larger counterparts (for obvious reasons) but they exist nonetheless. For example the way a building is painted, furnished and fitted are all expressions of creativity, so too are menus, styles of service and tariff structures. The point being that creativity in the small hospitality sector is often modest and may even use and build upon the ideas of others. This is especially true in a monopolistic business environment where many other similar firms are competing for business.

The following case provides a business example of what may be considered by some as modest creativity.

Creativity and the Freewheeling Entrepreneurial Spirit

By Nancy Chesworth, PhD

In 1987, Philip and Cathy Guest carefully considered the decision to turn a favourite sport into a business. In essence, it was a lifestyle choice. Recognizing that their working lives were taking them in different directions, the couple decided to put their relationship first, and became their own employers. The decision to find and operate the business was a very rational one. Both partners listed what they wanted out of life and reached the conclusion that cycle touring was the obvious choice.

Along with cycling for pleasure and mountain biking, Cathy was an experienced cycle racing enthusiast. Philip also enjoyed cycling and brought a wealth of experience as an adventure traveller. In addition, they were accustomed to organizing trips for family and friends. Ultimately, this combination led to the purchase of ten, top quality, state of the art bicycles, and Freewheeling Adventures was born.

Philip describes the venture as an 'educated gamble'. Among the early challenges were financing and finding a way to make a living while building a business. An optimist tempered by reality, he stated that a key factor was remaining confident that it could work, while not really knowing if it would. Another important issue for the couple was remaining financially independent. They avoided taking out loans or applying for government assistance, preferring instead to use savings, to mortgage their house, and later sell it, when a more desirable property became available. Meanwhile, Philip learnt carpentry skills and found a great deal of work refurbishing the interiors of yachts stored at local marinas. Cathy utilized her marketing knowledge to work promoting local businesses and charities.

The tourism season in Nova Scotia is short, thus, it was necessary to plan for slow but steady growth. This had been achieved through careful planning and dedication to the growth of the business. In many ways, Cathy and Philip epitomize the qualities they looked for in employees. Noting that multiple skills were needed to develop and grow a tourism company, they looked for employees who demonstrated energy, enthusiasm, high-level social skills and a genuine interest in other people as well as innate sales skills and the spirit of entrepreneurship.

Initially, Cathy baked all of the bread and made all of the lunches for each group. Eventually, a local source was found to take over this time consuming job, freeing Cathy to focus on other aspects of the business. Other local providers of various services have been added over the years as needed and when possible, local residents are hired as guides. Situated in the small rural community of Hubbards, with their home and business at the same location, this support of the local community, together with their two active sons, has made their property a sort of social centre. The addition of a skateboarding half- pipe provided the opportunity for their sons to learn carpentry skills as well as provide a safe and welcoming recreational opportunity for the boys and their friends.

In the past twenty years, kayaking trips have been added in the local area where the scenery, seals, sea birds and the occasional whale enhance the experience. Multi-sport adventures include combinations of cycling, hiking and kayaking. Van support is offered on all group trips, other than self-guided tours. Tours are offered for cyclists at every level of fitness and experience so as to enable anyone to participate. Accommodation is normally in comfortable inns that reflect the ambiance of the area. But some surprises await. Some accommodations are in castles and chateaux, adding a touch of elegance to the adventure. In the same vein, nutrition is carefully planned with healthy snacks and good quality restaurants part of the experience.

Making the business into a full-time, year round operation meant considering locations in other countries. As a result, Freewheeling Adventures now offers guided and self guided tours around the world in a wide variety of terrains. Each adventure is fully described both on-line and in the company's hard-copy brochure. The level of difficulty, an outline of the terrain and details of each adventure help the client make a well-informed choice.

Freewheeling adventures exemplifies the essence of entrepreneurship. The slow and steady growth of the company is the product of dedication, planning, flexibility, commitment and creativity. The result is a profitable business offering high quality adventures to happy, satisfied customers.

Questions

1. What role did creativity play in the founding of Philip and Cathy's original business?
2. What role did it play in establishing subsequent business activities and linked experiences such as kayaking and the provision of accommodation?
3. What role did 'preparation' play in their decision to become self-employed?
4. How innovative are these two entrepreneurs?

Source: Nancy Chesworth

This chapter introduces the notion of creativity and how it applies to the small hospitality entrepreneur. It is defined and considered a key entrepreneurial function. Creative idea generation is outlined together with a discussion of the nature of creativity and whether it is innate or an ability that can be learnt. The chapter continues by exploring stages of the creative process, identifying behavioural enhancers and barriers and concludes with some approaches and techniques designed to develop creative thinking in individuals.

Key point 4.1

The hospitality entrepreneur does not have to be totally original to be creative. Indeed, most creative business ideas are simply modifications of others.

CREATIVITY: TOWARDS A DEFINITION

The word innovation is often used interchangeably with creativity, however there is a difference between the two (see next chapter for a full discussion). In simple terms, both are important for entrepreneurs but innovation is more concerned with the logical steps involved in bringing a creative idea to market. In other words it is the process involved in actualizing creative ideas successfully (economically). Therefore creativity becomes the antecedent of innovation but it is no less important. If the hospitality entrepreneur fails to be creative or later does not implement creative decision-making, the firm will struggle to survive.

Definitions of creativity abound and as such we can conclude it is a tricky thing to be certain about. However, many use the word novel, new or original, for example, Kirby (2003) considers creativity to be the ability to think 'new' things. Similarly, *The Merriam-Webster Online Dictionary* (2008) defines the verb 'create' as:

■ to make or bring into existence something new.

More philosophically, Satre (1943) considers the act of creating as liberating and one where a state of 'nothingness' becomes 'somethingness'. Another thesis considers a creative human as Godlike. This follows the notion that if God is the creator, anyone engaged in the act of creation must therefore become God themselves because they have the power to change their fate. This is achieved by the individual moving beyond a passive resigned preordained existence into the active role of creation. We can see how this resonates with entrepreneurs as presented in Chapter 11 through the personality trait 'locus of control'! Many entrepreneurs truly believe that they alone are responsible for their success; context and good fortune make little or no contribution.

Reflective practice

1. How would you describe the relationship between innovation and creativity?

Leaving aside the above comparison with one deity or another, the link between creativity and entrepreneurship is not new. Schumpeter (1934) first made these assertions around eighty years ago describing the entrepreneur as an heroic creative artist and coining the phrase 'creative destruction'. Many still hold this as a 'truth' (for example, see Berglund, Dahlin, and Johansson, 2007) and consider creativity and the act of creation an essential element of

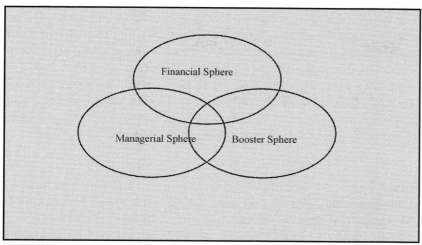

FIGURE 4.1   *The functional spheres of the entrepreneur.*
Source: Guzman (1994).

the entrepreneurial process. For example, Fontela, Guzman, Perez and Santos (2006) adopt Guzman's (1994) to identify creativity within one of three entrepreneurial 'spheres' shown in Figure 4.1.

The financial sphere is where the entrepreneur acts or responds to obligations as the financial owner of the firm. The management sphere concerns corporate direction and management duties. The booster sphere is where the founder assumes a more humanistic psycho-sociological and creative role within the organization.

Key point 4.2

Creativity is the process of generating a novel or useful idea of which opportunity recognition is part.

CREATIVITY: INNATE OR LEARNED

Paradoxically, evidence suggests that as small firms begin to develop and increase in size there is pressure for the entrepreneur to adopt more of a managerial role. Managing a small hospitality firm requires a number of complimentary skills but they are more administrative in nature and concern implementing policies, procedures, controls and so on (see Chapters 7 and 11 for a discussion). Accordingly, there is less time available to engage in creative behaviour (see Pinard and Allio, 2005). Fontela *et al.* (2006) agree that as firms grow entrepreneurial behaviour becomes 'rational' focusing on profit maximization rather than opportunity spotting and creation. However, does this necessarily have to be the case? Whilst there is clearly a requirement for hospitality founders to think logically when managing their business, they must also think laterally. Indeed, according to Fontela *et al.* (2006), founders need to understand that to be creative requires an effort to:

"... become less rational and more emotional" (p. 5).

In other words, in seeking to become creative and forward looking, entrepreneurs must attempt to contextualize their decision-making accordingly. Necessarily, this means that rationality is limited as the future has not yet been 'written' and so cannot be analyzed objectively. Decisions become bounded by uncertainty and as such require entrepreneurs to evaluate problems relying on lateral rather than rational thought processes. Fontela *et al*'s (2006) notion suggests that when hospitality founders think beyond the present they are not bound by rational certainties. Therefore, their capacity for creative effectiveness is enhanced once this is recognized. They also suggest that entrepreneurial thinking shares much with artists and that art is not mysterious but intuitive based on instrumental life experiences. In short, entrepreneurs must learn about ideas and how they are generated.

These authors also introduce the notion of 'intuition' into their argument. Not all commentators do this probably because currently intuition is treated much the same as creativity was some forty years ago. That is, the word has 'unscientific' connotations and cannot therefore be easily explained. Indeed, some argue that innovation is akin to the supernatural which of course also adds an implicit rational reason for not exploring the issue. Whilst we do not discuss intuition in depth here it is still something to note as Fontela *et al.* (2006, p. 8) consider it to be '... part of a legitimate chain of reasoning'. They also argue that in an artistic sense, any creation is a result of intuition if related to a person's intellect and emotions including the entrepreneur in terms of innovation/creativity. Whilst intuition is not fully understood, it is certainly not 'divine' but rather, has a possible fundamental relationship with opportunity spotting and creativity which has yet to be explored in any significant way.

In addition to the earlier definition of creativity *The Merriam-Webster Online Dictionary* (2008) also defines it as:

■ to produce through imaginative skill.

This is interesting as the definition uses the term 'imaginative skill' which suggests that whilst creativity may indeed be innate, it can also be learned. Until recently, this ability was often regarded as somewhat elusive or magical because it did not fit conveniently into logical and rational modes of management theory and practice. De Bono (1971) asserts that whilst creativity is surrounded by an aura of mystery, it remains a skill which can be learned using the appropriate techniques so long as rational and logical thinking are temporarily suspended by the individual. Creativity requires 'lateral' thinking which relies on previous experience and intuition. Essentially, lateral thinking is a way of framing the world, a problem or an issue.

Thus the notion that creativity is something either one has or has not is as ridiculous as the idea that all leaders are born and not made! Intuitively this sounds incorrect and an increasing body of scientific evidence concurs. Nonetheless, people have a natural tendency to think in a certain manner. Much of this depends on upbringing, culture, education and so on. Daft (2005) refers to this bias as a "cognitive difference" (p. 141) explaining it as the differences in the way people perceive and assimilate data, make their decisions and relate to other people. Essentially, the brain has two hemispheres. According to Ornstein (1975) the right side is associated with creativity and intuition and the left with logical analytical thinking. Herrmann (1996) has argued that the brain may be divided into four quadrants rather than two halves:

- Upper left
  - Logical – analytical – fact-based – quantitative

- Lower left
  - Organized – sequential – planned – detailed

- Upper right
  - Holistic – intuitive – integrating – synthesizing

- Lower right
  - Interpersonal – feelings-based – kinaesthetic – emotional

Adapted from Daft (2005, p. 144).

The fact of the matter is that with both the hemisphere and quadrant models the intuitive and logical thinking can still be metaphorically applied to the right and left hand sides of the brain respectively. If the entrepreneur understands her dominant hemisphere or quadrant, that is, how she makes sense of the world, other areas of the brain may be developed. In the present case we have an interest in the creative side of the brain. So can we increase someone's creativity? Well, according to Goodman (1997) and others the answer would seem to be 'yes' and there are a number of techniques available to do so.

Reflective practice

1. Interview a hospitality entrepreneur known to you and ask what role creativity played in their business success.
2. Ask them what they consider the word 'creative' to mean

IDEA GENERATION

To succeed in an ever frenetic and competitive hospitality industry business founders must be energetic, motivated and driven. Necessarily, the creation of new ways of doing things, new knowledge and satisfying customers is an essential skill which entrepreneurs must be able to develop. Indeed in small hospitality firms, creativity is probably the key competitive attribute possessed when vying for business against larger corporations; expensive marketing campaigns would not be possible or effective for example. Creative thinking may therefore be considered

> "... a core business skill and effective entrepreneurs lead the way in applying and developing that skill" (Zimmerer and Scarborough, 2002, p. 37).

Thus, hospitality entrepreneurs stand or fall by their capacity to create. Creativity comes in a number of guises and may not necessarily concern the invention of totally new services and products but may be a reconfiguration of resources and other inputs to develop, modify or customize existing commercial products. Is it easy to be creative? 'Yes' and 'no'; most people are, they just need a nudge to think about issues, situations and problems differently. Interestingly, few of us are exceptionally creative, around 10 percent are highly creative and 60 percent have moderate ability in this area (Morris, 1996).

The following case illustrates the role of prior knowledge on creativity and also provides implicit comment on whether 'degrees' of creativity are sufficient for business success.

Identifying Opportunities

It was spotting a gap in the market that gave Laurence Beere the impetus to open the Queensberry hotel in Bath four-and-a-half years ago. He knew the city well, having worked for the Savoy Group as operations director and having had a two-and-a-half-years stint as general manager of Bath's five-star Royal Crescent hotel. But when the Savoy Group sold up to Von Essen hotels, he took redundancy and found himself thinking about opening his own hotel.

Bath, he says, was an obvious location, not simply because he and his family were based there, but because he reckoned he knew what sort of property the city lacked. What he had in mind was a boutique hotel, combining modern design with an affordable price tag to appeal to a slightly younger clientele. He explains: "I knew the market well and there wasn't much competition - and still isn't - as Bath tends to deliver that chintzy, traditional style. I felt there was a real opportunity for something young and fresh."

Getting finance from the bank proved trickier than he had imagined, though. Beere says: "I was quite naive about what the banks wanted and, looking back, I'd advise using a broker, as it can save a lot of time."

To make an impact on Bath's competitive dining scene, they decided to refurbish the hotel's restaurant first, updating the decor and adding a bar, rather than upgrading less visible areas such as bedrooms. Doing this, he says, also earned the hotel valuable PR, which in turn paid off across the business. Occupancy is 83%, up from 69% when they bought the hotel.

"Plenty of people didn't think we were doing the right thing," Beere admits. "Our older guests looked at us as if we were young whippersnappers, changing what they were used to, but we always knew that the market was there to support it."

That understanding of a changing marketplace was something that spurred on Wendy Bartlett and Ian Mitchell when they set up their contract catering firm, Bartlett Mitchell. Bartlett feels that, as former Compass employees with years in the industry, they were well placed to develop their own niche. Bartlett also feels the company, as a smaller operator is able to adapt to new trends more readily than some of its competitors, keeping it ahead in the industry. "The sector has really changed in the past 10 years," she says. "Nowadays, people look for added value and passion - whether it's boutique hotels, retail or contract catering - and that's a big challenge for some of the bigger, more cumbersome firms."

Questions

1. Discuss the role played by prior knowledge in the success of Laurence Beere's Queensberry Hotel.
2. Comment on how it impacted on his creativity.

Sources: Caterer & Hotelkeeper, August 16, 2007, Institute of Hospitality eJournal Collection, Gale, Institute of Hospitality 28 Apr. 2008 & www.christie.com

---

Reflective practice

1. Interview a hospitality entrepreneur known to you and ask how they decided upon their original business idea.
2. Has their business changed since it started?
3. If yes, inquire how and why.

How Much is Too Much?

How creative does one need to be? This is difficult to answer but given that most small hospitality firms are under capitalized; the relative economy of lateral thinking and ability to create new innovations cannot be overstated. This applies to both individual firms and the sector as a whole. There are several self awareness tests available which help to determine one's inherent creative ability. Their reliability and robustness do not form part of this chapter, however, one should always exercise caution when using such diagnostic instruments. Figure 4.2 is an example of one such test.

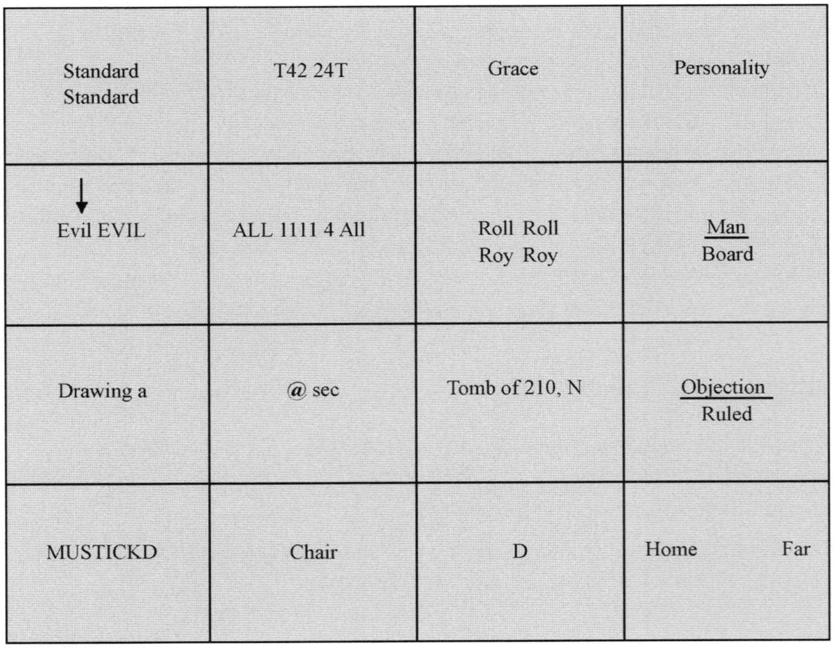

Standard Standard	T42 24T	Grace	Personality
↓ Evil EVIL	ALL 1111 4 All	Roll Roll Roy Roy	Man Board
Drawing a	@ sec	Tomb of 210, N	Objection Ruled
MUSTICKD	Chair	D	Home Far

FIGURE 4.2 *Recognition of common phrases represented as symbols.*
Adapted from: Zimmerer and Scarborough (2002, p. 40).

After reviewing the evidence, Robbins (2005) concludes that most people have the capacity for creativity so long as they are stimulated in the right way. He proposes that creativity is a function of:

■ Intrinsic motivation – the desire to apply oneself to a job because it is inherently interesting and satisfying;
■ Creative-thinking skills – personality characteristics associated with creativity including intelligence, independence, self-confidence, risk-taking, locus of control and a tolerance for ambiguity; and
■ Expertise – when the required technical ability, knowledge and other proficiencies are present in the individual.

Adapted from Robbins (2005).

The following extract from an address by astrophysicist and Nobel Laureate Padma Vibhushan Subrahmanyan Chandrasekhar illustrates the role of expertise in the creative process:

Shakespeare's education was simple, as Elizabethan education was. While it sufficed and stood him in good stead, Shakespeare was never persuaded by scholarship as such. Even so, when Shakespeare arrived in London in 1587, at the age of twenty-three, he had none of the advantages of a London background that Lodge and Kyd had, or the advantages of years at Oxford or Cambridge that Peele, Lyly, Greene, Marlowe, and Nashe had. There can be little doubt that Shakespeare was acutely aware of his shortcomings and his handicaps. He overcame them by reading and absorbing whatever came his way. The publication of the revised second edition of Holinshed's Chronicles of England, Scotland, and Ireland, was particularly timely: it provided Shakespeare with the inspiration for his chronicle plays yet to come (Chandrasekhar, 2001).

It is of course extremely important for the hospitality entrepreneur to keep abreast of all related business news and economic and political trends. Before engaging in techniques designed to enhance personal and organizational creativity, the entrepreneur needs to prepare. This is essential for anyone wishing to develop and enhance personal and organizational creativity. Kirby (2003) agrees noting that full benefits will only accrue if the entrepreneur indulges in:

■ reading,
■ attending associated conferences and trade events,
■ networking,
■ developing skills of listening,
■ questioning, and

■ becoming self-aware, that is, what skills does the entrepreneur possess and what does she need to do to bridge knowledge gaps.

Fontela *et al.* (2006) agree and the main characteristics of their 'Booster Sphere' in Figure 4.1 are consistent with Kirby's notion of preparation:

■ Motivation;
■ ambition;
■ innovation;
■ cooperation; and
■ proactivity.

Essentially, the entrepreneur must be motivated to create an ideal internal knowledge base and develop linked attitudes and behaviours in order to capitalize on their future creativity. Whilst subsequent 'good' ideas may appear to be spontaneous, the individual responsible with have engaged in a specific process; some stages of which are deliberate and others such as certain elements of incubation and illumination are not. This process of creativity is shown in Figure 4.3.

Whilst the above appears to follow a logical and orderly sequence, the reality is somewhat different. The creative process tends to be less systematized and more recursive. There are no set time limits (save self-imposed ones) and the entrepreneur may not always engage in every stage. Much will depend on the context, competing work pressures and the degree of expertise the individual already possesses in the field of creativity. For example, one person may be inherently more creative than another or may be more practiced at the process.

Key point 4.3

There is no secret to creativity; it can be learned. However, there is no substitute for sound preparation such as background reading and acquisition of related knowledge from other areas. This will help increase the chances of generating creative yet practical ideas.

Many of the above stages are illustrated in the following case but there is an emphasis on 'preparation'.

Close Contest (Management of Entrepreneurs).

By Emma Allen

Successful entrepreneurs rely on more than just flair to build their businesses. Most do a lot of local research, while some even set up on their former employer's doorstep.

Someone new to the area might have thought that the Lygon Arms (left) had the market sewn up in Broadway, but his local knowledge meant that Barry Hancox could see the gap in the market that allowed him to open his own venture, Russell's.

As any successful entrepreneur will tell you, one of the tricks to setting up a thriving business is to do your research first. However, no amount of investigation can beat having strong local knowledge built up by first-hand experience working in the area where you intend to buy. Knowing who your customers are, understanding trading patterns and, crucially, knowing whether there are any unfilled gaps in the local market will all give you a competitive edge. For hotelier Barry Hancox, being able to take advantage of all of these helped to establish his new venture when he opened Russell's, a restaurant with seven rooms in the quaint Worcestershire village of Broadway, nearly three years ago. The move was more a change of view than a relocation for Hancox. Before taking on Russell's, he had been general manager at the four-star Lygon Arms hotel, just 200 yards up the road, where he had worked for 16 years.

While Hancox hadn't planned it, having such a detailed understanding of the local market was, he says, invaluable. Not that the idea was to create a second Lygon Arms. He and his business partner, Andrew Riley – who previously owned the Broadway hotel, in the same village – had a clear vision of what they thought the market needed, and their focus was on a much more contemporary feel than the more traditional Lygon. Hancox explains: "We knew the village needed a good restaurant, and that people were looking for decent food without the stuffiness - we got in just at the right time. And because we had this huge space up-stairs, we decided to add bedrooms. The concept just snowballed."

There have been clear advantages, however, such as being on the spot to secure the site – an old design workshop on the village high street. Hancox and Riley say that understanding seasonal fluctuations in a touristy area was enormously helpful in their early days, while having good corporate contacts has been useful for building midweek trade. They both also feel that raising finance would have been much more difficult without their combined local knowledge. We weren't seen as such a risk."

Hancox also reckons that in some respects he and Riley have a bit of an edge over the Lygon Arms. "The Lygon never got that involved with the local trade," he explains. "It was probably seen as a bit intimidating, a bit stuffy, but we've always had strong support, which you need in a small place like this." Part of that has been down to well-pitched pricing, such as the restaurant's early-evening fixed-price dinner menu, which has drawn in the area's "silver" clientele. The accommodation is also doing well, with all seven rooms fully booked at weekends throughout the summer.

Questions

1. List and comment upon the preparation undertaken by Barry Hancox.
2. How did this impact upon his ability to be 'creative'?

Source: Caterer and Hotelkeeper, August 16, 2007.
COPYRIGHT 2007 Reed Business Information Ltd.

- Preparation

Formal education, training, experience, open mind, life-long learning perspective, open discussion with colleagues and interested others, join interest groups and trade associations, develop listening skills.

- Investigation

Develop sound understanding of the issues or problem.

- Transformation

Using convergent and divergent thinking to appreciate the similarities and differences between items under study by revisiting, rearranging and iteration.

- Incubation

Remove yourself from the problem to allow subconscious to work on problem. My PhD supervisor always used to say, 'If you come across an obstacle or 'write's block' go for a long walk on a windy hill'. It usually worked! Creativity can rarely be tapped when under pressure to generate new ideas.

- IIIumination

Happens some time during the earlier stage, known as the 'Eureka' factor. Many successful artists and musicians experience this whilst contemplating other unrelated things and even whilst in a state of dreaming.

- Verification

Validating the idea through successful pilots, protoypes, new menu items, new inclusive tour packages, new ways of satisfying customers, new operations and food production procedures and so on.

- Implementation

Transformation of idea into a viable reality

FIGURE 4.3 *The creative process.*
Adapted from: Zimmerer and Scarborough (2002, pp. 52–55).

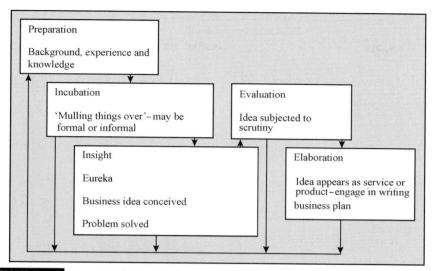

FIGURE 4.4   *Creative idea generation.*
Adapted from: Barringer and Ireland (2006, p. 38).

Similar to the above figure, Barringer and Ireland (2006) also consider creativity as a process noting that successful founders have the ability to recognize opportunities. They argue that creativity is the process of generating a novel or useful idea of which opportunity recognition is part and may therefore also be a creative process; this is shown in Figure 4.4.

Here the process is also viewed systematically moving from preparation to final elaboration with appropriate feedback loops. It also tacitly acknowledges that creativity is enhanced by the entrepreneur's prior experience, cognition, ability to network and their knowledge of the area. This makes absolute sense, for example, how can a chef patron create new and exciting dishes without understanding current eating out trends, fashionable menu items, what her market will stand and how to cook?

It is one thing for the hospitality founder to be creative when their business is small but quite another to maintain and encourage creativity in others as the hotel grows. Several 'creative' strategies and ideas can be implemented to keep the hospitality founder and her employees motivated. Figure 4.5 shows a number of key individual and organizational enhancers and detractors.

In addition to the specifics of the creative process shown in Figures 4.3 and 4.4, the above are other behaviours in which the hospitality entrepreneur may engage. These are designed to optimise individual creativity and to establish an organizational culture that incubates and perpetuates similarly across the whole firm. Many of the enhancers and barriers to creativity are

```
┌─────────────────────────────────────────────────────────────┐
│              Enchancers of creativity                        │
│  ┌──────────────────────────┐ ┌───────────────────────────┐ │
│  │ Individual               │ │ Organization              │ │
│  │ • Deal with employees as │ │ • Promote creativity at   │ │
│  │   equals                 │ │   org. level              │ │
│  │ • Speak with people you  │ │ • Establish diverse       │ │
│  │   do not usually have    │ │   labour force            │ │
│  │   the chance to          │ │ • Resource creativity     │ │
│  │ • Speculate, be open and │ │   training and reward     │ │
│  │   build on ideas of      │ │   novelty                 │ │
│  │   others                 │ │ • Model creativity        │ │
│  │ • Protect those who make │ │ • Support champions       │ │
│  │   honest mistakes        │ │ • Use diverse teams       │ │
│  │ • Embrace ambiguity      │ │ • Discourage written      │ │
│  │ • Recognize more than    │ │   proposals and replace   │ │
│  │   one solution           │ │   with protoypes and      │ │
│  │                          │ │   pilots                  │ │
│  │                          │ │ • learn fromother firms   │ │
│  │                          │ │   and adapt               │ │
│  └──────────────────────────┘ └───────────────────────────┘ │
│               Barriers to creativity                         │
│  ┌──────────────────────────┐ ┌───────────────────────────┐ │
│  │ Individual               │ │ Organization              │ │
│  │ • Pessimism, criticism,  │ │ • Not hiring creative     │ │
│  │   being judgmental       │ │   people                  │ │
│  │ • Being cynical or       │ │ • Intolerance of          │ │
│  │   negative               │ │   alternative behaviours  │ │
│  │ • Punishing mistakes or  │ │ • Reliance on former      │ │
│  │   failures               │ │   solutions to earlier    │ │
│  │ • Not engaging in open   │ │   problems                │ │
│  │   dialogue               │ │ • Keeping employees in    │ │
│  │ • Believing you are not  │ │   same job for lengthy    │ │
│  │   creative               │ │   periods                 │ │
│  │ • Focusing on logic and  │ │                           │ │
│  │   being practical        │ │                           │ │
│  │ • Fearing looking foolish│ │                           │ │
│  │ • Viewing play as        │ │                           │ │
│  │   frivolous              │ │                           │ │
│  └──────────────────────────┘ └───────────────────────────┘ │
└─────────────────────────────────────────────────────────────┘
```

FIGURE 4.5   *Barriers and enhancers: creativity.*
Adapted from: Barringer and Ireland (2006) and Kirby (2003).

intuitive and therefore not problematic to identify. Therefore with careful planning, they could be applied in small hospitality organizations without too much difficulty. Moreover, creative behaviours are not difficult to master and a number of techniques and exercises are available in several formats ranging from self-help to consultancy workshop formats.

Key point 4.4

In order to enhance creativity in the workplace the entrepreneur must develop an appropriate culture through engagement with employees and modelling the desired behaviours.

APPROACHES AND TECHNIQUES

It is important to recognize that thousands of people come up with thousands more ideas every day, not all are successful, nor will they be pursued. Entrepreneurs must therefore not only be creative but also innovative so that the idea may be applied and realize its full potential. In simple terms, creativity becomes the thinking part whereas innovation is the doing or undertaking of a creative idea. Innovation, its relationship with creativity and role within the creative process are discussed further in Chapter 5. Moreover, being creative is about more than coming up with one brilliant and insightful idea but rather about creative consistency of the founder and their employees. When hospitality entrepreneurs manage to gain competitive advantage over other organizations through implementing a creative idea it never lasts for long. The composite product (accommodation, food and beverage) is rather limited and there are only so many configurations available to the customer. It therefore becomes increasingly difficult to think of creative ways to secure business. However, the most successful entrepreneurs manage to spot opportunities and exploit them through creative thinking. Indeed, the hospitality industry typically progresses in a uniform manner for given periods of time and then 'spontaniously', someone introduces a new concept which is then adapted and customized by other founders; the pattern repeats itself. For example, the impact of MacDonald's on the restaurant industry was so profound that it gave birth to the fast food industry. Prior to this, diners had produced the same old fare in the same old manner since the turn of the last century. The MacDonald's concept remains vital today and has been adopted and adapted on an almost ongoing basis.

Key point 4.5

In order to be creative, entrepreneurs must develop the ability to think laterally.

Accor's concept and design of the Formula 1 accommodation some twenty years ago was an extension of the traditional Motel. However, the original hotels had an identifiable design with little in the way of luxury. This was entirely appropriate for an increasingly mobile and utilitarian customer base. Since the 1980s the design has been changed regionally to appeal to an international clientele in Belgium, Germany, Great Britain, The Netherlands, Spain, Sweden, Switzerland, South Africa, Australia, Brazil and Japan, but the core underlying principle of this brand remains.

Another example is the early success of 'conveyor belt' or Kaiten-zushi Japanese Sushi restaurants where food is delivered on a conveyor belt akin to a traditional automotive production line process. The original idea was born from a failure to recruit enough suitably qualified restaurant staff. The founder, Yoshiaki Shiraishi, was inspired by observing beer bottles moving around a Japanese brewery. The opening of the first restaurant in the late 1950s was followed a decade after by others numbering over 200. Since then these restaurants have enjoyed spells of popularity but all are based on Yoshiaki's original idea. A more recent and highly successful adaptation is the YO!Shushi chain. Ten years ago the founder British entrepreneur Simon Woodroffe established a number of modern hi-tech sushi restaurants in the UK; eleven more have opened internationally. Now he has diversified into the accommodation sector (YOTEL) and other retail areas. In true entrepreneurial fashion a portion of the YO! Company's website reads:

> *"YO! was always destined to be a retail brand and just happened to be a sushi bar in its first manifestation." (Mark Norton, designer of the original YO! Logo) http://www.yocompany.biz/retrieved May 2008.*

Interestingly, Woodroffe considers his business to be retail-based rather than hospitality oriented. In a sense this has allowed him to think unconventionally and creatively about his next venture which in turn has enhanced his ability to spot opportunities. Currently, his business interests range from restaurants to architecture and construction!

The following case also showcases creativity through opportunity spotting.

How we Got Started

Entrepreneur Margaret Dunford, 63, got her first taste of the licensed property market 27 years ago when she bought the lease to a run-down pub in Aldershot, Hampshire, with her then partner. For the first three months the business didn't make any money. However, having noticed that there were lots of bedsits in the area, Dunford decided to launch a take-out service providing cheap meals. Turnover quickly picked up after that. When the customers brought the plates back they would often stop for a drink. For her next business Dunford bought a house and turned it into a seven-bedroom B&B – "one of the easiest businesses to start" – having persuaded the bank to give her 100% financing.

An early guest at the B&B was a space shuttle engineer who was working on a simulator nearby. He liked it so much that he recommended it to his colleagues and she received a lot of trade from them after that, including the astronaut Bill Shepherd. Demand was such that she persuaded her bank to lend her the funds to open another B&B to cater for them. When the engineers' contract ended some six months later she promptly sold the second property for a profit. But the relationship didn't end there. NASA invited her over to Florida to see a shuttle launch and she would later buy a home and a motel business there.

Three years later Dunford sold the motel for a profit. Other properties followed when she returned to the UK, including a pub in Andover, Hampshire, which she later sold for [pounds sterling] 400,000, making [pounds sterling] 190,000. Her latest venture is the Woodlands Cheese & Cider Barn & Tea Rooms, situated at the foot of Cheddar Gorge, Somerset, which she recently bought through business transfer agent Redwoods. "Most people don't

RESEARCH AND EXERCISES

The ability to generate ideas is a key skill for the hospitality entrepreneur. This is not to say that all will develop into successful business opportunities but becoming practiced in creative techniques is essential. Some approaches are simply data collection procedures such as surveys where information is collected from a sample of individuals. Others focus on the individual through self-development exercises, some examples appear below.

- ■ Research oriented approaches

  - o Surveys

    When using research-oriented data collection approaches the normal protocols apply in order to ensure data is robust and reliable. For example, survey instruments used must be simple and questions should be easy for participants to understand. More fundamentally the sample should be selected randomly and be large enough to permit useful analysis. On the other hand and in a more practical sense, some information is better than none for the small hospitality entrepreneur. Indeed, small operators will not necessarily have the resources available for a full blown scientific survey; in a sense, this is not always appropriate anyway. The hospitality entrepreneur may be considering the introduction of a new menu for their small provincial restaurant. Would a random survey of thousands within a radius of 200 kilometres be appropriate in this instance? Probably not but an existing list of regular patrons could be used to good effect.

  - o Focus groups

    Another method of collecting large amounts of information efficiently is through the use of focus groups. It is normal to have no more than 12 group participants who have an interest in the matter being debated. This format allows open discussion and because it is a 'softer' way to elicit opinions and information, novel ideas will often emerge. The group usually has one or preferably two moderators. One tends to lead the discussion around a few carefully chosen themes whilst the other records the information on a flip chart or takes notes. There is little that cannot be debated in a focus group and the discussions contain much rich qualitative data. Questionnaire surveys do not always deliver data of this quality unless there are hundreds of questions being posed. Forms containing too many questions are cumbersome and therefore of limited value. However, focus groups have some negative associated outcomes if the entrepreneur is inexperienced at coordinating such events. For example, it is easy to miss key items of information due to the richness of the group debate. It is also possible for one or two members to dominate the discussion. Coordinators must be able to identify this behaviour early on in the session and take the appropriate remedial action.

o Other techniques

Approaches like the 'Delphi Technique' use the collective knowledge of industry experts to predict hospitality futures. These individuals would include senior members of allied international, national and regional associations like the World Tourism Association, the UK-based Institute of Hospitality, the Queensland Hotels Association (Australia), advisory board members, family, friends, local Chambers of Commerce and so on.

o Brainstorming

This is a common form of training in creativity and its practice is widespread. These events have the capacity to generate many ideas in a short space of time. The set up is similar to that used in focus groups with a moderator/coordinator, flip chart and so on. The thing which differentiates brainstorming is that no logical evaluation of ideas is permitted. Obviously, there will be some differences depending on context, specific purpose and actors but all forms forbid criticism of anyone's ideas. This is because first, criticism makes use of the non-creative left side of the brain; second, nothing is more effective in stifling ideas than criticism. The purpose during the early part of the session is quantity of ideas rather than quality. The more outrageous or seemingly bizarre ideas sometimes prove to be the most effective stimulators of creativity; carefree expression should be encouraged by the moderator. Sessions should also move along a fast pace, this encourages people to react to ideas of others without having the time to engage logically or rationally.

■ Self-development

These tests and exercises are not definitive but should be considered more as techniques and tools to help the process (making sure you select the most appropriate for the job in hand). For example, the techniques may be divided in to several categories ranging from defining a problem and idea generation to selection and implementation.

o   Boundary examination

An example of a technique designed to help define problems is known as 'Boundary Examination'. Essentially the problem boundary is the container, which separates highly relevant items existing inside the boundary from less relevant ones existing outside the boundary. If the boundary has been provided for you because another person has defined the problem it will be inherently skewed towards their understanding as well as your own. Thus the boundary setting itself may become part of the problem. De Bono (1994) recommends a method designed to bring potentially relevant aspects back into awareness.

- Write down an initial statement of the problem.
- Underline key words.
- Examine each key word for hidden assumptions. A good way to do this is to see how the meaning of the statement changes if you replace a key word by a synonym or near synonym.
- Having explored how the particular choice of key words affects the meaning of the statement, see if you can redefine the problem in a better way.
- The aim is not necessarily to change the position of the boundary but rather to understand more clearly how the wording of the problem is affecting our assumptions about the boundary.

Retrieved from ''http://www.mycoted.com/Boundary_ Examination'', May 2008

o   Talking pictures

Another technique, this time for idea generation is called 'Talking Pictures' (Clegg and Birch, 2008) and is most effective when groups are failing to come up with new business ideas. Individuals should be divided into teams with each being given a digital camera and access to a printer. Allow the teams a short fixed time away from their immediate area and ask to take pictures of unusual objects and from unusual angles. Reconvene the session with all teams and invite to distribute their pictures to the other groups. Advise each team to use the pictures provided to create associations that occur to them and then use these associations for idea generation. At the end of the session you can either collect all of the ideas together by writing them onto flipcharts or you can ask the groups to have listed their own and have these displayed for general perusal.

This technique uses random stimuli as an excursion with the advantage of a challenge/competition thrown in. The humour generated from the unusual objects/angles also raises the energy levels of the group, along with the fact that they have been up and moving about.

Retrieved from ''http://www.mycoted.com/Talking_Pictures'', May 2008

o Other random stimuli examples

Several authors recommend the use of random stimuli of various kinds and a formal approach may look like this:

- Identify your criteria for ideas – e.g. ideas for solving a problem or tackling some aspect of it, an idea to be built on, a hypothesis to be investigated, etc. Spend some time on this stage for better-quality outcomes later.
- Pick a stimulus at random, by looking or listening to everything around you indoors and outdoors, something that catches your attention, opening a newspaper, dictionary, catalogue, book of pictures, throwing a dice at random or any other method that appeals to you.
- You should now relate this random stimulus back to your original problem; this could be done using simple free association.
- On the other hand you could go for a full excursion by describing the stimulus (how it works, what it does, what effects it has, how it is used, size, position, etc.). Followed by 'force-fit' pieces of this. comprehensive description back to the problem to recommend relevant ideas.
- Should a random stimulus fail to work, pick another and keep trying.

■ Combining fixed and random elements

o Choose a specific element of the problem and name it the 'fixed element'.

o Now select a random stimulus via any chosen method and free-associate the way in which these elements could be combined. You can convey these directly to the problem, or use the 2-element combination itself to trigger additional ideas.

o Now select a new random stimulus, repeat the process with the same 'fixed element' and after several cycles of this choose a fresh fixed element and repeat.

■ Select two to three grammatically random stimuli

  o Noun + verb;
  o Adjective + noun;
  o Verb + adverb;
  o Noun + verb + noun.
  o Try to create an unusual phrase, for example if you observed a school and a plane flying overhead, that might yield phrases such as 'flying school' or 'teaching flying'. You could free associate further phrase combinations from the one created so 'flying school' might generate 'elevated learning', and so on.

Retrieved from ''http://www.mycoted.com/Random_Stimuli'', May 2008
Examples of other creativity exercises may be found at the following URLs:
http://www.lifehack.org/articles/lifehack/essential-resources-for-creativity-163-techniques-30-tips-books.html
http://www.brainstorming.co.uk/tutorials/creativethinkingcontents.html
http://www.members.optusnet.com.au/charles57/Creative/Techniques/index.html
http://www.virtualsalt.com/crebook2.htm

Reflective practice

1. Given the frenetic pace at which small hospitality firms operate, discuss how you would maintain personal and organizational creativity whilst engaged in managing the organization?

SUMMARY

Creativity or the ability to think creatively is an essential part of the small hospitality entrepreneur's toolkit. It plays the key role in differentiating one small firm from another. Indeed, it also allows small independent hospitality firms to compete with their larger affiliated counterparts. As such, entrepreneurs must have an innate or learned ability to think laterally and originally if they are to survive in the marketplace. Furthermore, being creative is not a temporary fix but rather a lifelong commitment to ensure the long term sustainable survival of the small hospitality business.

Few individuals are fortunate enough to possess significant amounts of innate creativity. However, evidence suggests that creativity can be learned provided the entrepreneur is motivated to do so and has the required knowledge and field expertise. This may be achieved by careful planning, attention to detail and preparation. Stages typically involved in this process are:

- preparation,
- investigation,
- transformation,
- incubation,
- illumination,
- verification, and
- implementation.

The creative process is not necessarily linear or logical but rather recursive and organic. In fact, the very act of being creative requires the entrepreneur to first think in a lateral fashion. For some this is a challenge as traditionally western management theories promote rational and analytical thought processes using the left hemisphere of the brain.

As small firms grow the founder often becomes compelled to act more as a manager than creator. This inevitable pressure to ensure policies, procedures and controls are in place tends to stifle lateral thinking and all but eradicate creativity. There are a number of simple behaviours in which the entrepreneur can engage to ensure that:

- they remain creative,
- individual workers remain creative, and
- the organization develops and maintains a culture of creativity.

Examples of each include dealing with employees as equals, protecting those who make honest mistakes and embracing ambiguity. The founder should also model creativity, support champions and use diversity in the workforce. Furthermore, the creative entrepreneur should beware of cynicism or negativity, intolerance of high spirits and 'play' in the workplace and relying on former solutions to earlier problems.

Specific techniques designed to promote creative thinking and decision-making are wide ranging but some of the more common ones include collecting stakeholder data via surveys, focus groups and use of Delphi-type techniques from industry experts and associated agencies and other international, national and regional organizations. Each of these approaches must be carefully planned and managed as each has inherent strengths and weaknesses. For example, focus groups are good for collecting qualitative (rich) data but facilitators must be experienced enough to prevent certain participants from dominating others in the session as information will be skewed. Similarly, surveys using questionnaires have the advantage of collecting large amounts of information but it may be of limited value particularly if the form is lengthy. This is because participants tire easily and often fail to take sufficient notice of questions towards the end of the survey. Telephone surveys also suffer from this problem especially if category choices have too many response options. Notwithstanding these challenges, the entrepreneur must ensure any research undertaken is appropriate for their business. Often a simple approach such as visits to competitors establishments may be sufficient for creative inspiration. At a self-development level, many creativity training courses are available should the hospitality entrepreneur wish to take advantage of them.

Case author
Nancy Chesworth
Department of Business and Tourism
Mount St. Vincent University
Canada

Innovation, Opportunity and Protection

After working through this chapter you should be able to:

- Understand the role innovation plays in the entrepreneurial process
- Recognize the relationship between creativity and innovation
- Understand the processes behind spotting opportunities and developing a new idea
- Recognize the importance of protecting intellectual property in the hospitality industry

Bannatyne Concept Hotel Launch

Bannatyne Hotels Ltd. has unveiled plans for an innovative concept in Norwich (UK) where guests can book rooms online for as little as $35 AUD a night.

The hotel, planned for the site adjacent to Bannatyne's Health Club in Thorpe St Andrews, will reverse the discount principle applied to late bookings.

Here, the earlier the booking, the cheaper the room will be.

The company opened its first early booking concept in Durham in early 2007, which is already proving a big hit with business travellers and tourists visiting the North East of England.

> *'Affordability is the key and there are not many hotels that offer guests modern and comfortable accommodation at such low prices,'* says Nigel Armstrong, managing director of Bannatyne Hotels Ltd.

Questions

1. What underpinned this innovation?
2. What role did creativity play in identifying and establishing a new reservations system?
3. Is the new reservations system an incremental or radical innovation?
4. How easy do you think the Bannatyne concept will be to imitate?

Source: Hospitality (2007, p. 8), reproduced with permission

TOWARDS INNOVATION

Most writers in the field of entrepreneurship recognize the importance of innovation in the business cycle, ranging from Schumpeter's (1934) 'creative destruction' thesis (see Chapter 1) to more contemporary individuals like Handy (1990) and Shane (2003). However according to Davila, Epsein and Sheltonet (2006) authors often use the term innovative and creative interchangeably. This suggests that innovation and creativity are linked in some way. Kirby (2003) notes that innovation it is difficult to define because it is a process that could apply across a range of entrepreneurial activities. These may be based on product or process such as the use of high production technology or implementing and observing a process of change. He concludes that innovation is best understood as a series of principles or steps by which an end product or service is created. Amabile, Conti and Coon (1996) lend some support to this idea and consider that:

> '*All innovation begins with creative ideas. . .We define innovation as the successful implementation of creative ideas within an organization. In this view, creativity by individuals and teams is a starting point for innovation; the first is necessary but not sufficient condition for the second*' *(pp. 1154–1155).*

By way of summary two notions of innovation are shown below:

- the successful exploitation of new ideas (*Department of Trade and Industry, UK*).
- A creative idea that is realized [(Frans Johansson)] (Harvard Business School Press, 2004) (http://en.wikipedia.org/wiki/Innovation, 2007)

Both the above suggest that innovation is a process by which creativity is harnessed and transformed. For an individual to be innovative they must first have creative insight and then the ability or tools to exploit the insight for profit. Thus, innovation is more rational than creativity or as Davila *et al.* (2006), write:

> '*Innovation, like many business functions, is a. . .process that requires specific tools, rules, and discipline*' *(p. xvii).*

How important is innovation in the entrepreneurial process? Drucker (1985) leaves us in no doubt and states:

> '*Innovation is the specific tool of entrepreneurs, the means by which they exploit change as an opportunity for a different business or a different service. It is capable of being presented as a discipline, capable*

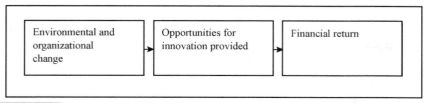

FIGURE 5.1 *The innovation process.*

of being learned, capable of being practiced ... And they need to know and to apply the principles of successful innovation'.

Although Drucker does not mention creativity above, in the present context innovation and creativity are inextricably linked in the entrepreneurial process with the aim of generating a profit. In short, contemporary innovation in organizations is about change. In such a fast-paced global trading environment, innovation is now a necessity rather than an optional extra and together with creativity is crucial elements of the entrepreneurial process. Thus, entrepreneurs should be both creative and innovative and have the ability to think laterally. Innovation is therefore the logical and systematic focus of the process because creative ideas do not automatically succeed nor do they take themselves to market. Drucker (1985) considers innovation as the process of 'opportunity spotting' and something that can be learned and practiced relatively easily because it is logical and systematic; no more, no less. Diagrammatically, it is shown in Figure 5.1.

Although the topic of creativity is dealt with elsewhere in this book, its relationship with innovation and entrepreneurship is worth revisiting.

Kirby (2003) considers that:

'... creativity is the ability to think new things whilst innovation is the ability to do new things' (p. 132).

CREATIVITY AND ENTREPRENEURSHIP

If individuals are to be successful entrepreneurs it seems clear that they need to be creative, innovative and entrepreneurial. This is a tall order because each of these elements require different (but overlapping) abilities and skills. Often, convening groups of individuals with these attributes can improve the chances of fashioning a creative idea into an innovative marketable product. This is

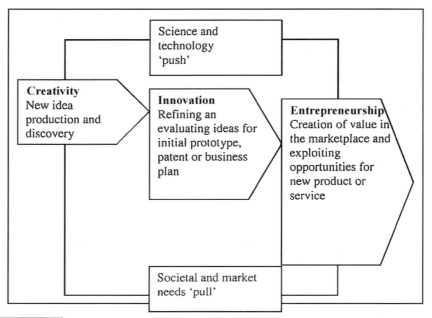

FIGURE 5.2   *A process model of creativity, innovation and entrepreneurship. Adapted from: Schaper and Volery (2004, p. 61).*

something that was recognized very earlier in the career of Bill Gates founder of Microsoft Corporation:

'We were young, but we had good advice and good ideas...Our success has really been based on partnerships from the very beginning.'

Source: http://entrepreneurs.about.com/od/famousentrepreneurs/a/quotations.htm, 2007.

However, whether team or individual-based, this does effect its relationship between with innovation and entrepreneurship. Several models are available and most view this association as a linear logical process as shown below in Figure 5.2.

In reality, the above is a simplified version of the complex interactions between and among the espoused three-stage process. Additionally, two environments areas of push and pull factors impact on creativity, innovation and entrepreneurship. For example, the former might consist of advances in science and technology (drugs, information communications technology and other developments) and the latter a combination of new market needs and societal necessities. For example, the above model helps us map the Landmark Hotel's (Landmark Hotel Company Ltd. UK) adoption of a fully integrated 'chip and Pin' management information solution to improve guest service, time and cost saving.

Pilot Rollout Proves Valuable

The Landmark Hotel Company Ltd. along with the Royal Lancaster and K-West, is one of the capital's exceptional five-star hotels and has been billed as the UK's first major hotel to go live with a fully integrated 'chip and Pin' solution in the hospitality sector.

'When chip and Pin was introduced in the UK in 2003, the card processing industry was simply not ready for hospitality' explains Alastair Brown, systems manager at the Landmark. 'As a result there was a huge amount of planning and testing to be done on already integrated systems which now had to work with chip and Pin.'

'The Landmark is unique in the UK in as much as we are the only major hotel, as yet, to have a fully integrated chip and Pin system for your MICROS-Fidelio property management system' explains Kevin Byrnes, reception manager. 'It is this integrated model which makes it so interesting and different.'

The fully PCI integrated PC-EFT (chip and Pin) solution was installed at the Landmark in February 2007 to handle the entire hotel's card processing – with bars and restaurants to follow at a later date. It is linked to the FidelioV.6 property management system and the MICROS 3700 Point of Sale system is to follow. In turn PC-EFT drives four pin entry devices at the front desk, handling check in and check out.

The solution uses the PC-EFT supervisor model to report on all transactions madder in the hotel providing a complete management and reporting package for the finance and accounting functions.

But both Brown and Byrne acknowledge that this point of difference between the Landmark and other hotels will be short-lived as the companies that installed the system have very long waiting lists.

Questions

1. In terms of creativity, what is the relationship between the Landmark Hotel's management and the manufacturer's of the 'chip and Pin' system?
2. In light of the above, which group is the more creative?
3. How are creativity and innovation linked in this case?

Source: Hospitality (2007, pp. 12–14), Reproduced with permission

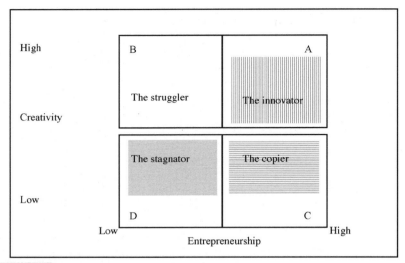

FIGURE 5.3 *Creativity and entrepreneurship.*
Adapted from: Burns (2001, p. 51).

Bolton and Thompson (2000) tie creativity with entrepreneurship as the appropriate context for ideas to become reality. Figure 5.3 helps to clarify their position through a matrix arrangement proposing a relationship between creativity and entrepreneurship.

Here the relationship between creativity, innovation and entrepreneurship is explained in terms of four quadrants. Quadrant B shows the entrepreneur as a struggler. Ideas are rampant but many are 'half-baked' with the individual having little innovative and entrepreneurial ability to turn ideas into marketable commercially exploitable products and services. In quadrant D, the individual has no innate ability to be creative, innovative nor entrepreneurial. In quadrant C, things area little different where the firm is not creative but has the ability to copy and perhaps be incrementally innovative to improve the product or service. Quadrant A is the only one of the four where creativity, innovation and entrepreneurship flourish.

Reflective practice

1. To which quadrant do you think most small and micro hospitality businesses belong? Explain your answer?

IDENTIFYING OPPORTUNITIES

Identifying opportunities for developing ideas is a key ability or skill which entrepreneurs must already have or acquire. Broad influences on opportunity identification include demographic changes, changes of public perceptions through shifting tastes, fashion and culture and new knowledge. Entrepreneurs must continually scan and observe environmental trends if they are to identify upcoming opportunities. Barringer and Ireland (2006) advocate the use of a PEST analysis shown in Figure 5.4 to help entrepreneurs in this quest.

This technique is incredibly powerful for environmental scanning. Obviously, a very detailed information requirement will need extra resources. However, this is a time consuming exercise and many entrepreneurs can instead use the services of dedicated research firms for their benefit. Services vary depending on which firms are used for this purpose but typically they should provide the entrepreneur with access to a wealth of information, opportunities to attend entrepreneurial conferences, lists of potential investors and so on. Rigorous application of such analyses has enabled certain entrepreneurs to flourish whilst others have failed.

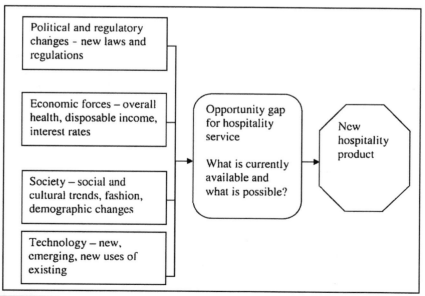

FIGURE 5.4 *PEST analysis for identifying a new hospitality product.*
Adapted from: Barringer and Ireland (2006, p. 31).

> **Hospitality Entrepreneur Leads the 'inn' Crowd**
>
> Years ago, Stephen Zimmerman discovered a formula for success in the volatile hotel business; think big, but stay small – six rooms small, to be exact. Add an exclusive French restaurant that caters to the romantic set, and the recipe is complete.
>
> 'Even with the ups and downs of this business, romance never goes out of style,' says Zimmerman, comfortably perched in the cozy library of his historic hotel, La Colombe d'Or. 'It's romance that sells.' More than two decades later, the formula still seems to be working for Zimmerman, whose European-style chateau has remained one of the most sought-after restaurants and inns in the city.
>
> Aside from servicing Houston's economic elite, the hotel has played host to a parade of glitterati running the gamut from former President Bush to Madonna to Bishop Desmond Tutu. Since it opened in 1980, La Colombe d'Or has, for the most part, flourished – a major feat in an industry laden with ups and downs in a city that has seen scores of hotels and restaurants go belly up.
>
> Through clever marketing campaigns, environmental scanning, consistent service and small, yet significant, improvements over the years, Zimmerman has accomplished what most all businesses look for – staying power. His friends chalk it up to foresight and vision. 'He's an up front guy who is mentally very agile,' says Dr. Malcolm Gillis, president of Rice University and a longtime friend of Zimmerman's. 'He has interesting ideas all of the time.'
>
> *Source*: Nancy Sarnoff, *Houston Business Journal*, May 23, 2003, http://www.bizjournals.com/houston/stories/2003/05/26/story5.html, 2007

Opportunities may also be viewed as symptoms of a problem emanating either from the hospitality firm or its industry. Typically these symptoms include the unexpected, incongruity, inadequacy of processes and changes in the industry or market. Vyakarnham and Leppard's (1999) 'Why Why?' technique may be applied to any of these symptoms to reveal the true problem. Essentially, a symptom is identified, for example, diminishing productivity in the restaurant kitchen. The question is 'why?' The symptom is then broken down into a number of composite possibilities, for example, 'untrained chefs,' 'untrained waiting staff,' 'poor quality raw materials' and so on. Each of these area in turn is then subjected to another round of 'why?' questions. Eventually when all rounds are exhausted the real problem emerges.

> **Key point 5.1**
>
> Creativity and innovation are linked but different. Innovation is a systematic and logical process with the aim of developing a creative idea into a commercially robust product or service.

There are other ways of identifying opportunities, however, and many entrepreneurs go with their instincts especially if they have had a number of earlier successes. However, initial accomplishments often breed an inflated sense of confidence and business invulnerability. The business world is full of failed enterprises because the individual was overly confident having a false notion of their ability to spot and exploit an opportunity. The following case underscores this point when Clive Sinclair tried to move his idea of a small electrically powered passenger vehicle to market.

The C5

Sir Clive Sinclair a British entrepreneur enjoyed significant success as inventor of the world's first electronic pocket calculator in 1972 and the UK's first mass market ZX80 home computer in the 1970s and ZX Spectrum early 1980s changing the face of home-based computer gaming. Sinclair was fascinated by electronics and miniaturization and some time after his initial successes embarked on development of the ill-fated Sinclair C5. This was a one-person, three-wheeled vehicle using a small motor powered by rechargeable batteries promoted by Sinclair as a revolutionary advance in personal transport with the potential to replace the car. In fact, it was not a car at all but was instead a glorified electric tricycle, powered by an electric battery with a supplementary pedal drive. The C5 was fraught with design flaws not well received by the press or the public and was not nearly as successful as Clive's earlier products. Attracting controversy and derision in equal measure, the C5 fiasco ended up having a catastrophic effect on Sinclair's finances. Losses of up to £7 million eventually forced the company to sell its computer business to Amstrad.

Adapted from:

http://www.thebubbleburst.co.uk/bb.php?entry=Clive%Sinclair, 2007
http://www.nvg.ntnu.no/sinclair/vehicles/c5.htm, 2007

However, opportunities are identified, they must be further explored prior to engaging in a full blown feasibility study. An idea can be explored initially using a concept model. This is not usually as detailed as the fuller feasibility study but at the very least must include four essential items. A concept model for a new intranet system in a hotel group is shown in Figure 5.5.

Once the idea has been expressed it may be tested or 'piloted' on people known to you such as family and friends. Issues which detract from the idea are every bit as important as those which appear to support it; therefore, both need careful consideration. How are you going to achieve this? At this stage, entrepreneurs also need to be totally honest with themselves asking critical questions such as:

■ How interesting is this idea to me?
■ How interesting is it likely to be to others such as investors?

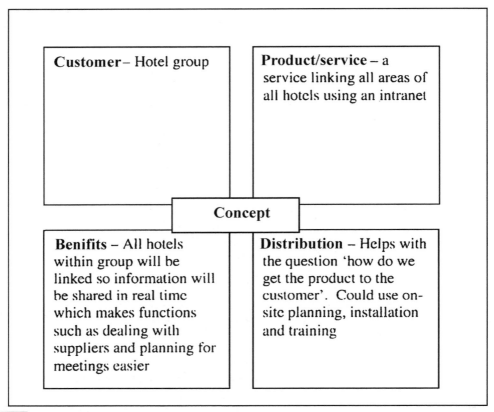

FIGURE 5.5 *Concept model.*
Adapted from: Allen (1999, p. 32).

Introspection at this stage is vital. Be honest, are you being overly subjective with this idea? A simple cautionary note here should not be underestimated and whilst you need to be motivated intrinsically:

do not fall in love with your own business idea.

There are many pet projects pursued by entrepreneurs against the advice of others. Whilst it cannot be denied some are successful they are significantly outweighed by those doomed to failure. Interestingly, these casualties are frequent in the resort sector of the UK hospitality industry and there are likely to be myriad of reasons for poor performance. UK seaside resorts are dominated by small hospitality businesses. The town of Blackpool is representative of this sector with a profile of micro firms managed by 'one-property' owners employing one or two family members. As such, their owners are not motivated by classical entrepreneurial ambitions of growth (Rowson and Lashley,

2007) but rather are happy for their hotels to simply support their lifestyle. With this kind of 'lifestyle' firm, entrepreneurs have little knowledge of even the basics of running a successful business and frequently succumb to the 'deadly sins' of entrepreneurship. Lashley and Rowson (2006) note that matters of basic service quality, marketing, business strategy are at worst, non existent and at best 'informal' (p. 1) in these hospitality micro-firms. Business success in this sector is also hindered because setting up is straightforward and unencumbered relative to other business areas. For example, no qualifications are needed, there are no regulatory bodies or special legal requirements (except those which apply to all business sectors) and private dwellings are easy to convert into business premises.

Regional trading conditions notwithstanding, the failure rate of small UK hospitality firms is noteworthy because it appears to contradict some espoused wisdom. Overall, entrepreneurial behaviour is motivated by two dimensions. The first is 'push' or necessity-driven and the other is 'pull' or opportunity-driven (see Chapter 1). Relative to other nation states, the UK has a well developed system of alternative incomes and safety nets such as its welfare system and a diversified labour market. According to Minniti, Bygrave and Autio (2006), wherever such economic conditions exist, opportunity-driven entrepreneurship is more common that the alternative. Additionally, there is also a tendency for fewer entrepreneurial failures because business conditions are conducive and supportive of new ventures.

Key point 5.2

Before realizing a entrepreneurial idea undertake rigorous research; do not fall in love with your own business.

Why then are there so many failures? Clearly, a lack of business skills helps to explain the situation. It is also the case that many individuals expressing the desire to become hospitality entrepreneurs appears to be in search of an 'ideal' or dream of owning their own hotel or restaurant. Examples of this abound (see Getz, Carlsen and Morrison, 2004) and popular television programmes such as ''No Going Back'' serve to illustrate the point. Typically, couples are featured who, for some reason best known to themselves, truly believe they can run a small hospitality firm easily with no prior qualifications, skills or related experience. In most cases, the programme is a sad but revealing insight into how not to run a business. However, this is only one explanation. There is also the restaurant entrepreneur who has no idea of what customers require. Often this person is male, qualified as a chef with a notion that the market requires a 'top quality', high price, high 'mark up' *a la carte* or equivalent operation (consistent with his training). Often these craft individuals have been trained at the top level perhaps working for a number of years in leading metropolitan hotels and Michelin-rated restaurants. Many UK seaside resorts have witnessed multiple failures of this kind of restaurant entrepreneur.

Lifestyle Proprietorship and Seasonal Trading: Findings from Scotland

In much of Scotland, especially rural areas away from the urbanized Glasgow-Edinburgh Central Belt, seasonally operating accommodation businesses remain prevalent. This is despite advances in off-season trade through increasingly more creative destination marketing campaigns, investment in year round amenities and the gradual spread of low cost air routes, among other facilitating factors. Yet few direct empirical links have been established between lifestyle proprietorship and the seasonal operation of hospitality businesses. Indeed, there is a fundamental issue as to whether operating an accommodation establishment in a seasonal business environment is a 'lifestyle choice' or simply a pragmatic response to prevailing conditions.

A recent large scale survey of independent, seasonally run accommodation businesses in Scotland including bed and breakfast, guest house, small hotel, holiday park and self-catering operators aimed to explore associations between seasonal trading and lifestyle attributes. The study captured all known Scottish tourist establishments operating to a defined sub-annual 'season'. Among the 700+ respondents, two-thirds of proprietors claimed to prefer to operate their business seasonally rather than be open year round, whilst half the proprietors claimed they choose the length of their operating season to fit in with their lifestyle (Goulding, 2006).

Of course 'lifestyle proprietorship' is a subjective and potentially vague notion. However, underlying the high incidence of seasonal trading preference and lifestyle choice expressed within the study is a range of intrinsic personal variables which fall into six distinct clusters. These include:

■ 'work-life balance' factors, in which the need for rest, relaxation, 'getting away' and free time are paramount;
■ social priorities, including family commitments and broader socialization activities;
■ 'internalized' factors around the home environment, including privacy, self-occupancy, having space back;
■ lifecycle, health and wellbeing, including both physical and mental health, energy and retirement;
■ migration, in which operating a part-time business fits in with enjoyment of an idealized physical environment;
■ altruism, including concern for the natural environment and local community impacts;

The study also observed that lifestyle proprietorship based on preference and choice, is an entrenched condition and mindset among Scotland's small seasonal accommodation operators. The great majority in the study claimed to have always operated seasonally from business start-up, many of whom were recent entrants into the industry. Neither revenue maximization nor significant market expansion beyond his/her temporal boundaries appear to be top priorities for the seasonally trading lifestyle proprietor.

Whilst many external factors are clearly influential in determining supply-side seasonality, the lifestyle-oriented, seasonally-predisposed small-scale accommodation operator is a fact of life in the make-up of Scotland's tourism sector.

Philip Goulding, June 2007

Reflective practice

Approach a small business owner in the small hospitality sector and enquire how they identified an opportunity for their successful enterprise.

INNOVATIONS BIG AND SMALL

Interestingly, there is a widely held notion that innovation concerns significant change or novel concepts; this is not necessarily so. In the majority of cases, innovations are little more than a repackaging or reconfiguration of elements into a new format giving rise to an amended process or product often through identifying problems and solving them. According to Kottler (2003) 'Every problem is a disguised opportunity' (p. 128).

The advantage of minor innovations is that they usually have a low risk factor, carry a degree of certainty and yield speedy results. They can be adopted and implemented at relatively little cost and disruption to foregoing technologies and processes. However, they often only provide small financial advantage for whoever adopts the idea. Volery and Schaper (2004) classify innovations as 'incremental' or 'radical'. Incremental innovation is not uncommon in hospitality organizations, for example, consider the efficiency differences between a full *a la carte* 'silver service' compared with the less labour intensive and relatively uncomplicated production and service style of a *table d'hôte* system. A similar benefit can be observed when comparing the table d'hote service with fully 'plated' food service. Obviously, before the decision is taken to replace the full silver service with something less theatrical, the entrepreneur must be sure that the market will accept the innovation. Similarly, in the public and large-scale catering sectors innovations of cook-freeze and chill-freeze food service styles have become increasingly popular. Not only are these systems more cost saving than a more traditional style of production and delivery but they are also alleged to preserve more nutrients in the food which has obvious benefits for recovering patients.

Another example of innovation linked to the hospitality sector is that of the 'laundry service'. In the hospitality industry firms often take advantage of an 'external' laundry service; especially in the small to medium-sized sector where staffing, wear and tear, machine maintenance and other associated costs are at best irksome, at worst prohibitive. Many enterprising individuals have seized the opportunity to provide a worthwhile laundry service by observing the above problems. Like other contract services which hotels do not consider worth investing their own time and energy on for example. Maintenance, cleaning, interior decorating and so on, a laundry service could not be considered a radical innovation but many 'service' firms of this nature have emerged because owners identified a timely market need or 'problem to be solved'.

However, the operation of these organizations is easy to copy and as regional markets mature, less opportunity exists for similar products unless they offer something over and above their nearest competitors. Firms like these are continually striving to differentiate themselves in the marketplace and there is a continual ebb and flow of failures and new entrants.

On the other hand and as the name suggests, radical innovations can be extremely disruptive, require much 'nursing' to get over teething problems but can potentially bestow significant advantages. According to Burns (2001) new knowledge is probably the least predictable source of innovation but it is the area which receives most entrepreneurial and media attention because it is incredibly glamorous. The obvious example here is McDonald's in the 1950s as creator and innovator of a new fast food industry having a product featuring unique systematized preparation and cooking procedures. Radical innovations represent real breakthroughs and have the potential to earn appreciable profits and establish strategic competitive advantage for individuals and firms. Quite how long these advantages can be maintained depends on whether the product or service can be easily copied by others; competitive advantage is notoriously difficult to sustain. For example, McDonald's now has many competitors, Burger King/Hungry Jack's, KFC, Red Rooster have all copied and amended the McDonald's system. Each uses similar 'formula' standardized production and delivery systems rooted in those devised by the pioneering McDonald's brothers and Ray Croc.

The McDonald's Story

The McDonald's story started in 1940 when two brothers, Dick and Mac McDonald opened a highly successful barbecue restaurant in California. After WWII, they noticed that families were concerned about value for money and that the USA was investing in a more comprehensive road infrastructure system. They thought this would make future customers interested in speed of service and so temporarily closed their restaurant. The newly adapted one featured a simplified menu based around their most popular products with a more efficient interior. In short, they invented the self-service, drive-in concept that comprised a limited-menu, paper-service, hand-out operation, featuring cheap hamburgers, cheeseburgers, soft drinks and French fries. This new concept proved so successful that they quickly opened eight more restaurants.

In the mid 1950s, a food service equipment salesman named Ray Kroc became involved at first as someone who simply owned the national marketing rights to the five-spindle Multimixers the brothers used to make their milkshakes. His interest in the McDonald's business was kindled because they bought 10 of these machines to cater for their successful business. Ray was subsequently granted exclusive rights to develop and franchise McDonald's drive-ins for the United States and opened the 9th McDonald's restaurant in Illinios, 1955. Some 6 years later Ray bought the proprietary rights to the McDonald's system, including all rights to the rest of the world. The organization that Ray founded proceeded to add more than 23 000 McDonald's restaurants and 4500 franchisees across more than 111 countries around the world.

Questions

1. Who were the creators and who were the innovators in the McDonald's story?
2. Who were the entrepreneurs?
3. How important was the role of Ray Croc in the success of the McDonald's Corporation?
4. Can you think of some hospitality examples of:

   radical innovation and
   incremental innovation?

In order to create a sustainable competitive advantage through innovation, entrepreneurs must utilize strategic resources, that is, those that form the basis of an entrepreneur's market position/advantage[1]. By definition, strategic resources have four dimensions and allow the entrepreneur to implement strategy by:

■ exploiting opportunities,
■ being non-substitutable,

---

[1] Strategic resources differ from common resources in that the latter enable the firm's usual activities but provide no particular advantage against other organisations. Common resources include financial, physical, human, technological, reputation and organizational (structure, systems and procedures).

TABLE 5.1 Characteristics of innovation	
Incremental innovation	**Radical innovation**
Uniform improvements	Novel improvements
Uses existing technologies and processes	Uses new technologies and processes
Quick to implement	Extended periods of piloting
Immediate gains	No short-term gains but long-term advantage
Strengthens customer loyalty	Also exploits new markets

Adapted from: Volery and Schaper (2004, p. 57).

■ being rare, that is, not available to competitors, and
■ being difficult to copy.

Controlling all of the above dimensions is very difficult to achieve. That is why ultimately most firms fail to hang on to any competitive advantage they might have enjoyed in the short-term.

The characteristics of incremental and radical innovations are summarized in Table 5.1.

> **Key point 5.3**
> Most innovations are small using only amended processes and procedure. Whilst the economic returns are relatively small, they are more assured and cause less organizational disruption and carry less risk than large innovations.

THE INNOVATIVE SMALL HOSPITALITY BUSINESS

Whilst it can be agreed that innovations are the lifeblood of mature economies whether big or small, radical or incremental, just how easy is it for entrepreneurs to come up with ideas and innovations? According to Kirby (2003) and others, the odds are stacked against them when compared with the scope large organizations have for developing new and innovative ideas. In short, this is a resource-based perspective of entrepreneurship and it considers that creative and novel innovations, no matter how good, will fail unless adequate resources are applied. Moreover, large firms also enjoy economies of scale and are therefore likely to develop new ideas and innovations more cheaply than their small business entrepreneurial counterparts. Intuitively this seems to make sense as does its accompanying credo shown in Figure 5.6.

The key issue for the entrepreneur is to take advantage of imperfect information about price whilst going through the process shown above and a tacit

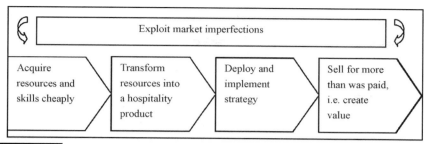

FIGURE 5.6 *The process of a resource-based perspective of entrepreneurship. Adapted from: Schaper and Volery (2004, p. 63).*

recognition that large firms have better access to most resources. These used to be expressed as the 'Four Ms', that is, men, machines, materials and money. Wickham (2001) prefers to group all into three categories of financial, human and operating. A more descriptive classification might further divide categories into:

- financial,
- physical,
- technological,
- human,
- reputation, and
- organizational.

However, for firms to establish and retain sustainable competitive advantage, their resources must not be available to others, non-substitutable. Company culture may be considered a unique resource in this case, for example, a team of hotel managers may have been trained and nurtured to perpetuate company values as they are highly complex, somewhat intangible and thus difficult to copy. However, the fact that top managers and executives can be attracted to other companies through better pay and working conditions cannot be ignored.

According to the resource-based perspective most significant innovations are more likely to originate with large companies who have abundant required inputs to take an idea, develop it, innovate and produce. But surely this is not how large companies work, is it? Derived wisdom suggests that large corporations are monolithic, lumbering organizations which are often slow on the uptake or rather inflexible and not particularly good at responding to an increasingly competitive and fast-paced trading environment. In a contemporary environment, this is only partially true. Many large firms now recognize the inherent structural advantages of small organizational structures such as enhanced flexibility, less bureaucracy, fewer levels of management proximity to customers and so on. The 'small' firm model is also alleged to engender human resource development, creativity with customers and to hold innovation as the key to optimum entrepreneurial development of the organization (see Robbins, Barrett and Storey (2000) and one more. Thus, large companies now spin off much smaller, flexible and organic organizational structures within the overall design of the firm. An example of this is the rise in popularity of the intrapreneur (see Chapter 1). This is a person (or persons) charged with the responsibility of identifying opportunities and applying their creativity to innovate through developing new products and services. In other words, these individuals act as 'company entrepreneurs'. In some respects this has similarities with the more traditional Research and Development departments used by virtually all major corporations. However, a key difference with the intrapreneurial initiative is that it represents more than just another department. Of course, people are still charged with their entrepreneurial responsibilities much as the former R&D centres were but the real difference is the 'cultural shift' adopted. Rather than being seen as another separate company dimension of their operations, the intrepreneur initiative is viewed more strategically with appropriate support structures in place. Even as early as 1994, Naisbitt identifies a number of large companies who have 'deconstructed' in line with the above logic including ABB and Grand Metropolitan.

In his influential book *Thriving on Chaos*, Peters (1987) proposes the following support model shown in Figure 5.7.

Whilst independent small firms also take advantage of their structural advantages they do not have the physical and economic resources and capacity to create, innovate, produce and market a novel product or service. Kirby (2003) also adds this lack of capacity is a direct result of having no new available capital. He cites four main reasons for this and they include the unwillingness of bank lending, uncertainty of new products especially those with a significant technological orientation. Others are that traditionally lending institutions such as bank do not consider research and development as anything other than an intangible which may not be able to be protected through copyright and patenting. However some evidence suggests that despite the odds, small hospitality organizations survive because reinvention may not necessarily be overly costly (depending on the magnitude of the change) and is effective over short periods. Indeed, common themes of flexibility and short run planning (1 year) characterizes small hospitality firms which means they have an innate capability for innovation (Edgar and Nisbet, 1996). In this sense they do so by providing a continually differentiated product (sometimes small, sometimes large) on a seasonal basis in many resort

Strategies			
Piloting should replace written proposals and 'champions' should test ideas away from company HQ	Use teams drawn from a diverse company background for all developmental activities also use suppliers, distributor and customers	Copy from international product leaders but adapt in novel ways	Promote the importance of word-of-mouth marketing
Tactics			
• Support those with passion for the new ideas and encourage 'champions' from all over organization • Managers must practice and encourage what they preach • Support the many failures that will occur as this will shorten organizational learning • Establish accurate and meaningful metrics			

FIGURE 5.7 *Corporate support for intrapreneurs.*
Adapted from: Kirby (pp. 2003, pp. 135–136).

towns globally. According to Augustyn (2004) tourism firms succeed precisely because their resources are in short supply as this situation together with high entrepreneurial aspirations drives the firm innovatively and creatively. "Needs must when the devil drives". Russell and Faulkener (2004) are of a similar opinion and consider that small hospitality operators thrive on conditions of uncertainty as they tend to have an ability to effectively identify opportunities amongst conditions of chaos.

Reflective practice

1. Identify a local entrepreneur or someone you know in the small hospitality sector. Ask them how innovative they had to be for their business to succeed and remain successful. Also, how did they deal with other hospitality organizations that may have imitated their product.

In a more general sense, the effectiveness and advantages of the small firm are clearly evident in the modern global economy where small businesses dominate in almost every nation whether they are part of a large company or a truly small firm owned and operated by a few individuals. Indeed, much evidence suggests that entrepreneurship and small firms are on the increase with their underpinning economic role being recognized as imperative for future growth by all major governments (see Chapter 1).

Seaside Tourism Planning Officer

You know, if I were to pick say, 20 member hotels and restaurants from our local hospitality and tourism employers association, most owners would be from away (other parts of the country). You asked me earlier why this is the case; I think there are several reasons but first you had need to understand a bit of the history about this seaside town – I'll give you a potted version. This town once had enormous wealth from its fishing industry, Herrings to be precise. It began a couple of hundred years ago and lasted through probably until the early 1960s although most of the Herring grounds had been fished out by that time. With the development of the fishing industry came a supporting infrastructure that early tourists and providers could use. With the advent of the railway system in the 1800s, we had a perfect mode of transport which tourists used to literally flood into the town. In those days, the industrial heartlands of the UK provided almost all of the tourist market. Midland factories would shut down for two or three weeks at a time and all of their workers would jump on the train at their end and jump off at ours. You can actually see how the hotels, shops and other key enabling elements of infrastructure developed. Most were originally constructed near to the railway station with other buildings being added a little further away to take advantage of the town's major attraction, the esplanade. There is no real difference between most of the UK's seaside towns in terms of layout apart from the market they catered for. For example, Great Yarmouth, Blackpool and Margate tourists were mainly working class whereas tourists frequenting Brighton and Bournemouth tended to be from the middle classes. I do not believe there has been much significant change in markets for the last hundred years or so.

Of course things are different now as we do not have anywhere near the number of tourists we used to. It all started around the mid 1960s with the advent of the cheap 'continental' package tour to places like Benidorm and Majorca. Ever since then, towns like ours have had to fight tooth a nail to keep the tourists coming. Some have succeeded by differentiating their 'promise', others have not done so well; I had count ours in the latter category. You only have to walk around the town to see once profitable small hotels and guest houses boarded up, empty or given over for another use. Setting up rest homes for the elderly was a popular alternative use for these establishments. I remember in the early 1980s it seemed like everyone had either set one up or was giving it serious consideration. The local council soon got wise and put a stop to it though.

If I compare the town's current operating capacity with say 1970, we probably only have twenty percent of hotels and restaurants trading in the summer season. Of course the trouble is, tourism is the lifeblood of this region and without it, other businesses have gone under; everything from local retailers and DIY stores to garages and Taxi firms; we have all suffered. In the very early days there were only a few hotels in the town; perhaps four or five. The oldest purpose built hotel was here long before the advent of the railway. In fact it was a 'coaching house' and used to take regular delivery of the mail and provided accommodation for the coachmen and passengers prior to the emergence of Post Offices in the region. Once the railways arrived, hotels popped up all over the place with most being converted from private dwellings. Interestingly, one of the largest hotels on the seafront with 150 rooms is a conversion of several Victorian Villas. You have never seen such a thing. It is a complete labyrinth of passageways and corridors.

Getting back to my earlier point, many hoteliers and restaurateurs were born outside the region. This is an interesting demographic and you will find similar in other seaside resorts, especially where local industry pay is low compared to elsewhere in the UK. Here for example, agriculture was the major employer and locals found it difficult to raise the initial capital to purchase even the smallest guesthouse. Wages of factory workers from the midlands were relatively handsome in comparison. So, surprise surprise, many erstwhile tourists saw the opportunities available to them whilst enjoying their holidays and snapped up the relatively low costs housing converting to small hospitality operations. This is something of a flashpoint with the local community even now. Incomers tend to view the locals as lazy and non-entrepreneurial; locals view incomers as having an unfair advantage.

Questions

1. Identify where entrepreneurial innovation occurs in this case
2. How would you classify the innovations shown in the case?
3. How easy was it for the innovations to be copied?
4. Discuss how this seaside resort could innovate as a collective tourist destination

PROTECTING YOUR INTELLECTUAL PROPERTY

Intellectual property may be defined as, '...any product of human intellect...that is through imagination, creativity and inventiveness, that is intangible but has value in the marketplace' (Barringer and Ireland (2006, p. 278). With the advent of information communication technology and *e*-commerce, intellectual property is probably more valuable than a firms physical assets. This importance is compounded by the increasing use of the internet for a plethora of *e* transactions, reservation systems, website designs, domain names and the rise of *e*-tourism[2] and the companies that operate in this environment. Essentially there are four types of intellectual property:

- A patent – government confers the originator a right to exclude others from making, selling or using an invention for the term of the patent

---

[2] *e*-Tourism enables direct booking, easy payment for end-user, business-to-business trading for product providers, travel agents and resellers. With application of e-tourism, amongst other things, travellers are able to make online reservations, bookings and receive immediate confirmation.

and allows them to make and sell the invention so long as no other patents are infringed. For example, a new beverage dispenser may require an element of an earlier (say) patented Hobart food processing machine. The inventor would need permission from the Hobart company to make and sell the new machine. They could refuse, agree or insist on a licensing fee for the use of its technology.

■ Trademark – a word, name, symbol used to identify the origin of a service/product, for example, Travel Lodge, Ibis, Hyatt and so on.

■ Copyright – protects the owner/author of a literary work, software, drama, music, lyrics, other works of art, sound recordings and architecture and affords them the legal right to determine how the work is used for economic benefit. Appropriate items include company specific training manuals and other media used exclusively by one company.

■ Trade secret – essentially this is information that does not require the above types of protection (although this is not always the case) but is important if a small hospitality firm wishes to establish and maintain competitive advantage. For example, if a hotel wants to exploit the potential benefits of a customer loyalty scheme it will need to keep details of all customers in order to establish more intimate and frequent contact via online news letters and emails. This a powerful way for small hotels to compete directly and successfully with their larger counterparts. Not all information can be classified as a trade secret and if information is disclosed in error or overheard by a competitor it ceases to remain a trade secret. There is much confusion over this dimension of intellectual property but in general, the law will not protect a trade secret unless its owner first does so (Barringer and Ireland, 2006, pp. 282–295).

Innovations in the tourism and hospitality industry (as in others) have the potential to bestow significant benefits upon the entrepreneur in terms of economic returns. However, to create a real competitive advantage they must be difficult to replicate, copy or imitate. One way of sustaining competitive edge by minimizing the opportunity for replication by competitors is to 'protect' the innovation legally. Indeed, it may also be the case that an innovator/entrepreneur wishes to share their intellectual property for financial gain through franchising their innovation (examples include, McDonald's, KFC, Domino's Pizzas).

In the case of tangible manufactured products, intellectual property issues are relatively straightforward but for hospitality services this is not the case. This is why the most common forms of legal protection in the hospitality area are for products which are manufactured. For example, fast food restaurants are really nothing more than a production line operating according to strict guidelines. On the other hand many hotels and restaurants are commonly differentiated by their location and by the individuals who deliver the service. The much quoted 'location, location, location' byte springs to mind here as a region simply cannot be copyrighted. Effectively, all hospitality organizations near to a location of outstanding natural beauty will benefit as these natural assets will create a competitive advantage for the region but not between each hotel in the area. However, controllable aspects such as hotel design, service style, appearance and so on may well qualify as intellectual property and become appropriate for legal protection. Nonetheless, the very intangible nature of service and 'atmosphere' of some establishments is impossible to capture and replicate exactly. In part this helps explain why so many independent small hotels and restaurants remain popular with customers despite the ever increasing presence of hospitality brands like Hilton, Shangri-La and Hyatt.

There are a variety of ways to protect intellectual property but the laws surrounding the issue are in constant flux and differ between countries. They key consideration for entrepreneurs is to recognize the importance of legal protection for their innovations and pursue the matter sooner rather than later to avoid wasted time and missed registration deadlines. Some practical steps for protecting your hospitality firm are detailed at this site:

http://www.restaurant.org/legal/law_trademark.cfm

Before they can do this hospitality entrepreneurs must understand of what their intellectual property is comprised, its value and the role it plays in their potential business success. How can this be achieved when potentially all aspects of the business has intellectual property? This can be a tricky process but there are two questions entrepreneurs must ask themselves to determine which aspects of their business require legal protection (Barringer and Ireland, 2006):

- Is the intellectual property related directly to achieving and sustaining competitive advantage? For example, all major international hotel chains such as Hyatt, Hilton and Regal have their own logos which differentiate them from each other (at least in theory!) as they strive to convey recognizable and consistent global standards thus creating customer loyalty. This is also the case with groups of smaller independent hotels and accommodation providers including Best Western, Golden Chain Motels, Preferred Hotels & Resorts Worldwide and Leading Small Hotels of the World.

■ Is the item valuable in the marketplace? In other words, the hospitality entrepreneur should test their business idea before investing a considerable amount of time and effort developing and protecting it.

Figure 5.8 shows a summary of intellectual properties linked to the hospitality industry.

Conduct your Own Intellectual Property Audit

The hospitality industry is dynamic in terms of demand and supply, mergers, acquisitions and takeovers. Indeed, there are many examples of small firm takeovers by national and multinational companies. Amongst other things, the avaricious chains buy out their smaller counterparts because they are interested in their intellectual capital. They are only too aware that the small firms sector provides a much sought after, intimate service product that is often missing from the large and sometimes impersonal atmosphere found in large hotels. Entrepreneurs should therefore ensure they are fully aware of their intellectual property and its value when large companies come door-knocking. It is therefore a good idea to conduct an intellectual property audit. The audit *proforma* shown below details some key questions for the procedure, some of them are more appropriate for the hospitality industry than others

Patents

- ■ Are services, products and packages under development that warrant protection?
- ■ Do we have any day-to-day or strategic processes that should be protected?
- ■ Are our current patent maintenance fees up to date?
- ■ Has our business changed so much that we do not require any of our existing patents?
- ■ Do we have accurate documentation about our patents?

Copyrights

- ■ Do we comply with the copyright license agreements we have entered into, for example, do we have a music/Performing Rights Society license for our entertainers?
- ■ Do we have a policy about when copyrightable material should be registered?
- ■ Do we know where to obtain our licenses?
- ■ Is there documentation in place protecting our rights to use material we create or pays to have created?

Trademarks

- ■ Are we using any slogans, logos, signage that requires trademark protection?
- ■ Are we going to expand the use of our trademarks elsewhere?
- ■ Do we need any more trademarks to cover new services?
- ■ Do we know whether our trademarks are being infringed and, if so, by whom?

	What is protected	How to protect	Who applies	Term of protection	Protection provided	Enforcement	Federal or state law	Example
Trade mark	Words, phrases and logos as a trademark (on tangible goods), service mark (with services), trade dress (visual appearance)	Apply for federal or state registration	User or licensor of user	Unlimited until abandoned, federal registration may vary but usually 10 years (renewable)	Right to exclude others whose use may cause confusion	Suit for infringement – federal court	Federal and state common low/statute	Sofitel, Novotel (Accor), Akzent Hotels (Germany), Amanresorts (small luxury international resorts, Johnny Rocket's (1950's themed restaurants), Red Rooster (Australian fast-food restaurants)
Trade secret	Secret technical or business information	Use reasonable measures to keep secret–no registration available information	No application process	Unlimited until no longer a secret	Right to prevent unlawful use or disclosure	State or federal court	State common law/statute	Radisson's "Look to Book" travel reservation marketing system.
Patent	A process, machine, a made item or an improvement	Apply for patent	First inventor or designate	20 years from filing of first application	Right to exclude other from making, using,	Suit for infringement – federal court	Federal	Geronimo Inns (high quality food public house - Uk) pioneer in the neighborhood pub concept, Sous Vide cook chill and other specific food production equipment manufacturers

[3] In many instances methods of protection are numerous, for example, trademark, copyright, trade secret would all be appropriate for recruiting pamphlets, company-specific training literature and manuals, website design, slogans, customer lists, contractual forms etc.

FIGURE 5.8   *Intellectual properties linked to the hospitality industry.*[3]
Adapted from: Kaplan (2033, p. 226).

> **Trade secrets**
>
> ■ Is there leakage of our firms trade secrets by accident or by design?
> ■ Do we have a policy governing nondisclosure
> ■ How much information are our employees exposed to and could this be limited?
> ■ Are our intellectual property security arrangements effective?

Adapted from: Barringer and Ireland (2006, p. 298).

SUMMARY

There is a common misunderstanding of the terms creativity and innovation not least because several writers and pundits use the terms to mean the same thing. Whilst they are similar they actually mean two different things. Creativity is the laterally-oriented antecedent of innovation; innovation is a systematic logical exercise designed to harness the creative idea and bring it to a successful entrepreneurial conclusion in the marketplace. This possible in two ways; the first is a sheer seat of the pants, intuitive and sometimes lucky hunch (not recommended); the second is a more methodical systematic process of environmental scanning and strategic and tactical planning. There are a number of approaches and techniques that can be used to help the entrepreneur through this process. It is also a good idea to use 'concept' models to pilot an idea prior to a full feasibility study.

Much of the hospitality sector is dominated by small and micro firms. These organizations are operated by entrepreneurs who often have no prior experience or skills in the hospitality area. Many of these operations fail for this reason together with unrealistic expectations of the owners. However, the structure of small hospitality firms has a number of advantages over the large organization including flexibility, proximity to the customer and adaptability to prevailing economic conditions. Some evidence suggests that despite limited resources available to small hospitality firms, they succeed because of these structurally inherent capabilities. Indeed, large organizations now recognize that 'small is beautiful' and many have created small more organic organizational structures within their superstructures giving rise to 'intrapreneurs'.

Protecting intellectual property in the small firms sector of the hospitality industry is important as many customers value the personal intimate experience. However, there are many intangibles that cannot be claimed and protected by any operator, as such the independent entrepreneur-run hotel is still very much in demand; so too are regions of outstanding natural beauty and their hotels. Nonetheless, large operators engaging in acquisitions of small firms will only do so because of the intellectual property the take over bestows. Entrepreneurs should therefore be familiar with their intellectual property and take steps to guard it through one or more of the four types of protection available - patent, copyright, trademark and or trade secret. Entrepreneurs should also be mindful that the laws governing intellectual property vary, to a lesser or greater extent, by country.

CHAPTER 6

The Feasibility Analysis

After working through this chapter you should be able to:

- Understand the term 'feasibility analysis' and how it applies in maximizing the chance of entrepreneurial success.
- Discuss the limited value of intuition and gut reaction when planning to launch a new hospitality venture.
- Understand the role of research in entrepreneurial success.
- Apply the tenets of Porter's Five Forces model in a feasibility analysis.

INTRODUCTION

According to the *Merriam-Webster Online Dictionary*, the word 'feasible' means 'capable of being done or carried out'. In a business or entrepreneurial sense, a feasibility study or analysis may therefore be understood as an investigation into something which is capable (or not) of being successful, such as the initiation and continuation of a new business venture based on a creative or novel idea. Barringer and Ireland (2006) propose a simpler explanation:

"*[Feasibility analysis is] a process of determining if a business idea is viable*" *(p. 52).*

According to White (2007):

"*A feasibility study isn't magic, although it can have a magical effect on... profitability... Rather, a feasibility study provides you with data that replace wishful thinking. The study gives you a rich, detailed and accurate picture that includes information you really need to know, rather than information that's just easily available*".

Whatever the semantics and whether we are considering starting or buying and developing an existing business, serious consideration should first be given to its potential. In other words, the question becomes, 'Is the idea worth pursuing?' In a sense, these considerations will depend on individual preferences and personal circumstances. For example, someone sacrificing paid employment of 30k will be more likely to proceed, all other things being equal, with a business idea than another who may be sacrificing a salary of 120k.

The aim of this chapter is to introduce the concept of a feasibility analysis (or study) and to discuss the basic steps involved. It does this first by considering the role of feasibility analysis in the context of the hospitality industry. Then each element of service/product, industry/market, personal/organization, and finance is introduced and explained. Further discussion is left until elsewhere in the book where each is expanded and developed.

Key point 6.1

A feasibility analysis provides essential information to determine whether a business idea is viable and is an important precursor the business plan.

HOSPITALITY ENTREPRENEURS AND THE ROLE OF FEASIBILITY ANALYSIS

Whilst the provision of hospitality and tourism services is probably one of the world's oldest industries, many entrepreneurs still rely on gut reaction and intuition as a method of determining whether their venture will be successful. As discussed in Chapter 1, some hospitality entrepreneurs[1] have a tendency to be swept away by enthusiasm for their own ideas and launch into a new business before carefully considering whether:

- there is a market for their service;
- there are adequate sources of start-up and continuing finances; and
- they have the skills to deliver such a service.

Barringer and Ireland (2006) refer to this somewhat cavalier approach as the 'ready, fire, aim' syndrome where the business is launched prematurely. This almost certainly guarantees ultimate failure or an inordinate amount of subsequent iteration to (re)establish business objectives. In a sense, the overconfidence and willingness to follow intuition is not really surprising. After all, successful entrepreneurs take risks, trust their own judgement and have a clear vision of the way their business ought to be; do they not? Well actually, yes, but the successful business person takes 'measured' risks, makes a judgement and

---

[1] This behaviour is not uncommon amongst entrepreneurs in other sectors (see Bhide, 2000).

forms a business vision in a less haphazard fashion. Unfortunately, the popular media loves a winner and goes to great lengths to ensure that the public shares the enthusiasm and success without showing the extensive preparatory planning involved. Whilst it is true that occasionally mavericks appear in the limelight, for us lesser mortals a reliance on carefully collected facts and figures is the sensible way to maximize the chances of entrepreneurial success. Thus, intuition alone is an unreliable way of ascertaining future success of a hospitality venture.

In order to gain a more reliable picture of whether a business idea is likely to be successful requires a dispassionate and systematic approach through a feasibility study. There are a number of techniques associated models and approaches which may be used for this purpose. All include a requirement for information about selecting an appropriate site, market analysis, concept and mix development and financial feasibility. This does not necessarily have to be conducted by the entrepreneurs; instead professionally performed analyses may be commissioned. However, these services can be costly and so long as a few simple rules are followed most people are perfectly capable of conducting an adequate and systematic feasibility study. Figure 6.1 shows the main elements of a feasibility analysis and where it features in the overall planning process.

Many entrepreneurs in the micro seasonal sector of the hospitality industry have objectives which are not always consistent with those usually ascribed to

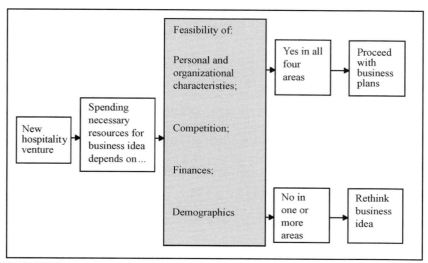

FIGURE 6.1 *The role of feasibility analysis in developing successful business ideas. Adapted from: Barringer and Ireland (2006, p. 54).*

founders of 'growth firms'. Instead, the aspirations and skill sets of these entrepreneurs are modest, preferring 'lifestyle proprietorship' with neither revenue maximization or market expansion as priorities. Business objectives tend to be personally defined. Goulding's (2006) study of UK-based small hospitality firms concurs and concludes that instead of clear commercial objectives, operations are inextricably linked to intrinsic personal variables emphasizing the need for rest and relaxation, social priorities, family commitments and privacy. The above positioning of the analyses, elements and process hold true irrespective of whether entrepreneurs are keen to set up growth or lifestyle firms.

However, there are a number of reasons why many hospitality entrepreneurs might (erroneously) consider the above figure redundant when planning for a new business. These including ease of entry into the industry and a perception that required skills are little more than an extension of those used in a domestic setting. There is much to be said for intuition as a partial driver of management decision-making but the feasibility stage of a new venture is probably not best suited to this approach. The latter point is important because some evidence (reference) suggests that many hospitality entrepreneurs do not have industry-specific skills or qualifications and lack basic business knowledge. Moreover, the industry demands little in the way of special legal requirements to start trading and there are precious few regulatory industry bodies. It is therefore unsurprising to learn that conversion of private dwellings into business premises remains a common route to entrepreneurship in the hospitality industry (Lashley and Rowson, 2006). The following vignette based on the BBC's (UK) *From Hell to Hotel* television broadcast illustrates the impetuous nature of some would be hospitality entrepreneurs.

The St. Giles House Hotel

At the turn of this century, a rather well-off (financially secure) husband and wife team decided to purchase a dilapidated shell of a building in the city of Norwich in the UK. The defunct General Post Office construction site was deemed ideal for a high-class luxury hotel. The main investors for the initiative were family members who ultimately financed the project to the tune of several millions. During the refurbishment the couple had to persuade family benefactors to reinvest significant extra sums in order for the hotel to open.

During the course of the broadcasts viewers witnessed the highs but mainly lows of the conversion process up until the grand opening of the hotel. During early stage-setting broadcasts, interviewers were keen to know about the impetus for the idea and how data was obtained about the primary market segment for the St. Giles. The couple indicated that owning and running a hotel had always been a dream and they felt that the time was right to embark on their venture. The process of identifying a primary market for the hotel was similarly idiosyncratic. The couple felt that customers' tastes and preferences would mirror their own somewhat ostentatious expectations. Moreover, when enquiries were made about the husband and wife's hospitality training and expertise, none was forthcoming. Indeed, their total sum of knowledge appeared to be based on a former cosmopolitan lifestyle which included extensive travel and international hotel patronage. They agreed that these experiences had equipped them with knowledge sufficient to own and run their own hotel successfully.

The remainder of the broadcasts journalled a litany of mistakes, crises and errors arguably rooted in a complete lack of management, people and operational skills. Many staff were treated in a questionable manner and expected to take on other duties besides those hospitality-related. As a result many staff left or where asked to leave including managers. After missing several launch deadlines, the hotel was finally opened with an almost completely new staff profile. Once the 'honeymoon' period subsided, occupancy and restaurant bookings declined significantly. At this point the television series ended and viewers were left wondering about the future of the St. Giles House Hotel. In 2007 the predictable fate of the venture was made clear. Shortly after the hotel was opened, the original investors withdrew and it was taken over by a new company. The husband and wife team still remain but have no strategic decision-making autonomy and play a minimal role in the operation of the enterprise.

Questions

1. List and explain the mistakes made by this entrepreneurial couple.
2. How would a feasibility analysis have helped them avoid some of the pitfalls seen above?
3. Give three examples of research methods which could have been used to help the St. Giles House Hotel identify its niche market.

Reflective practice

1. How would you ensure emotional detachment from your business idea to improve its chances of success?
2. Contact successful hospitality entrepreneurs known to you and ask whether they used intuition or feasibility exclusively or a combination of both methods when deciding on launching their business.

PERSONAL CHARACTERISTICS

In order to run a hospitality business successfully individuals need appropriate skills and, some argue, specific characteristics. The preferable scenario is when the founder already possesses them. For example, to run a restaurant, food preparation and service skills are key. Of course as an owner-operator there will be a wide range of other skills necessary ranging from how to change beer kegs to book-keeping. If, after a while a decision is made to expand the business or relocate to a bigger premises, there may be good reason to employ people to take care of these operational tasks on your behalf. In this instance, alternative skills such as those of basic management and marketing will be required. However, whether you already have appropriate abilities or a willingness to embrace them depends to an extent on personal characteristics such as stamina, commitment and dedication. There is overwhelming evidence to suggest that many businesses fail soon after opening due to a lack of them (see Chapter 1). Entrepreneurial traits/characteristics have already been introduced as important predictors of success in Chapter 2, and here Burns (2001) considers them as:

- stamina;
- commitment and dedication;
- opportunism;
- ability to bounce back;
- motivation to excel; and
- tolerance of risk, ambiguity and uncertainty.

Table 6.1 shows a feasibility checklist abstracted from the *Canada Business Network* (2007) website and contains questions pertaining to some of Burn's entrepreneurial characteristics.[2]

This type of analysis does not stop with the entrepreneur (although for micro businesses it is likely to in the first instance) but may be expanded to encompass the whole organization to determine an overall organizational competency. The process of introspection and diagnosing allows the entrepreneur to determine their 'suitability' before embarking on their business journey. If resulting gaps are exposed it may reveal a shortfall of skills or traits but does not necessarily guarantee business failure. It is simply a technique which may be used so that the entrepreneur becomes self-aware of potential weaknesses. It is then up to the individual to take remedial action in the form of personal education and skilling or even a shift of focus to the abilities of others by establishing a network of business friends and colleagues. In fact this is a basic requirement of effective entrepreneurship. Establishing extensive networks allows some personal capability gaps to be 'managed' by using the attributes of others. In exchange for external advice and experience, the entrepreneur may extend an invitation to the colleague; perhaps a place on the board of directors or advisors would be appropriate.

---

[2] This reproduction is not represented as an official version of the materials reproduced, nor as having been made in affiliation with or with the endorsement of *Canada Business*.

TABLE 6.1	Feasibility characteristics checklist		

The product or service

		Yes	No
Do you like to make your own decision?			
Do you enjoy competition?			
Do you have will power and self-discipline?			
Do you plan ahead?			
Do you get things done on time?			
Can you take advice from others?			
Are you adaptable to changing conditions?			

The next series of questions stress the physical, emotional and financial strains of a new business

		Yes	No
Do you understand that owning your own business may entail working 12–16 h a day, probably 6 days a week, and maybe on holidays?			
Do you have the physical stamina to handle a business?			
Do you have the emotional strength to withstand the strain?			
Are you prepared to lower your standard of living for several months or years?			
Are you prepared to lose your savings?			

Specific personal considerations

		Yes	No
Do you know which skills and areas of expertise are critical to the success of your project?			
Do you have these skills?			
Does your idea effectively utilize your own skills and abilities?			
Can you find personnel that have the expertise you lack?			
Do you know why you are considering this project?			
Will your project effectively meet your career aspirations?			

Key point 6.2

There are certain entrepreneurial characteristics including stamina, commitment dedication which are important in optimizing chances of new business success.

Networking may also give rise to 'clustering' or collaboration co-existing with competition in some sectors. In short, clustering invites firms to focus on their core activities but also to collaborate and build relationships with others to access, develop and share internal resources. This approach allows companies to build collectively on their strengths. The benefits of this ongoing dialogue and information exchange between firms allows them to improvise, innovate and accelerate their development much more effectively than if each was operating independently. They also benefit from 'knowledge bleeds or 'spill over' by virtue of being in close proximity and enhanced flexibility to react quickly to shifts in customer demands. This enhanced form of networking extends beyond industry sector to include broader memberships extended to industry suppliers, research and development institutions and government departments providing development and extension services. Hospitality clusters are typically found in resort towns of the UK and Europe for example Aviemore, Bath, Lausanne and Cannes.

Reflective practice

1. Discuss which personal characteristics and skills you believe important for launching a successful hospitality venture.
2. Using the above questionnaire, reflect on your strengths and weaknesses.
3. Can missing characteristics be learned?
4. How important is it to learn them?

COMPETITION

New business entrepreneurs could do worse than follow a key piece of advice from Tzun Zu's Chinese military treatise written during the 6th century, that is, 'know your enemy'. In other words, how does your service compare or differ from that of the your competition? How can this information be obtained and used? It will depend very much on the exact nature of the business and how much can be afforded. For example, if the trading environment is slow and predictable with only a few competitors research can be relatively simple and rudimentary. However, this environment is extremely rare in hospitality and tourism except in brand new locations in developing global regions. Even here, multinational players soon recognize the potential for business and seek to dominate the market. This is an interesting point because, all things being equal, entering a market with fewer competitors would seem more favorable than one which economists refer to as 'monopolistic competition' where many small operators are vying for business. Unfortunately, the trading environment is rarely simple. Whilst one would seek to avoid this situation as a new entrant, entering a market with only a few players is also unwise as a first step. The key issue here is how substantial are the few? In other words, a market highly concentrated by say three large organizations will confer benefits to them due to their independent and combined strength, established market position and relatively abundant resource base. Whilst one only has to observe that large and small hospitality organizations do indeed exist in resorts internationally with many enjoying business success, it is more difficult to succeed and sustain (despite the natural locational advantages bestowed on all hospitality organizations in the region). The following case illustrates some of the opportunities and challenges faced by entrepreneurs entering a market.

Small and Medium Hospitality Enterprises in New Zealand: too Many New Entrants?

New Zealand's hospitality industry has grown significantly in the last decade, confirming its importance for the nation's economy. The number of restaurant, café, and accommodation operations grew by almost 40 per cent between 1999 and 2005; equally as impressive is the growth (76.4 per cent) in the number of full-time employees in the industry during the same period (Statistics New Zealand, 1999, 2005). These developments suggest potential opportunities for current and future hospitality businesses. For example, it is no secret that New Zealand has recently become a more known tourist destination, possibly with some collaboration from the movie industry, and that the international tourist market has increased.

However, despite such positive outlook, there are a number of issues that demonstrate the challenges that small and medium enterprises (SMEs) in the hospitality as well as in other industries face. For example, reports suggest that on average 5.75 times more newcomers start their ventures than what New Zealand's economy can actually sustain (Pinfold, 2001). The number of new start ups in already saturated industries, or the level of owners' preparedness to start a venture can have a direct impact on the lifetime of SMEs. Challenges may be more severe for hospitality business owners, as these have to wrestle with a wide array of bureaucratic, economic, and labour issues, and in recent years with consistent decreases of returns (Stewart, 2006).

To investigate challenges and other business related areas of concern, a study was conducted with the assistance of owners of small and medium hospitality operations in Christchurch and Wellington. A total of 255 hospitality enterprises that included cafes, motels, restaurants, bars and bakeries were approached in these two cities, and invited to participate completing a questionnaire sent to them. In total, 62 (24.3 per cent) responses were obtained.

It was found that 51.6 per cent of the participating businesses had been operating for three years or less, and within this group, 22 (68.8 per cent) had been operating for two years or less. This finding suggests a high per centage of new entrants in the small sample of this study. Several reasons might be behind owners' decision to abandon or sell their hospitality business. For example, the most pressing challenges among participants were lack of skilled labour, with 56.5 per cent of responses, competition from other hospitality businesses (41.9 per cent), and local authorities' rules, including signage and/or costs of compliance (40.3 per cent). In contrast, lack of customers was the least important issue for participants, with only 19.4 per cent of responses.

Interestingly, when ownership structures of the hospitality operators were investigated, it became clear that most operations (74.2 per cent) had already existed prior to being taken over or purchased by the current owner(s). Adding this to the large per centage of participating businesses that had been operating for three years or less (51.6 per cent) provides further evidence of the high ownership mobility among hospitality SMEs. That only 12 (19.4 per cent) of all respondents in this study started their hospitality operations from scratch only confirms the difficulties among many businesses to survive in a very challenging environment.

Participants worked on average 60.6 h per week. Not surprisingly, on average their hospitality businesses represented 84.3 per cent of their yearly income. To be independent or to be one's own boss (83.9 per cent), to make money (72.6 per cent), to change lifestyle (62.9 per cent) and passion for the hospitality industry (58 per cent) are participants' main reasons for starting their hospitality business. In contrast, as it would be expected, working in the hospitality industry 'as a hobby' (4.8 per cent) is participants' least important reason for being in this industry.

While future research could further investigate the overall validity of this study, or if any changes have occurred in the business structure of hospitality SMEs, the overall findings suggest a number of areas that new entrants, or even those already in the hospitality industry, should closely pay attention to.

Questions

1. What challenges other than the ones discussed in this case do you think are affecting hospitality SMEs as we speak? Think about your own suburb, city, or country.
2. What potential strategies, if any, would you suggest for hospitality SMEs in this study to minimise the apparent high per centage of 'casualties' among businesses?

Possible answers

1. A number of individuals may be entering the hospitality industry to make an investment they expect to recover, or reap benefits from, quickly. As positive results in the form of high profits, or even beyond break-even point, are not to materialise within a short-term, disillusion or disappointment may set in among new entrants, persuading a number of them to sell their businesses, or simply abandon the hospitality industry altogether.
2. While it is a complex issue with no simple solution, assistance should be made available by local chambers of commerce, the hospitality industry itself through a task force advising new entrants, or government agencies. Educational institutions (degree providers) could also significantly contribute educating and advising would be entrants about industry requirements so that these would be better equipped, and about potential challenges they might face in the industry.

Source: Alonso (2007).

Understanding the market and its exact competitive nature relative to your service is quite clearly fraught with difficulty. Hospitality entrepreneurs need many answers before they can even think about starting a business or approaching potential investors for start-up funding. The $64 000 question becomes:

■ When is the best time for launching the new business?

This seems straight forward enough as an enquiry but the answer can appear somewhat inexact as it depends on a myriad of environmental and contextual conditions and variables. However, these answers are worthwhile pursuing to optimize the chances of entrepreneurial success.

Key point 6.3

In general, markets are most attractive when they contain only a few competitors. However, this very much depends on the degree of market concentration.

Some commentators speak of 'industry attractiveness'. Simply, if it is attractive it would be reasonable to enter and *vice versa* but how does one measure 'attractiveness'. Linked to this is whether the industry will remain attractive and for how long? This depends on its inherent dynamism, for example, information communication technology is notoriously fast-moving compared to say that of the museum curator. So too, industries such as hospitality will have sectors which are more or less dynamic. The key is to take a strategic perspective, focus on the appropriate areas and ask the right questions. Barringer and Ireland (2006, p. 61) consider an industry to be attractive according to a 'must' list:

■ must be large and growing and important to customers that is 'must' have rather than 'would like';
■ must not be 'mature' where product is tired and price competition is intense;
■ must have high operating margins; and
■ must not be 'crowded' as crowding gives rise to fierce price competition and low margins.

Another useful way to ascertain attractiveness is by brainstorming all of the likely information you are likely to need for the potential business. There are also a number of business models available for guidance; a popular one is Michael Porter's Five Forces Model and it is shown below (Figure 6.2).

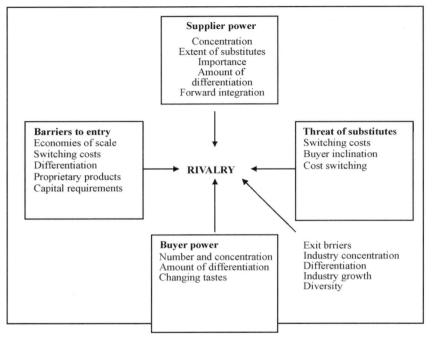

FIGURE 6.2 *Porter's five forces.*
Source: Porter (1985, p. 6).

The construct has value because it alerts the nascent entrepreneur to several key areas prior to market entry. These may be considered as 'information requirements' and once established may be pursued via a number of sources; some examples are shown in Table 6.2.

The World Wide Web is also an excellent source of market information and many of the above have their own sites. It is also worthwhile conducting online searches via an appropriate search engine. However, the entrepreneur must not take this intelligence unquestioningly. Its credibility depends on a number of factors such as why the research was commissioned, who commissioned it and why. All information is political and will therefore have an inherent bias. Entrepreneurs must avail themselves of this background information whenever possible if they are to make balanced informed business decisions. However, even seemingly objective and unbiased information may be based on questionable premises and therefore have weaknesses.

TABLE 6.2 Information sources for feasibility analysis		
Source	**Example**	**Information**
Publications	Books, professional and industry journals, business magazines and daily broadsheet newspapers that is *Hospitality, Economist, In Touch in Business, Management Today, HR Monthly*	Overviews of general economic trends, features on specific industries and regions, service and product intelligence
Databases	Independent vendors, market consultants in possession of consumer lists, telephone and business directories from extant businesses	Electoral registers, property ownership, purchasing behaviour
Government	Central and state government and government agencies	Regulated industries and sectors, Hansard, commissioned inquiries
International, national and regional trade associations, chambers of commerce, trade shows	World Tourism Organization, Institute of Hospitality, Australian Hotels Association	Published surveys and other research related to business interests of members
Annual company reports	All publicly listed organizations	Financial performance, goals, profile of executives and senior management, forecasting and comments on state of industry
Universities and other educational institutions	Rigorous published academic research, opportunity-spotting for innovative business ideas	Tourism Management, International Journal of Hospitality Management, Journal of Management Development, Journal of Small Business and Enterprise Development

Adapted from: Schaper and Volery (2004).

Reflective practice

1. To what extent do you believe Michael Porter's five forces model is a practical option for the hospitality entrepreneur?
2. Discuss why you think this is so.

Complimentary sources of information are those which the entrepreneur may elicit themselves using any number of research methods. Indeed, it is most unlikely that secondary data (even if reliable) will be sufficient for fully informed decision-making. Despite the fact that no one ever has 'perfect' information, the gap often inherent in the avilable secondary data can be filled (at least in part) by the entrepreneur gathering data themselves or commission someone else to do it. In fact, it would be unwise for any business to proceed without this sort of knowledge input as potential sites, markets and so on all have their own idiosyncracies by virtue of context and timing. Simple examples of primary data collection methods include observing how other similar establishments operate by visitation. Nothing could be simpler that booking reservations at nearby restaurants or accommodation in hotels within your vicinity. A wealth of information can be collected in this way including staffing, style of service, interior design, menu style, pricing and so on. Entrepreneurs looking for more 'scientific' and potentially richer information could use interviewing and focus groups techniques or alternatively use trained rearchers.

Similar to the judicious use of secondary data, primary data must also be treated cautiously due to a number of potential biases and inaccuracies which could affect its value. According to Schaper and Volery (2004), the main causes or error are:

- Nature of the sample – is it of the general population or the intended market?
- Is the research method appropriate for the respondents and nature of the research question?
- Are the questions appropriate – do tyey allow respondents to really give their own opinion or do they only allow a response to be categorized into one or two categories when clearly more should be used?
- How high is the response rate?
- Has the research been conducted that can be repeated by someone else – reliability
- Does the information measure what it is supposed to. For example, if a respondent is asked about their preference for a particular variety of tea can this be generalized to their propensity to consume it and other hot and cold beverages?
- Can these results be generalized to other groups of people not included in the study?

Reflective practice

1. You have an idea to open a small bed and breakfast in a popular resort destination. With limited resources, what primary form(s) of data collection would you use for your feasibility study?
2. Same question for a small bistro in a city centre location.
3. Same question for a small hotel on a tropical resort island.

ORIGINATING OR FOLLOWING?

When planning to introduce products and services, the entrepreneur needs to consider whether they are new or simply augmentations of existing ones. If the former, there will be no secondary data available on which to identify a likely demand. A comprehensive understanding of primary data-gathering research techniques and methods is therefore of primary importance. In this situation, other considerations are also important such as whether the innovator wants to deal with issues that arise from being the first operator in a particular field including lengthy lead times prior to profit-making, ease of immitation by competitors and significantly higher costs to bring the service to market.

On the other hand, analyzing markets for services that already exist is much easier than for those that do not and usually less costly. It is certainly more common as most new services are simply an addition or augmentation of other preexisting ones (Audretsch, 1995). For example, some styles of food service delivery require chefs to both prepare and then arrange/present food on the plate to be delivered to the customer by the food server. Others such as *Gueridon* service, sees the food server preparing the dish in front of customers and then serving the finished item (although this style of service is becoming increasingly rare). Breakthrough hospitality services are uncommon but one example would be the 'stone grill' concept where restaurant customers cook the food themselves. Another (and more significant) example is that of the MacDonald's hamburger. Although the food item itself was not novel, the actual service concept underpinning the item was groundbreaking and the owner, Ray Croc, enjoyed what Barringer and Ireland (2006) refer to as 'first mover advantage' for a considerable amount of time before the concept was copied by other organizations. Table 6.3 shows some examples of competitive innovations in hotels in the most recent 15 years.

Being the first to offer a service or product means that the originator can enjoy dominance over the whole market including a powerful and recognizable brand image. On the other hand, disadvantages include costly set up costs and

TABLE 6.3 Range of innovations in hotels	
Frequent guest programs	**Database management**
Strategic alliances	Direct to consumer marketing
Computer reservations systems	Internet
Branding	Travel agent valuation
Service quality management	In-room sales and entertainment
Franchising and management fee	Core business management

Adapted from: Lewis and Chambers (2000).

greater risk of failure. It may also be the case that even if the first mover manages to build market share, business success is not always forthcoming. Moreover, some industries are not structured in a way that rewards first movers. The hospitality industry is one such sector where 'second movers' are often, after studying the originator, able to move in quickly with a refined and potentially more successful product. Besides, hospitality customers are typically diverse with a broad range of tastes and preferences which cannot be satisfied by one service type or where one can be substituted for another.

An important element of market feasibility is successfully identifying a niche for the entrepreneur's product. Essentially, a market segment or niche is a specific subgroup of individuals with a set of characteristics which differentiate them (or the niche) from other consumers (Frederick, Kuratko and Hodgetts, 2007). As an example, these authors note that specific segments exist amongst Australian wine drinkers. A similar classification could be applied to beer drinkers in the UK particularly if 'Real Ale' enthusiasts are included in the total market for beer consumption. These might be ritual-oriented drinkers; premium inconspicuous drinkers; fashion-oriented drinkers and social beer drinkers.

Small hospitality business often begin by selling to niche markets before broadening their horizons. The key is to identify a segment that is large enough to enable entrepreneurial success without invoking direct competition. The paradox is that the more successful a niche, the more limited the time frame for the entrepreneur to remain successful without expanding significantly to combat increased competition. An example here is where ethnic entrepreneurs initially cater for people sharing their own same cultural background, that is, their intended market (see Chapter 2). For example, in the city of Birmingham, UK, a few Pakistani entrepreneurs established the first 'Balti' curry houses in the mid 1970s to satisfy a small and culturally defined demand. Thirty years later, the popularity of these restaurants and demand therefore has expanded to such an extent that the term Balti house is common parlance country-wide amongst the ethnic and non-ethnic groups alike with many original recipes now appearing in generic and dedicated published cookbooks (for example, see Chapman, 1998).

Reflective practice

1 What advantages and disadvantages would face the entrepreneur introducing a new hospitality service?

2 What advantages and disadvantages would face the entrepreneur introducing an imitation or copied hospitality service?

FINANCES

An important stage of the feasibility analysis concerns finances. A detailed analysis is not usually required here as we simply want to gain an impression of whether the idea is likely to be a success or not. Therefore, it is wholly appropriate not to get bogged down in minutiae and financial forecasting but rather, focus on the main areas of:

- capital requirements,
- rate of return, and
- breaking even and other positive aspects associated with the business.

Once these preliminary analyses have been completed and the idea remains a reasonable prospect, financial projection statements can be completed, usually for the first three years of the operation. Usually, these details are included in the business plan (see Chapter 9).

In plain English, a capital requirement simply means how much money (capital) will the business need to start up and from where will it come? An exact amount is not necessary for a feasibility analysis but the estimate should be realistic and account for all likely financial requirements. Typically, they might inlcude cost of premises purchase, staff hire, equipment costs, training, marketing, business launches and so on. A full discussion on raising capital is not appropriate here but some sources include:

- personal savings/assets;
- loans from family, friends, banks or similar institutions;
- business 'angels' and venture capitalists.

In the SME sector of the hospitality and tourism industry, most sources of capital are from personal assets and from family and friends. Conversion of private dwellings remains one of the most common routes for industry entrance. These sources of start-up capital are common elsewhere and reflect the current position in the generic small business sector.

Whilst securing sufficient funding is clearly important, the actual sources of capital also warrant serious consideration. The saying, 'There is no such thing as a free lunch' could not be more appropriate. Capital for start-up will have an associated 'cost' and more 'risky' ventures attract higher costs for the entrepreneur. A useful metaphor here is Marlowe's play *The Tragical History of Doctor Faustus* based on the original Faust story where, in exchange for power and knowledge, the main character sells his soul to the devil. The moral in an entrepreneurial sense is that financiers want a return on their investment and the more substantial the investment the more they will require as a reward for their risk. This does not only apply in a strict financial sense but may also influence the way a business is managed and operated. For example, a family member providing 75 per cent of all start-up funding may waive a financial reward (return on investment) in favour of having a stake in the business which translates into (but not limited to) making most of the strategic business decisions. Indeed, this may even happen tacitly in that a family benefactor may feel 'entitled' to have a significant input into running the business by virtue of their financial contribution and also by dint of their position in the family hierarchy! Obviously, there are a myriad of these configurations and sometimes small family businesses become challenged less by the act of trading and more by the complex interfamily relationships and power structures. The moral here is that for the entrepreneur there are always strings attached when seeking start-up capital whether emotional and/or financial.

The emotional side of capital funding has warranted little attention by commentators but all rightly note that understanding and forecasting a financial rate of return is essential. Typically, projections calculated include 'return on assets', 'return on equity' and 'return on investment' (see Chapter 9) and are used to see whether the projections are appropriate, that is, do they justify pursuing the business idea. Whilst there is a degree of subjectivity involved several issues must be considered ranging from the actual amount of capital required and the time it will take to obtain the return to inherent risks and what economists refer to as the opportunity costs involved. For example, is there a better investment alternative such as a high interest bank or building society account? In other words, what would the potential investor stand to gain (or lose) by investing in your hotel or restaurant in preference to other available investment opportunities?

Key point 6.5

Sometimes small family businesses become challenged less by the act of trading and more by the complex interfamily relationships and power structures. The moral here is that for the entrepreneur there are always strings attached when seeking start-up capital whether emotional and/or financial.

Another key set of questions must be addressed at this stage of the feasibility analysis. According to Schaper and Volery (2004) they can be summarized as:

- How long will it take before the venture reaches break even point?
- How long before cash returns exceed disbursements?
- When will the business be profitable? If this takes too long, the venture will fail.

Barringer and Ireland (2006) draw attention to other issues related to financial feasibility:

- steady and rapid sales growth during the initial five years ina defined market segment or niche;
- high percentege of repeat business;
- ability to forecast income and expenditure;
- internally generated funds to finance and sustain growth;
- availability of an exit opportunity for investors to convert equity into cash (an acquisition or initial public offering).

Reflective practice

1. Interview a hospitality entrepreneur known to you asking for an estimation of when their new venture began to break even?
2. How did they cope financially before their business became profitable?
3. Now they operate a successful business, what is their most significant ongoing cost(s)?

DEMOGRAPHICS

Demographic data is a key part of any feasibility analysis and is reasonably inexpensive to obtain and fairly straightforward, right? Wrong. As with all data in raw form it forms a collection of numbers which can be interpreted in a variety of ways. Typically demographic studies illustrate findings as circles at specific kilometre intervals around a region (like a dartboard without the number segments). According to White (2007) these areas rarely form neat and tidy concentric circles as consumers are not attracted equally from all points of the compass. So what is the best way to identify a market for a restaurant for example?

Around 80 per cent of the restaurant's custom will come from local residents, the remainder will come from those living outside the primary and secondary areas. Understandably, the primary market is likely to be bigger than the secondary market and a feasibility analysis must scrutinize a number of factors to determine the size and shape of the market areas and how much business the restaurant is likely to generate. Table 6.4 contains an indicative summary of what factors to include in the analysis.

Whilst the above serves as a useful checklist, these items are by no means exclusive and other equally important aspects must be considered including the size of restaurant's geographic market, who is attracted, how often they visit and how much they spend. Restaurant design is also a key issue. Will the

TABLE 6.4	Summary and considerations of a feasibility analysis

■ Exact location and site remembering that only a short distance can have an effect on the size of the market area and the amount of business

■ Visibility of signage, major road attractiveness and access

■ Co-tenancies, which includes other tenants or uses in the shopping center or in surrounding properties

■ Layout of the site and relationship of the entrances and parking to the building's entrance

■ Natural and man-made physical features make act as barriers. For example, as rivers and mountains, cemeteries and industrial areas may require potential customers to travel a considerable distance to your restaurant even if they only live a few kilometers away

   o Other barriers tend to be psychological in nature and concern how your business is perceived by association with proximal physical features, often man-made, ranging from unsightly and run-down buildings to the quality of residential estates

   o These psychological barriers can be alternately viewed as opportunities. They key is to know your market and establish your business objectives accordingly. For example, a fine-dining restaurant would find little success on a city-based light industrial estate. However, a medium-priced take-away operation in this location would have a better chance of doing well because its fare would be more appropriate to its primary market – that is industrial workers

   o In a city or town centre location, shopping and entertainment nodes create patterns of travel. These influence the restaurant's exposure to residents in their non-working hours. However, being improperly located within a node could be problematic as being located in a mall may render the restaurant inconvenient to visit

   o Travel patterns are important as if the population normally travels in a southerly direction for entertainment and dining, they may resist going north or west to get to your restaurant. Travel times are also key as they are more important than travel distance. Moreover, traffic density also has a psychological impact on peoples' willingness to drive to particular locations. For example, a longer route which has less traffic and is therefore less stressful is often preferred to a shorter high density trip

Adapted from: White (2007).

operation have a theme? If so how will it be incorporated into the layout and quality of internal fixtures and fittings? Feasibility analyses therefore must be able to target the socio-economic lifestyles of its market(s) in preference to simply identifying an 'average customer' demographically; this is too simplistic. When calculating patronage, spend, and intended restaurant design/ambience the entrepreneur needs more detailed knowledge including Table 6.4:

■ customer values, lifestyles and actual behaviour;
■ with whom they associate or avoid; and
■ of which socio-economic lifestyle groups is your primary market comprised?

For example, knowing that the income of one particular male demographic is between $50 000AU and $60 000AU tells nothing of food-related tastes and buying behaviour. One particular restaurant design or concept may attract a particular group but not another. Not knowing about their preferences and behaviour will prevent the entrepreneur from operating optimally; relying on gut reaction here will just not do. In the hospitality industry amongst chef restaurateurs (particularly amongst those with limited resources and business savvy), it is often believed that customers share the same love of food and wine as themselves. In some cases, chefs believe they can 'educate' their customers out of their preferences for less ostentatious dishes. Whilst this is commendable in one sense it is also incredibly arrogant and fool hardy in another. Occasionally, there may be an isolated success story or two. However in the main, businesses started intuitively with little more than the entrepreneur's belief that others share their predispositions are doomed to failure as many anecdotal tales from the hospitality industry will attest.

Key point 6.4

Typically demographic studies illustrate findings as circles at specific kilometre intervals around a region (like a dartboard without the number segments), these areas rarely form neat and tidy concentric circles as consumers are not attracted equally from all points of the compass.

SUMMARY

Feasibility analyses determine whether a business idea is worth pursuing or not. This can be framed in a number of ways but answers key questions such as:

- Is there a market for the considered service or business idea?
- Are there adequate sources of start-up and continuing funds? and
- Does the entrepreneur have the skills or other means to deliver this service?

In the hospitality industry (but not exclusively) there is a tendency for entrepreneurs to commit emotionally to a new venture and launch before first conducting a thorough and systematic analysis of all pertinent factors. This process is key to optimise chances of business success irrespective of whether the venture is of the 'lifestyle' or 'growth' types.

Feasibility analyses should be comprehensive but appropriate to the new venture focussing on areas of:

- personal characteristics of the entrepreneur;
- nature of the competition;
- availability of start-up and continuing finances including rate of return and breaking even; and
- demographic information.

This information can be obtained from a variety of sources including that which has already been published and also by a process of primary data collection. The latter is particularly important if the new service is a truly novel concept because in these circumstances data will not be readily available given the originality of the idea. However, making sense of secondary data and collecting reliable primary data is fraught with difficulty. The former type will almost certainly contain errors and biases to a lesser or greater extent depending on who commissioned the research, why and how the data was gathered and interpreted. Collection of original data requires a full understanding of appropriate research methods to avoid drawing inappropriate conclusions. This research may be either commissioned from a dedicated professional organization or undertaken by the entrepreneur. The choice most often depends on available resources but the process itself does not necessarily have to be overly onerous. Ultimately, the amount of data required on which to base an initial 'yes' or 'no' decision rests with the entrepreneur. However at the very least, they should be confident that most bases are covered. Nascent entrepreneurs should speak with experts and or familiariz themselves with at least one construct (checklist) designed to ascertain 'industry attractiveness'. This should allow an educated estimate of whether the venture is likely to be a success. The following stage is a more detailed inspection of the market, finances, organizational readiness and so on in the form of business plan.

Case author
Small and medium hospitality enterprises in New Zealand: too many new entrants?
Dr Abel D Alonso
Edith Cowan University
School of Marketing, Tourism and Leisure
Australia

CHAPTER 7

The Family Business: Who's to Bless and Who's to Blame?

After working through this chapter you should be able to:

- Identify the inherent advantages family firms have over non-family firms
- Understand the roles of key individuals in the family firm
- Discuss the nature of conflict in family businesses
- Identify why a significant number of family businesses fail to be transferred successfully

INTRODUCTION

The *Collins English Dictionary and Thesaurus* (1992) defines 'Family' as '[a] parent and children or near relatives'. A family business is more difficult to classify. According to Litz (1997) and Sharma (2004) this is because the field itself is still relatively new and under-researched; therefore, several definitions exist. Litz (1995) suggests that a business can be defined as 'family' when its ownership and management are concentrated within a family unit.

Shanker and Astrachan (1996) are more prescriptive and note that the criteria used to define a family business can include:

- Percentage of ownership;
- Voting control;
- Power over strategic decisions;
- Involvement of multiple generations; and
- Active management of family members.

The *Australian Family and Private Business* Survey of 1997 classifies a business as 'family' when any one or more of the four following criteria are met:

- More than 50 per cent of the ownership is held by a single family;
- More than 50 per cent of the ownership is held by more than one family;

143

■ A single family group effectively controls the business; or

■ The majority of senior management is drawn from the same family.

In 2003 the same survey opted for a self-identification method, asking businesses to nominate whether they thought they were either a family or non-family business (Smyrnios, Walker, Le, Phan, Vuong, and Young, 2003). Currently, *Entrepreneur.com*, defines a family firm as:

> *A business actively owned and/or managed by more than one member of the same family, http://www.entrepreneur.com/encyclopedia/term/ 82060.html, retrieved February 2008.*

These definitions are unhelpful in terms of furthering scientific research in the field as they do not allow direct comparison between studies. However, they are useful here as they have a commonality and introduce the notion of 'family control' or dominance of the business by one or more family members which is appropriate for this chapter. Nonetheless, an assessment of the extent to which family businesses exists cannot be accurate due to definitional differences but we can make some reasonable assumptions. For example after reviewing the evidence, the Centre for Labor Research concluded that 67 per cent of Australian firms consider themselves to be family businesses (Spoehr, Nukic and Robertson, 2005). In the US, around 92 per cent of American businesses are classified as family businesses (Shanker and Astrachan, 1996). This makes the sector significant in terms of employment provision and wealth generation.

Reflective practice

1. How would you help overcome the challenge of defining small family hospitality firms?

This chapter identifies the difficulties in obtaining an accurate profile of small family owned hospitality firms and continues by discussing some typical roles played by family members in new hospitality businesses. A notion of new venture teams is introduced and the use of 'external' advisors outlined including governmental and non-governmental sources. The chapter continues by discussing the advantages that small hospitality family firms have over those managed by others and how conflict may be recognized and addressed. Finally, transferring the family business and succession planning are introduced with some suggestions how the complex process may be managed effectively.

HOSPITALITY AND TOURISM

Most hospitality and tourism enterprises fall into the small or micro firm category. Unfortunately, it is difficult to be entirely accurate due to the non-uniform manner in which the information is collected. However, aggregated data suggests that internationally most hotels are small to medium-sized (Lee-Ross, 1999). In Australia, they form 90 per cent of total hotel stock (Lee-Ross, 1998). Similarly, in the UK around 85 per cent of hotel firms are small (Sheldon, 1993). The Australian and UK profiles are reflected globally and Morisson (1998) comments that internationally, 'The small firm continues to play a significant role within the hotel industry . . .' (p. 191). Moreover, owner-operators account for 85 per cent of all hotels (MSI, 1996). This is confirmed by Wanhill (1997) who notes that the small and medium-sized hospitality sector is dominated by family businesses. It may therefore be concluded that family plays a vital role in the hospitality and tourism industry and that to understand entrepreneurship therein necessarily requires an understanding of how families think, interact and operate.

When it comes to starting a new hospitality business, there is a temptation to rush headlong into the process without first giving due consideration to those who will actually be involved. Often at start-up there may only be one person, the founder, and perhaps a 'significant' other who will probably be holding down a job elsewhere to ensure an income stream at this crucial early stage of the business. Assuming the entrepreneur wishes to grow the firm (not all do) creates a situation where one individual simply cannot undertake all the required activities, certainly not in the long-term. So who exactly becomes involved in running small hospitality firms? The following hypothetical case helps us to identify some key people and also highlights other issues including poor planning, impoverished knowledge of alternative sources of finance, role ambiguity and obligations of family members.

The 'Sea View' Bed and Breakfast

Stella and Gary Slack purchased a B & B in a UK seasonal seaside town. Formerly, they were locals living elsewhere in the town and so had a reasonable understanding of the tourist demand for accommodation during the busy summer months.

Stella held down a job in a local retail outlet whilst Gary worked for a gas and oil rig maintenance company. Tired of his 'two weeks on' and 'two weeks off' shift-working arrangements both he and Stella decided to start afresh as small hoteliers. After giving notice, Gary quit his job and they purchased and an existing B & B business in need of some 'tender loving care'; Stella remained employed elsewhere as they would have to rely on her job for income during the 'off-season' when the business was closed.

After extensive refurbishment during the winter months, Stella and Gary opened their doors for business in June of the following year. At first, trade was slow but they had received a number of bookings from the regular trade established by their predecessors. Stereotypically, Stella did much of the cooking and Gary looked after general maintenance and some waiting at tables. As the summer season began to gather pace, their B & B became busy with many 'walk-ins' and increased prior bookings. This demand meant that for a period of around six 'peak' weeks, they managed to let all eight of their bedrooms almost every night.

Understandably, this created extra work; far more than they could deal with by themselves. So like many new entrepreneurs they relied on family members, friends and locals to fill positions including, room attendants, wait staff and kitchen assistant. All individuals were paid the going rate for the job including family and friends. Some were *bona* fide employees whilst other were paid 'cash in hand'. As the season started to become quieter, some staff were no longer required.

After several successful Summer seasons, Stella and Gary decided to expand their business premises. Luckily the adjacent B & B was up for sale and the couple were most keen on making a purchase. However, they could not raise enough capital to secure the deal so they approached family members in the hope of an interest free loan. Much to their delight a brother and sister in law came to the rescue but with one condition. The new couple wanted joint ownership and, occupying similar roles, to work alongside Stella and Gary in the new venture.

After little thought, virtually no negotiation or scenario planning, Stella and Gary agreed to the condition. Soon after the house was purchased both converted into one large B & B with 16 bedrooms. After decorating and renaming the new B & B, all was set for their first busy summer season.

1. How would employing these individuals have affected the running of Stella and Gary's B & B and how should they have planned for the busy period?
2. How would the founders have advertised these employment positions?
3. What knowledge would Stella and Gary have needed to ensure their staff were enjoying fair and legal employment conditions?
4. What impact would the new couple have on the operation of the B & B?
5. Take an educated guess at some of the opportunities and challenges associated with joint ownerships and working with partners.

Source: the authors

Key point 7.1

Family plays a vital role in the hospitality and tourism industry and that to understand entrepreneurship therein necessarily requires an understanding of how families think, interact and operate.

THE CHOSEN FEW

As discussed in Chapter 1, many hospitality enterprises fail in the first year or so of operating. Reasons cited include poor marketing, inability to innovate, poor business planning, failure to delegate responsibility and so on. These shortcomings are essentially people-related, that is, many entrepreneurs lack relevant expertise and experience. Barringer and Ireland (2006) refer to this as the '... liability of newness ...' (p. 127) where firms struggle because of inexperienced and inflexible founders and associates. One of the biggest hurdles is for the entrepreneur to identify their weaknesses and be totally honest about it. This is important when starting a business and questions the founder needs to ask herself include:

1. What do I know?
2. What don't I know?
3. What do I need to know?
4. Who has this expertise and knowledge?
5. How do I access and use these skills?

Satisfying these questions for some may be difficult, because entrepreneurs typically have a strong 'locus of control' (see Chapter 2) and as such, may not like to admit their shortcomings. However even before start-up, it is essential that founders are smart enough to realize that they may not have all of the answers and relevant business experience to run a small hospitality firm successfully. They may be deficient in a number of areas and require the advice and expertise of others. The best situation is where the family group is heterogeneous (within reason) and all individuals bring different knowledge and experience to bear on the new firm. However, a more usual scenario is where family members only possess a few complimentary skills or where the family group is so small (two people) that neither person has the required business knowledge.

So what can entrepreneurs do to address these knowledge and skill gaps? Fortunately, free advice is usually available from an array of public agencies and interest groups. Local tourism and hospitality associations are good places to seek advice. Several examples of generic small business services are shown below:

■ Australian government sites - http://www.business.gov.au/Business+Entry+Point/How-to+guides/Thinking+of+starting+a+business/& http://www.australia.gov.au/Small_Business
■ www.business.qld.gov.au/mentoring

- National Network of Area Consultative Committees funded by the Australian Government, working to promote regional development www.fnqacc.com;
- Council of Small Business of Australia Ltd. - http://www.cosboa.org/webs/cosboa/cosboaweb.nsf/
- Small Enterprise Association of Australia and New Zealand - http://www.seaanz.asn.au/
- UK Government - http://www.businesslink.gov.uk/bdotg/action/home?domain=www.businesslink.gov.uk&target=http://www.businesslink.gov.uk/
- Advice for small business (UK) - http://www.smallbusiness.co.uk/ & http://www.smallbusinessadvice.org.uk/sbas.asp
- US Small Business Administration - http://www.sba.gov/
- European Small Business Advice - http://www.esba-europe.org/
- Small Business Europe - http://www.smallbusinesseurope.org/en/

Similar services are offered in other countries and are free with advice being offered on all aspects of running a small business including, staffing, strategies for growth, marketing, sources of finance, strategic planning and so on. Alternatively entrepreneurs can avail themselves of similar services from private firms who charge for such a service.

Another option for hospitality founders is to acquire and apply knowledge but this could take time and prove costly in the long run. Networking with others in industry associations and elsewhere through social outlets may also allow the entrepreneur access to business knowledge and information. Wherever the hospitality founder seeks information she must be eager and quick to learn if it is to be used effectively and developed. Family businesses are often at an advantage here as the knowledge acquired stays within the firm and grows organically over time with the addition of new family members. Whilst focused industry-relevant acumen is advantageous, prior generic business savvy is also important when starting a new business. So too is an awareness of funding availability. The following case illustrates this point.

How I Got Started

Nantwich-based entrepreneur Andrew Donaldson was running storage businesses in and around Manchester when he decided to get into the hotels business.

He began by setting up his own company, The Egryn, to buy the Egryn hotel in the North Wales seaside resort of Abersoch. And he quickly secured [pounds sterling] 450 000 of financing from Bank of Scotland Corporate, which was recommended to him by his accountants.

Donaldson's main aim was to attract young families and budget travellers by offering cost-effective, comfortable rooms on a sliding price scale. Although there are numerous hotels and B&Bs in the area, he felt that holiday-makers on a tighter budget were not really catered for, leaving a lucrative gap in the market. Fortunately, Bank of Scotland Corporate shared his vision.

Having bought the hotel, Donaldson used the remainder of the cash to refurbish and extend the property, turning the former owner's accommodation into a three-bedroom, self-catered chalet, bringing the total number of bedrooms available to 10, along with one-bedroom staff accommodation.

And he certainly didn't hang about. Contractors were lined up and waiting and, after Donaldson got the keys on 1 July, 'with a lot of hard work and endeavour' the new-look Egryn was open for business within 48 hours.

Occupancy rates have been good so far, with the self-catering chalet let out for the whole of the summer. If the project continues to be a success, Donaldson, who set up his first business in 1991 with a loan from the Prince's Trust, aims to develop further sites in the area, making the most of his storage knowhow.

> 'Buying a hotel is a first for me,' he says, laughing, 'although the two companies both work along the same principle of letting out space.'

Source: Donaldson, A. (2004) How I got started, *Caterer and Hotelkeeper*, Sept. 2, p. 105.

Reflective practice

1. Interview a entrepreneur known to you asking how they identified their knowledge and skills gap and how they addressed the problem.

A checklist of those who may be involved directly and indirectly in a new venture is shown in Table 7.1. Clearly some roles apply to family members whereas other more specialized ones do not.

The above list is by no means exhaustive, for example, the last category of 'Other professionals' is vast as each person offers a different service. Moreover, a decision to hire such people must not be taken lightly, a variety of issues need to be considered beforehand. Shaper and Volery (2004) caution that business consultants must not be considered a panacea for all business challenges and the founder should engage in their own research before using such services. These authors provide a useful summary of criteria which must be addressed prior to engaging the services of business consultants; they are shown in Figure 7.1.

TABLE 7.1	New venturers

Players	Details
Founding team	■ Can be more effective than individual entrepreneur as mutual psychological support offered to each member; ■ Past successes are a good predictor of new venture also allows trust to be developed; ■ Heterogeneity provides good basis for inter team debate provided individuals are significantly different to each other; ■ Power struggles may ensue as venture develops; ■ Members must have appropriate skills, knowledge and experience and operational ability linked to the venture. Restaurateurs should ideally have food production and service abilities in addition to higher management capabilities.
Key employees	■ Decision to hire based on solid planning, some founders may play key staffing roles, especially in a family business where flexibility is key; ■ Good 'job fit' is essential, recruited through existing founder network, advertisements in various media, executive search firms for management staff.
Board of directors	■ Necessary when firm becomes incorporated, not usual in hospitality SMEs especially at start-up; ■ Directors add 'legitimacy' to firm, sends signals to customers, employees and investors; ■ May be founders or external who oversee appointment of managers, declaration of dividends and affairs of the firm, usually meet quarterly ■ Other key role is ongoing support and guidance for founders and managers, therefore essential that directors have appropriate experience.
Advisory board	■ Ongoing panel of experts, similar role to directors but has no legal responsibility for firm
Lenders and investors	■ In the family firm these will probably be relatives and friends. May also be keen to observe the hotel closely and to become involved depending on the significance of the investment; ■ Can be a cause of conflict where investor has different ideas of operating compared with founders and managers; ■ Can provide invaluable help and advice in areas including recruitment, market knowledge, as directors or advisors.
Other professionals	■ These include, lawyers, accountants, architects, business consultants and so on; ■ Small hospitality businesses might use a consultant for advice in several areas as employing one person in each designated area would be too costly.

Source: Adapted from Barringer and Ireland (2006, pp. 128–140).

An important issue not shown above is that of entrepreneurial confidence. Often the founders of small hospitality firms have technical knowledge and little else. It is vital that rapport is established between founder and consultant if the bases of the new firm are to be established to optimize its chances of future success. Some consultants are passive whereby the client is assisted in finding their own solutions. Others adopt a more dominant role as problem-solver (solicitor or accountant), whilst some challenges are of a more fixed nature. For example, a hotelier might decide to adopt computer software to deal with guest reservations. In this instance the consultant may be an

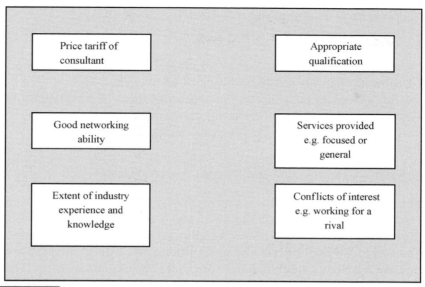

FIGURE 7.1   *Key selection criteria.*
Adapted from: Shaper and Volery (2004, p. 232).

employee of the software manufacturing firm hired to give specific instructions about how to use the new system. In any event, the type of problem usually dictates the consultancy style.

Key point 7.2

Before opting to use a consultant for business advice founders must engage in their own research to establish the credibility of the potential advisor.

ADVANTAGES OF THE FAMILY BUSINESS

Leach (1996) cites seven advantages enjoyed by family firms:

- Specialist knowledge and know-how protected and retained by the family;
- Free advice from experienced family members;
- Extensive business and social networks;
- Extensive knowledge of markets, suppliers etc;
- Commitment through family ties;
- Cultural long-term stability and positivity relative to non family firms;
- Reliability and pride building strong relationships with customers;

- Short-lines of communication allows fast decision-making;
- Family usually willing to advance loans at zero or low interest with 'flexible' repayments;
- Initial passion of founder may be transferred inter-generationally;
- Resilience of family members during times of crisis;
- Long-range planning although not necessarily of the 'formal type'; and
- Employment flexibility in terms of time and effort and whether to accept a full salary all of the time especially when business is not performing.

Adapted from: Leach (1996) and Deakins and Freel (2006).

Sirmon and Hitt (2003) also consider the family firm to have several inherent advantages noting that success depends on the management of a few unique resources. The first is how complimentary the skill sets of immediate family are. Second, a recognition that individual family members are likely to have a variety of complimentary external networks and linkages. The third resource is the nature of family capital which is often unfettered by red tape, is 'flexible' (in some cases interest-free!), and may be relied on in cases of emergency (including free labour). Finally because of the trust element present in family firms, much of the costs associated with 'official' policies, procedures, security systems and so on are at a minimum. Burns (2001, p. 359) agrees noting that a business culture characterized by task orientation, and performance management is at a disadvantage because it lacks a strong sense of emotional attachment which characterizes the family-firm.

However, family businesses also have their problems, the most obvious being nepotism. Deakins and Freel (2006) consider that the overarching management style exhibited in small firms tends to be autocratic and malignantly paternalistic. Overwhelming evidence suggests that this is also the case in the hospitality and tourism industry. Family firms are prone to conflict for a number of reasons which are discussed in the next section.

Reflective practice

1. Through either desk research or by interviewing a hospitality entrepreneur known to you, identify some key inherent advantages that family businesses enjoy.

FAMILY CONFLICT

Business founders typically experience higher workloads than virtually all categories of employee (Harris, Saltstone and Fabroni, 1999). It would therefore be reasonable to expect high stress levels amongst these individuals. Furthermore, these extreme conditions are likely to engender conflict in the workplace. This may also be compounded by other issues if working closely with family members. Conflict within the family is likely to negatively impact on venture performance by lowering the well-being of the founder and subsequently hinders work performance (Sheldon, 1993, p. 289). Shelton (2006) defines work–family conflict as:

> 'A form of inter-role conflict arising because pressures emanating from one role are incompatible with those from another role' (p. 288).

So does this mean that conflict is reduced when the work/life interface is managed appropriately? The answer is 'yes' but there appear to be other challenges and nuances within the family group which must also be considered.

So how is conflict best reduced in family businesses? The evidence is conflicting but some cautious generalizations can be made. In small to medium-sized hospitality firms, co-founders are often family members. However, convening the family team or rather the appropriate configuration thereof is essential and may be challenging due to the inherent roles played by individuals as family members. For example, who will be the leader of the family business, the child, father, mother, uncle etc.? The extra dynamic here is that of the 'traditional' hierarchical structure of the family and the culturally bound relationships between members. Lambing and Kuehl (2007) note that family businesses are complex precisely because they are based on family relationships rather than the relatively simple notion of making money. There may be cases of nepotism, sibling rivalry for the top job and disharmony between parents and children. These challenges may be exacerbated when offspring marry and the family becomes extended. Not to mention the extra financial burden accompanying the advent of more members joining the business.

What about the relatively simpler family profile of only two members? Many small hospitality firms are comprised of only husband and wife (or similar) and employ others only during the busy periods. Even this situation may create a double edged sword. Figure 7.2 identifies some related advantages and disadvantages.

Essentially, the issue here is 'business creep', that is, when work and family life become merged. This often happens during the early stages because couples (and other members) are intent on making their business successful to the exclusion of everything else; family life therefore takes second place. In extreme cases, this can continue until it is hard to distinguish the family from the firm. Anxieties and work-related stress can manifest in the home environment. Ultimately, these pressures can result in couples divorcing and other family members becoming estranged. Interestingly, divorce rates and/

Advantages	Disadvantages
Both partners/spouses work long hours to make the hospitality business a success	Too much time spent together
Partners/spouses can rearrange working conditions to account for domestic chores	Conversations and activities in domestic setting are dominated by business issues
Marriage/relationship and careers and intertwined	Divorce/separation may cause loss of business for at least one of the partners
Trust	

FIGURE 7.2 *Advantages and disadvantages of family 'couples'.*
Adapted from: Lambing and Kuehl (2007, p. 95).

or separations amongst hospitality managers are high at 33 per cent (Shrimpton, 2002). So too is alcoholism which may also reflect the significant stress levels under which family members work (Crosland, 2007).

So how can the impact of business creep be mitigated? Several coping strategies exist and they fall into two categories. The first considers psychological coping responses to negative emotions surrounding work–family conflict (see Ashforth, 2000). For example, suppression of behaviour and thoughts between the work and family domain, fixation and significant focus on only one domain to counteract the negative consequences of the other and limited involvement in one area to cope with demands from the other.

There are a number of practical steps which may help limit the negative effects of working side by side with a partner. Probably the easiest to implement is establishing separate times to discuss business and personal matters. A somewhat more challenging practice is to describe each partner's behaviour and then discuss it. If all else fails, a family business consultant may be used or even a family relationships counsellor! (Lambing and Kuehl, 2007).

The second strategy looks at role manipulation. Rooted in the earlier work of Moen and Yu (2000), Shelton (2006) advances the notion that role elimination, role reduction and role-sharing are key considerations for high performing family businesses (particularly for female entrepreneurs). Evidence suggests that work-family conflict may be lowered more effectively (than internal coping mechanisms) by adopting appropriate work-family management strategies as they can reduce conflict by changing the configuration of competing family and work demands. Moreover, if used judiciously these measures can also reduce the requirement for psychological coping mechanisms (Shelton, 2006). The strategies shown below help lower family conflict by organizing, sequencing and delegating work and family activities:

- Role elimination – no role in family
- Role reduction – smaller family role or deferring a family until business is established
- Role sharing
  - o delegation of role played in the venture (participative management techniques)
  - o delegation of family role by outsourcing family obligations

The actual strategy chosen will depend on the salience of work and family roles (i.e. which is most important) and the type and quality of external resources available. The founder has to find an optimum 'fit' taking these factors into consideration. Shelton (2006) advances the idea that salience may be mapped against external resources as shown in Table 7.2.

It also goes without saying that in a business sense, both partners must share goals for the growth and development of the firm and allocation of roles. Furthermore, these issues are seldom static and may change over time as the business changes and matures. It is essential to revisit any original agreements on a regular basis.

The road is obviously fraught with difficulties and some commentators, in a general sense, recommend the use of a 'family council' whereby members meet regularly to discuss and debate major issues. Advisory boards may also be used to help ameliorate the inherent problems of governing a family business. Burns (2001) advises a four-step approach to resolving conflict within the family:

- Address the critical issues relating to family involvement in the business, that is, how does the business relate to the family and vice versa;
- Establish a family council to express views and set ground rules;

TABLE 7.2 Optimal work-family management strategy choices

		Internal family salience	
		Low	**High**
External resources	High	Delegate family role (role-share)	Delegate venture role (role share)
	Low	No family (role elimination)	Defer family
			Smaller family (role reduction)

Source: Shelton (2006, p. 292).

■ Construct a family constitution by developing a written statement of the family's values, beliefs and objectives; and

■ Monitoring progress and maintaining regular communication through council meetings.

Adapted from: Burns (2001, p. 367).

In a practical sense resolving family conflict is unlikely to be as smooth as suggested by the above model but these elements are important and the wise family business founder(s) would be advised to give each adequate attention.

Key point 7.3

There are two overall strategies for mitigating the negative impacts of business creep. The first considers psychological coping responses to negative emotions surrounding work-family conflict. The second is the manipulation of the work-family situation by role elimination, role reduction and role-sharing.

Reflective practice

1. What strategy would you adopt to avoid business creep in the small family owned and run hospitality firm and why?

SUCCESSION PLANNING IN THE FAMILY BUSINESS

The effective transference of the small hospitality firm from one generation to another (i.e. succession) is a direct result of thorough planning and communication as it addresses a number of key questions including:

■ Will the business be transferred on a certain date or by a certain date? The former is immediate whilst the other is a longer term option and, all things being equal, the preferable pathway;

■ Who will be the successor and are they ready and capable of running the business successfully? If not, how will the transition period be managed and by whom until the 'heir' is sufficiently skilled?

■ Does the heir want to take over the hospitality enterprise?

■ Do they know that parents are planning to hand it over? and

■ When will the business be transferred?

The following case illustrates some of the above issues.

A Success Story

Like many hotel owners, long-time Best Western member Don Seaton grew up in a lodging industry family. More than 50 years ago, his parents owned a small, independent property in the Lake Tahoe region of California.

> *'I started out when I was eight years old, doing the laundry,' Seaton said. 'We didn't have dryers back then, so my job also involved taking the clothes to the back line, drying and folding them.'*

Looking at a career in education, Seaton went on to college, but after graduation, he found it difficult to make ends meet on a teacher's salary. In 1960, his father offered him a full-time marketing position at the property, which by then was a Travelodge. Seaton then started out on his own, acquiring a Travelodge in Clearwater Beach, Fla. Seaton sold the property, but by 1973, his family had acquired a membership for the 110-room Best Western Seawake Inn, also in Clearwater Beach.

Now, almost 30 years later, his daughter Wendy Damsker is manager of the Seawake. His other two children also have worked in the lodging industry. And Seaton's Best Western portfolio now includes the 116-room Best Western Crystal River Resort in Crystal River, Fla., and the 124-room Best Western Harbor View in Melbourne, Fla.

As the son of a hotelier and father of children who wish to continue in the business, Seaton typifies the 'sandwich generation.'

When it came time for Seaton to take over the business, he chose not to accept the inheritance of his parent's stock, but to acquire their interest equally with his wife. Seaton and his wife now own 50 per cent, with the remaining 50 per cent split among his three children. In part, this has been undertaken as a strategy to blunt the otherwise significant impact of inheritance taxes.

> *'In our kind of business, it's very important that the next generation doesn't get clobbered by these taxes,' said Seaton, who also has six grandchildren-none of which has shown an interest to make lodging their career choice.*

When imparting grandfatherly advice, Seaton encourages them to be flexible. Like family entrepreneurs in other industries, he knows the fourth generation of a hotel family doesn't tend to be locked into the family tradition.

Sid Friedman is president and CEO of Philadelphia-based Corporate Financial Services, a consulting firm that helps manage the generational transition in hospitality industry families. Friedman said he believes successful succession planning is an art comprising prudent financial planning and managing the human relationships and pride that come into play as part of family life.

When it comes to the financial aspects, Friedman is a big believer in family-limited partnerships.

'When you start bringing your kids into the business, the growth is in your kids' names, not in yours,' he said.
Gift taxes on bequeathed-limited partnerships are significantly lower than estate taxes.

'Limited partnerships help get the assets out of the estate,' said Bill Meyer, co-owner of Meyer Jabara Hotels, a company based in West Palm Beach, Fla., with a 25-hotel portfolio. 'The [Internal Revenue Service] will attribute the limited-partnership interest with a 25-per cent discounted value for estate-tax purposes. Gifts of a limited-partnership interest don't have control aspects, which is why the IRS discounts the value of that gift.'

Meyer's father and the father of his business partner, Bill Jabara, are 40-year veterans who still play important roles in their hotel businesses. Their franchises include Holiday Inn, Sheraton, Marriott and Hilton.

Family matters come into play when heirs who have been substantially vested feel they should have the major say in day-to-day hotel-management affairs. Friedman said disputes might result if the parents don't want to cede control. He recommends setting up two classes of stock, with parents retaining a majority of voting shares.

Friedman said that while some children in a given family might be interested in continuing in the hotel business, others might not. In such cases, he suggested awarding ownership with a ratio partially determined by each child's degree of interest.

Michael Gulesarian is certainly an interested member of a second-generation hotel family. His father, 68-year-old Ed Gulesarian, owns a 175-room Sheraton Commander hotel in Cambridge, Mass. Trained as an engineer, Ed Gulesarian has been with the property since 1969. That year, his own father, who started in the residential suites business in 1946 and acquired the Commander in 1960, brought him into the business.

Ed Gulesarian still owns the 75-year-old Sheraton Commander, but his son Michael is general manager. At times, this can lead to generational disputes about how much authority the offspring has.

'He is basically running the place and really doing an excellent job,' Ed Gulesarian said. 'I have given the reins to him, but sometimes I stick my nose in things. I find it difficult to let go.'

Gulesarian has yet to work out the financial aspects of generational transfer.

'We have to do some more estate planning,' he said. 'Three weeks ago, the sermon in church was, 'Do what you can do today, and don't leave it to tomorrow.' That's probably right.'

Cendant Corp. franchisee Rick Williams also grew up in the hospitality industry as one of three brothers in an entrepreneurial family that first owned several motels in Georgia during the 1960s. He recalled overhearing conversations about the business as a child, but his education didn't stop there.

'Throughout the years, my exposure went beyond the dinner table,' Williams said. *'I bell-hopped, checked rooms and desk-clerked.'*

Williams is responsible for the 10-property hotel arm of Adel, Ga.-based Williams Investment Co. Because Williams was more interested in the hospitality business than his siblings, he said they have complemented each other. His father, John Williams, still drops by the office. *Source*: Shaw (2002) Successful succession transfers take prudent financial planning, *Hotel & Motel Management*, http://www.hotelmotel.com/hotelmotel/article/articleDetail.jsp?id=37172, Retrieved February 2008.

Unfortunately succession planning in small family firms is an area which is often haphazard and 'organic'. Smyrnios *et al.* (2003) note that amongst first generation family firms in Australia, only just over half survive into second generation with around a quarter of this proportion following through to the third generation. North American succession statistics are similar with only 30 per cent of businesses surviving the first generation (Ward, 1988) with a mere 15 per cent passing to the third generation (Morris, Williams, Jeffrey and Avila, 1997). These authors consider a lack of planning as the major reason for failure including family quarrels leading to poor decision-making or no decision-making, irrational division of family assets, appointment of incompetent managers and so on. The hypothetical case below illustrates some of these challenges.

Growing Pains

David and Ruth Edwards were a successful entrepreneurial couple who owned a seventy-bedroom seaside hotel. Originally some 25 years earlier, they bought into an equal partnership arrangement with four existing partners. After a couple of years, they raised enough capital to buy out all of them and became proud sole owners of their establishment. In their late thirties at the time of purchase, they had a son Eric aged 16 who began to work in various roles. Eric continued to gain operational hospitality skills and experience, even working for short periods in other hotels, up until he left the region to attend university. During this time Eric returned during vacations to work for his parents in the family business. After graduation, he returned to work full-time in the hotel but now as a supervisor/junior manager. Happy to be working in this new capacity, Eric was keen to be given more responsibility for the strategic side of the business. He and his father also now broached the idea of succession once David and Ruth neared retirement age. Eric greeted this with enthusiasm but was disappointed with the outcome. Discussions simply consisted of ill-focused exchanges about what might or might not happen in the future with his father constantly stating that 'One day son, all of this will be yours'. This was rather frustrating for Eric but he was unsure what he should do next, after all it was his parent's business and they could really do what they liked with it.

As the years went by Eric's role as manager really amounted to nothing more than providing emergency cover across most departments when staff failed to turn in for work. In fact, the only time Eric was granted any managerial responsibility was on his parent's one day off every week. And on these days he would receive a constant stream of telephone calls from his mother telling him what he should and should not be doing when dealing with issues that may arise on that day.

On a more personal level, Eric was feeling discontented as recently he sought to move out of the family home into a place of his own. Much to his disappointment he was unable to arrange a mortgage for a nearby house because his salary was relatively low in comparison with other paid employment for a man of his qualifications and experience. Begrudgingly he had to approach his parents to raise extra capital for the purchase. They of course were more than happy to do so but Eric was starting to feel beholden to them and began to question his financial worth and as a member of the family business. After undertaking desk research on salary levels for comparable occupations he became even more disgruntled.

A couple of years later Eric got married to Layla. She had extensive management experience in hotels but left her most recent position to accompany Eric in the family business. All four family members now worked together and Eric hoped that this new situation would tacitly persuade his parents to give him and Layla more real managerial responsibilities in the hotel. In more private moments, Eric and Layla saw that the business was doing reasonably well but there was much room for improvement, particularly in the area of banqueting and weddings. Fortunately, they could cater for these events with virtually no disruption to the ongoing business of the hotel as it had several kitchens and function rooms which could be easily cordoned off whilst events were taking place. After much discussion, from their notes, they drew up a comprehensive business plan and presented it to David and Ruth. It was received rather coldly and unenthusiastically despite their being few costs apart from employing a limited number of wait staff as and when the situation demanded. After the ensuing discussions where the parents were non-committal, nothing more was said about the matter. Six months later Eric once again tried to convince his parents about the worth of the idea. He was informed that while the scheme seemed reasonable, both David and Ruth were quite happy with the way things were and could not really see anything other than extra work being created for everyone, if the new idea was pursued.

Eric and Layla felt that this response was not only typical of people entrenched in a particular way of thinking and working but also short-sighted. After all, the family business would soon be expected to support four people rather than David, Ruth and, to some extent, Eric. They also considered his father's attitude to be rather disrespectful of their feelings and abilities. Later that year Eric and Layla found paid employment elsewhere and moved to a different region.

Some ten years later, David and Ruth decided to sell the family business and retire. After a lengthy five years on the real estate market, the hotel was purchased by a Chinese consortium for a vastly reduced price.

1. Discuss the important succession planning and issues revealed in this case.
2. Identify the major problems from the perspectives of Eric; and his parents.
3. Suggest how things could have been managed more effectively.

Source: the authors

Unfortunately, this case reflects a common situation where there is unclear communication between the founders and their children. It also highlights the common entrepreneurial challenge of an inability or unwillingness to delegate responsibility. Finally, it exposes how unsatisfactory transferring (or not as the case may be!) a business can be if succession plans are not seriously considered well in advance of retirement. There is really no substitute for careful planning when family businesses are passed from generation to generation. However, even with a succession plan in place, transferring a family business is challenging.

The following case similarly illustrates the often 'unspoken' and un-planned process of succession.

Kingtree Lodge: Savouring Success

Website: http://www.kingtreelodge.com.au

David and Cheryl Rourke are the original start-up owners of Kingtree Lodge and Kingtree Wines in the Ferguson Valley. This valley is a lush and verdant part of the Geographe Wine Region, 38 kms east of the regional port city of Bunbury and some 200 kms south of the state capital Perth, Western Australia. The decision to move to Ferguson Valley was in part a 'tree-change' for the couple since the valley is a certainly a wonderful place to live, work or visit. In this context, their investment decision did have a lifestyle aspect to it which is reflected in the way they have structured the business.

Built in 1991, the property consists of a federation style award winning two storey lodge built from beautiful local polished hardwood timbers. The main building is over 950 square metres in size and is situated high up overlooking 100 acres of prime valley land. The property was purpose-built to accommodate the family and up to eight guests in separate areas of the two storey structure. The business mix includes a vineyard, café and the hosted accommodation, all of which this couple run with some help from their eldest son Peter.

The wines from the vineyard have collected many awards including the Gold Medal at the Qantas/Mount Barker Show, Silver and Bronze Medals at the Perth Royal Show and Silver and Bronze Medals at the Geographe Wine Show. This entrepreneurial couple have built up the property to now be worth in excess of AUD$2,500,000 with no debts to external parties. It is all too easy for the casual observer to forget that they work long hours and have all the market and seasonal risks attendant with running a hospitality and viticulture business. Success has come through hard work, attention to detail and a positive 'can do' approach to life and business.

At the time of writing this case Cheryl was 52 years of age and David was 74, they have two children aged 22 (Peter) and 11 (Olivia) from their marriage of 24 years. Considering their age, it is apparent that the Rourkes have already given considerable thought to who will inherit the property if something were to happen to them. Olivia is too young to consider her future career and Peter is still undecided about the long term viability of working on the farm. The vision that the Rourkes now articulate is one where son Peter and his new wife will work the vineyard part-time, build a home on the property and perhaps continue to work off-farm. At present Peter and his wife are trying life off the farm, working in higher paid opportunities that are the result of the mining boom happening in the northern parts of Western Australia. Until Peter returns home and makes a career decision the future of the winery remains in limbo, to sell or to pass on to the children. With father David now having turned 75 he wants to retire in the near future, so some tough decisions are needed.

It seems unlikely that the hosted accommodation business will be viable once Cheryl decides to retire because they need and want to continue living in the property. When discussions of succession switch to the hosted accommodation Cheryl quips that her 'retirement plan was death'. The top floor of the lodge was designed as a retirement space for the Rourkes. Once they retire, the downstairs hosted accommodation area will be used to vacation the family they now have, and any new grand children. So, even as they plan for the possible end of one component of the business they look forward to enjoying new beginnings.

Source: Weber, 2007

Burns (2001) explains the succession process through a model based on that of Churchill and Hatten (1987). Essentially there are four stages involved in the transfer of power:

- Owner managed firm – early stage when founder has control and son/daughter are introduced to the business permanently;
- Training and development – decision is made to pass business on to heir and process of training and development takes place;
- Partnership – heir shows enough acumen and knowledge and founder relinquishes some control and engages in more delegation and power sharing; and
- Power transfer – strategic planning, management control and operational responsibility shifts to the incoming generation with founder playing a less active role in business and ultimately retiring.

Adapted from: Burns (2001, p. 362)

Key point 7.4

Amongst first generation family firms in Australia, only just over half survive into second generation with around a quarter of this proportion following through to the third generation.

In reality, handovers are not quite as prescriptive or systematic as the model suggests and conflicts may be frequent taking a variety of forms with a number of behavioural outcomes. These include the orientation of the founder which, according to Lambing and Kuehl (2007), is linked with their strong locus of control. This means they are loath to relinquish control of their business to anyone including their children. This may manifest as jealousy as the entrepreneur's control ebbs away. The founder may also ensure boundaries are unclear so that they can still exert significant power in the decision-making process. A less extreme version is where the original owner expects their offspring to manage the business in exactly the same manner as they have done. This can create enormous problems where second generation family members have different ambitions and attitudes (Deakins and Freel, 2006). Managing a family business with limited autonomy where major decisions are still being taken by the founder is a recipe for disaster (as illustrated by the 'Growing pains' case).

There may also be the issue of sibling rivalry (O'Brien, 1998). What happens when there are many children, power-sharing? This sounds like a reasonable solution but it does not always work especially if the founders make no distinction between heirs active in the firm and those who are not. Perhaps appointing the most qualified sibling as leader could help but what constitutes 'most qualified'? Will the remaining siblings accept this decision as fair? Martin, Martin, Martin, and Mabbert (2002) identify the following 'succession risk factors':

- firms where there is no distinct management team and employing between 10 and 50 employees;
- where business success is attributable to owner's personal goals;
- where founder is unable to delegate decision-making effectively;
- an absence of an internal successor; and
- when owner ignores the need for succession.

The key for successful transition is to begin planning early so that transference is a gradual process rather than one 'transplanted' onto the heir. Moreover, the planning process should be intergenerational and involve both active and non-active family members. It is often useful to develop something in writing which sets out roles, responsibilities, objectives and a management framework. It is also important to remember that transferring a small hospitality firm will have financial and tax implications. Call in solicitors and accountants to give expert legal and financial advice. For example, in many countries, founders can 'gift' business assets up to a certain sum per annum to the next generation without incurring financial penalties and minimize inheritance tax upon the death of the founder. Planning for retirement is also an important but often overlooked element in the context of business transference. This will have positive financial and emotional outcomes so long as the decision to retire is resolute (Burns, 2001).

Reflective practice

1. Through desk research, identify two successful intergenerational hospitality firms and discuss the reasons for their accomplishments. Now repeat the exercise for two family firms who have not enjoyed similar success.

Assuming heirs do not want to establish different careers, Deakins and Freel (2006) advance the notion that for successful transition, founders must have a full understanding of their situation and ensure that the successor receives appropriate training. In order to ensure clarity of roles and responsibilities it is a good idea to include such in the firm's business plan to avoid squabbles but also to inform potential investors should this be desired in the future.

Harvey (2004) concurs and identifies several key factors in successful transitions including:

- Understanding the need for change and planning for it;
- Willingness of founder to foresee retirement;
- Recognising the importance of business education amongst heirs;
- Making sure individuals are trained;
- Ensuring heirs work elsewhere to broaden their business experience and aspirations;
- Ensuring heirs have a comprehensive knowledge of the family business where possible; and
- Engendering motivation amongst heirs to run the business.

Adapted from: Deakins and Freel (2006)

Manikutty (2004) proposes that for a family firm to be successful after transferral it must focus on several independent variables grouped under three headings of governance, business philosophy and culture and managerial practices. Specifically, the variables are:

- Governance
  - o A greater number of external members serving on the board of directors;
  - o Decisions being taken collectively rather than the Chief Executive Officer; and
  - o Having a clear succession plan.

- Business philosophy and culture

  - o A continuation of the founder's business philosophy by the subsequent generation; and
  - o An adherence by subsequent family members to the cultural norms of the founder.

- Management practices

  - o Delegation of important decisions to lower levels;
  - o Prioritization of team management as preferred practice;
  - o Focus on strategy; and
  - o Sophisticated and systematic financial, marketing and operational planning; and a use of outside services of consultants and advisors.

Adapted from: Manikutty (2004).

SUMMARY

Notwithstanding the difficulties of defining and therefore establishing an accurate quantum of family owned and operated hospitality firms, they would appear to dominate the hospitality industry internationally. Many fail within their first few years of operation but others succeed. This chapter has over-viewed some of the probable causes for these outcomes.

There can be no doubt that many small family owned hospitality businesses become established due to the enthusiasm and sheer hard work of the founders. However, the ability and willingness of these individuals to engage in appropriate planning would appear less than forthcoming. Before start-up, founders need to identify their own strengths and weaknesses to determine who will actually be involved in the business. Many small hospitality enterprises are family run and for this reason have a number of potential advantages of those operated by managers and employees. A few of these are:

- Commitment;
- Resilience;
- A cheap or even free labour force;
- Long-term stability; and
- 'Flexible' financing.

However, the above benefits will only occur provided account is taken of the attributes each family member brings to the firm, that is, they must be complimentary to avoid role conflict and duplication. Moreover, other challenges arise including a potential for nepotism, sibling rivalry, exploitation and so on.

A common problem encountered in small hospitality firms especially in the early stages is 'business creep' where work and family life become merged. New entrepreneurs have a tendency to devote all of their time and effort to the new business and relegate or put family life on hold. This is understandable during start up but if allowed to perpetuate can have a number of negative outcomes including divorce or separation for couples, estranged family members and ultimate failure of the small hospitality firm. There are some practical measures and coping strategies which if adopted may help mitigate business creep including:

- limiting involvement in either work or family domain to cope with the demands from either area;
- establishing separate times to discuss business and personal matters; and
- delegation of family responsibility to another person and so on.

An overall strategy is to establish a family council where members meet regularly and discuss major issues.

One could be forgiven for thinking handing over a family business to successive generations is a fairly straightforward affair. However, this is not the case and succession planning or transferring the family firm is an area where careful planning is an absolute must. Aggregated evidence suggests that between 30 and 50 per cent of all small businesses survive into second generation, with significantly fewer following through into the successive generation. There are a variety of challenges to the smooth handover of a family business; some concern issues of financial planning but many more surround the emotions of the founders and heir(s). For example, some owners tend to resent losing power after transferring the firm and actively seek to limit the decision making autonomy of the new family member. Similarly, founders may have not considered the matter of retirement to any great extent and are left making decisions for which they nor their successors are prepared. Other challenges where founders have more than one child include sibling rivalry, identifying criteria most effective when delegating power and control and whether to include children who are not already active in the business.

Proceeding on the basis that family members do not see employment elsewhere and are internally motivated to take over the firm, there are some key issues which founders need to consider to increase the likelihood of successful transitions:

- An understanding of the need for change and planning for it (including foreseeing retirement);

- Ensuring heirs receive appropriate prior business and skills training including acquisition of experience outside the family firm; and
- Ensuring heirs have a comprehensive knowledge of the family business.

Case author
Dr Paull Weber
Curtin University of Technology
Australia

CHAPTER 8

Hospitality, Commercial Homes and Entrepreneurship

After working through the chapter you should be able to:

- Critically discuss hospitality and hospitableness in the context of small firms
- Recognise the attractiveness of commercial hospitality to owner/managers
- Evaluate the linkages between commercial homes and hospitality businesses
- Recognise the tensions and dilemmas inherent in commercial homes

INTRODUCTION

The prevalence of small firms in the hospitality and tourism sector is a dominant feature of the international industry. Even in advanced market economies where a small number of firms dominate most markets, most individual hotels restaurants and bars are owned and managed by small firms. Whilst recognizing that a small number of hotel groups, restaurant groups and some country pub groups, do control a disproportionately large share of these markets, most premises are owned by small firms. Frequently, these are micro firms, employing fewer than 10 staff, and in many cases they employ none, other than family members who 'help out' as needed (Lashley and Rowson, 2003, 2005, 2007).

Whilst there are clearly economic and location factors which limit opportunities for economies of scale and require the location of hotels, restaurants and bars to be close to their markets, the sector has attractions for the small firm entrepreneurs. The nature of hospitality, its cultural meanings and links to domestic experiences suggest for many would be entrepreneurs that they have the skills needed to offer hospitality services commercially (Lashley and Rowson, 2008). The 'commercial home' provides a setting for a number of levels of commercial engagement. Also, and perhaps more importantly, it allows different levels of engagements as host. This chapter suggests that hospitality and opportunities for engagement with hospitality and acts of hospitableness is a significant attraction to those looking for business opportunities, for working closely with the family, or for undertaking work which limits engagement with the labour market. The chapter explore some of the emergent issues and debates surrounding hospitality and hospitableness before going on to discuss issues and dynamics flowing from studies of the commercial home.

Reflective practice 8.1

Describe your most memorable experience of being a guest in a hospitality setting. This may be in a private dwelling or in a commercial setting. What makes it memorable.

ON HOSPITALITY AND HOSPITABLENESS

The emergence of the *hospitality* to describe commercial service delivery in bars, hotels, restaurants and other catering activities provides a chance to look at these commercial operations with a more critical eye because of the implied meaning that these businesses provide more than services for monetary exchange. Hospitality has deep cultural significances across the globe. Although there may be some cultural variations, hospitality implies:

- altruistic giving,
- welcome for strangers, and
- feeling of safety and security.

Certainly, recent academic enquiry and debate amongst academics suggest that hospitality and hospitableness are worthy avenues of study in their own right (Lashley and Morrison, 2000; Lashley, Lynch, and Morrison, 2007; Molz and Gibson, 2007). The study of hospitality from social science perspectives has enabled a better understanding of host–guest relationships in an array of

- commercial,
- non-commercial, and
- domestic settings.

In some cases, social scientists have used hospitality as a metaphor for understanding societal interactions between host communities and the guests who come as tourists, asylum seekers, foreign workers, or migrants. In the case of entrepreneurial firms, hospitality can be studied to the extent that it persuades individuals that there are opportunities to generate income. Many seem to think they have the necessary skills to provide commercial hospitality. In some cases, the perceptions are that the provision of food, drink and bed spaces requires no skill. It is something they do at home (Lashley and Rowson, 2008).

Key point 8.1

Studying hospitality as a wider social phenomenon helps explain why so many would be entrepreneurs consider that they have the skills necessary for business success providing commercial hospitality services.

Lashley (2000) initially proposed that a three domain model helped to set the context of hospitality using a Venn diagram to distinguish between cultural/social; private/domestic and commercial domains but to also show how the domains potentially overlap and influence each other Figure 8.1.

Whilst it was recognized that the Venn diagram was unsophisticated, it did allow a discussion of the three domains to take place and the following will highlight some of the emerging issues that have implications for the management of hospitality and tourism. The Venn diagram also suggested a way of thinking about hospitality that looked beyond the immediate commercial activities in hotels, restaurants, bars and cafes, etc.

■ Hospitality was also likely to be practiced in private domestic settings, and this was likely to be a site of learning about hospitality that might ultimately inform hospitality practitioners in commercial settings.

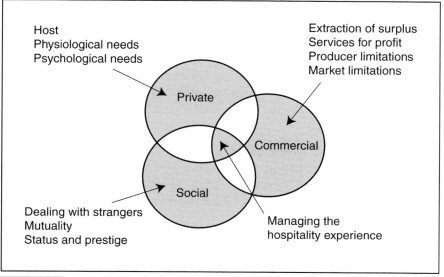

FIGURE 8.1   *The three domains of hospitality.*

- Both would be set within a social and cultural setting that would inform expectations of both guests and hosts about hospitality transactions.
- The social and cultural domain provides the setting in which both the private expectations of hospitality and commercial delivery of hospitality goods and service take place.

The French philosopher Jacques Derrida said,

'Not only is there a culture of hospitality, but there is no culture that is not also a culture of hospitality. All cultures compete in this regard and present themselves as more hospitable than the others. Hospitality – this is culture itself.' (2002: 361).

The social/cultural domain

The quotation from Derrida (2002) suggests that these are claims made by all cultures, and are indications of the human decency with which a society seeks to define itself. Derrida tends to assume a timeless and unchanging aspect of hospitality.

- It is clear that modern industrialized societies do not have the same cultural and religious obligations to be hospitable to strangers.
- There is not now, as there would have been in medieval England (Heal, 1990), or Austinia Rome (Lomaine, 2005), ancient Greece or Judea (O'Gorman, 2007) a need to offer shelter, food and drink to strangers.
- Nor is there a widely held social intention to 'turn strangers into friends' (Selwyn, 2000).

That is not to say that these obligations do not exist in contemporary societies across the globe, as will be discuss later, there are examples of societies where these obligations on both guests and hosts are taken very seriously, and in some cases with deadly consequences when transgressions occur (Lashley, 2008).

- A common theme in all these settings is that the obligation to offer hospitality to strangers was both cultural and religious.
- Socially defined meanings of decency included requirements to offer shelter to strangers, to provide food and drink and protection from danger.
- These obligations extended to all, irrespective of status or origins.
- These social and cultural obligations were reinforced by religious strictures and in both Greek and Roman, and later Christian parables suggested that the Gods, or Jesus, often assumed a disguise as a poor

traveller, so as to test the hospitality offered to strangers by hosts, and woe-betide any host who refused a request for hospitality.

■ In all these Greek, Roman and Christian contexts, the parables suggest that a failure to be hospitable would result in all worldly goods being taken away from the inhospitable wrongdoer.

Writing about hospitality in the early medieval England, Heal (1990) suggests that there were strong moral cultural obligations to offer hospitality to travellers, strangers and the homeless. The host was to offer protection and safety as well as nourishment and a place to sleep. She says these obligations were founded on five underlying principles:

1. that the relationship between host and guest is a 'natural' one (i.e. that it is grounded in the nature of social life);
2. that an intrinsic part of being a host is having regard for the *sacred nature* of the guest (which refers, broadly, to the honour and status to which a guest may bring to the host);
3. that hospitality is noble;
4. that *altruistic giving* is an established and expected part of English social life;
5. that hospitality and the social relationships and exchanges it engenders are at least as important as those formed in the market place (22).

Although the obligations to be hospitable no longer have the moral authority they once had in advanced industrial societies, moralists continued to make reference to them throughout the 20th Century. Selwyn (2000) traces sermons by religious leaders stretching into the nineteenth and twentieth centuries which were extolling the virtues of giving hospitality. Even in 1930s USA the Catholic Workers movement advocated re-engaging with medieval ideas of hospitality as a way of providing support for unemployed and poverty stricken people (Selwyn, 2000). Writing form a Christian perspective, Nouwen (1975) argues that hospitality should consist of the following facets:

■ Free and friendly space – creating physical, emotional and spiritual space for the stranger.
■ Stranger becomes a guest – treated as a guest and potential 'friend'.
■ Guest protected – offer sanctuary to the guest
■ Host give gifts – the host welcomes the guest by providing the best gifts possible.
■ Guest gives gifts – the guest reciprocates and gives gifts to host.
■ All guests are important and gifted – the host values the guest and gains value from them.

- Acceptance, not hostility – especially the kinds of subtle hostility, which makes fun of strangers or puts them into embarrassing situations.
- Compassion – hospitality is basically a sense of compassion.

Whilst these obligations to offer hospitality do not have the same social and cultural force that they once had, many individuals are still concerned about hospitality and being good hosts, and also we must not forget, good guests. Sherringham and Daruwalla (2007) remind us of an old Italian saying, which roughly translates as, 'Guests are like fish, after three days they stink'.

These obligations to offer hospitality to strangers are of interest for a number of reasons.

- First, the moral and ethical dimensions of hospitality provide an interesting point of comparison with the current commercial delivery of hospitality goods and service. 'Treat the customers as though he/she was guest in your own home' (Lashley, 2000: 13) is how one restaurant company attempted to instruct staff in the levels of service required. Of course this instruction only applied if the customer was able to pay.
- Second, these moral, ethical and personal commitments to provide hospitality, although not so widely held across the society promoted as they were in the past, may well be held by individuals who want to make a living out their passion to entertain in a hospitable way. Hence the sector may be attractive to entrepreneurs with a specific interest in hospitality, learnt through the wider culture or through religious teaching.
- Third, the models of hospitality from the past or through ethical teaching may help entrepreneurs to be gain competitive advantage by adapting the principals of hospitality to inform service deliver and build customer relationships, 'Turning customers into friends' (Lashley and Morrison, 2004).

Key point 8.2

Cultural obligations to offer hospitality and to be hospitable provide important ethical modes which can guide contemporary entrepreneurial practice.

On hospitableness

Typically hospitality and hospitableness are expressions of altruistic generosity driven by pure motives and a desire to serve others without immediate promise of reward. Telfer (2000) considers the philosophy of hospitality, and suggests that there is a distinction between hospitality and hospitableness. Telfer's work suggests that the motives of hospitality are what defines whether hospitality is genuine or not. Providing hospitality because the host has an ulterior motive or for personal gain, is not said to be true hospitality.

Interestingly this raises an issue of interesting debate about the meaning of true hospitality and the role of reciprocity. Hospitality practiced by elite families in Augustinian Rome was founded on the principle of reciprocity as an early form of tourism (Lomaine, 2005). Affluent Romans developed networks of relationships with other families with whom they stayed as guests and then acted as hosts when their former hosts were intending to travel.

For Telfer (2000), these reciprocal arrangements do suggest ulterior motives and question the nature of the hospitality. This does also raise issues about the nature of commercial hospitality because one reading of Telfer's assessment is that commercial hospitality is not likely to be hospitable because of the provision of hospitality being linked to the ulterior motive of profit generation.

Telfer (2000) suggests truly hospitable behaviour is motivated by genuine needs to please and care for others, and should not be practiced to deliberately impress the guest or for the expectation of repayment. She says hospitable motives include the following:

- the desire to please others, stemming from general friendliness and benevolence or from affection for particular people; concern or compassion;
- the desire to meet another's need;
- a desire to entertain one's friends or to help those in trouble.
- a desire to have company or to make friends, and the desire for the pleasures of entertaining – what we may call the wish to entertain as a pastime.

Key point 8.3

Truly hospitable behaviour is different from offering hospitality because it is motivated by genuine needs to meet the needs of others and hospitableness.

Consideration of hospitableness is valuable to hospitality operators because it can provide a model for staff training as well as service quality definition and management which can build a genuine competitive advantage for hospitality entrepreneurs. If strangers/customers can be converted to friends they are likely to be much more loyal customers.

The private/domestic domain

Whilst there are cultural and social expectations about hospitality which set the broad rules about both the treatment of guests by hosts, and the behaviour of guests when they are being hosted, the practice of practical hospitality is experienced mostly in domestic private settings.

■ Entertaining family and friends for dinner, offering drinks to visitors and even accommodating them are activities that are widespread in most societies.

■ Typically individuals would therefore experience being guests in other families' homes, and being hosts when others come to their home.

The rituals associated with hosts and hosting behaviour is itself a topic worthy of study. Rules about guests making contributions to the host in the form of wine, gifts, or dishes to be consumed are worthy of study across communities.

■ In some cases, the guest who turns up for dinner without a contribution of a bottle of wine would be regarded as lacking generosity and taking advantage of the host.

■ In other cases, hosts might be offended by the guest who arrives with wine, food, etc. because it suggests that the hosts cannot afford to entertain the guest.

Certainly, these obligations and expectations will be largely shared through the sharing of cultural and social norms of what is appropriate (Lashley *et al.*, 2007).

The key concern for hospitality and tourism operators is the extent that these motives and desire can be captured, promoted and delivered in a commercial context. In principle, Telfer suggests that where hosts are offering hospitality for personal gain, or for vanity or solely out of a sense of duty the actions are not genuinely hospitable. Warde and Martens (2000) research on 'dining out' suggested that dinners interview about their experiences of dining in commercial and domestic setting stated that the experiences in domestic setting was more authentic than those in commercial restaurants.

■ The domestic/private domain of hospitality provides a bench mark against which commercial hospitality is judged.

■ Respondents often use the language of domestic hospitality to evaluate their experiences in commercial settings (Lashley *et al.*, 2005)

■ It is also a source of learning about host and guest relations which can be used during communications with guests and with staff in commercial operations. For example, one UK based restaurant group required service workers to 'treat customers as though they are guests in your own home' (Lashley, 2001: 70).

The link between the private domestic domain and commercial activities as a source of learning also extends to career choice as many subsequent chefs initially take their inspiration from within the home (O'Mahony, 2003).

- Research on top award winning chefs by O'Mahony suggests that a common theme with all the winners was that they had developed their love of cooking and entertaining with a mother or grandmother.
- Lashley's (1985) research into leading hotel and restaurant chef profiles also revealed that they typically developed an enjoyment of food and cooking in the home with a mother, grandmother, or other significant female family member.

Furthermore, the link between the domestic domain of hospitality and commercial activities has a major influence on hospitality entrepreneurial activity. This occurs in two ways.

First, many commercial hospitality activities are set in domestic dwellings. The 'commercial home' in the small hotel and bed and breakfast sector, or in farm stay settings involve guests entering the private domestic dwelling.

- Often the decision has involved selling domestic home to buy the hotel. Lashley and Rowson (2005, 2007) found that over 70 per cent of hotel owners in Blackpool's small hotel sector had sold a house in order to purchase the hotel.

Lynch and MacWhannell (2000), Lynch (2005), and Sweeney and Lynch (2006) have undertaken research exploring the relationship between commercial hosts and their paying guests. There appear to be different levels of engagement with between hosts and guest.

- In some cases, hosts accept and treat paying guest as they would family and friends. In other words, there are few 'no go areas'; guests and hosts dine together, use the same sitting room and sleep in bedrooms still adorned with family bric-a-brac.
- At the other end of the scale, guests and hosts occupy different parts of the property, eating in separate dining rooms, sitting different in rooms and guest sleep in bedrooms which have been made to be depersonalized. Lynch (2005) points to some important tensions in the expectations of guest in these small properties compared with hosts and their advisors.

Overseas visitors often choose these smaller hotels and guest house precisely because they want to live with a 'real family'. However, the hotel proprietor wants to establish some distance from their paying customers, and tourism official frequently advise them to professionalize their relationship with guests, making it less friendly and more anonymous like a traditional larger hotel.

The second link to between domestic and commercial domains of hospitality is in the nature of the assumed skill sets required to operate a commercial hotel, bar or restaurants. Through the domestic nature of providing sleeping accommodation, food and drink many new business start ups underestimate the skills needed for successful commercial hospitality operations (Lashley and Rowson, 2007).

The domestic/private domain of hospitality provides valuable insights for those interested in marketing commercial hospitality experiences. It establishes a context in which individuals perform acts of hospitality and display their qualities of hospitableness. The domain also establishes the sense of authenticity of the hospitality experience. The assumption being that those who invite guests to stay or dine, in their home are motivated by the desire to entertain, though as Telfer (2000) shows, these motives may not always be genuine. Individuals may be offering hospitality out of a sense of vanity, for ulterior motives or because they feel an obligation to do so. Certainly, the domestic/private domain is an important setting for both learning the obligations to be a good host and guest, and the specific skills need to run accommodation, bar and restaurant operations.

Key point 8.4

The private/domestic domain of hospitality provides a key learning environment for learning social and cultural expectations of hospitality and it can provide a basis for learning skills relevant to commercial hospitality.

The commercial domain

One of the key issues relating to hospitality provision in the commercial sector relates to the authenticity of the hospitality provided.

- Are commercial hospitality products and services merely another service?
- Can commercial hospitality ever be genuinely hospitable?
- Are models of cultural and privates hospitality of any value?

Slattery (2002) and Jones (2004) argues that restaurant, bar and hotel services are essentially economic and involve a management activity. The study of hospitality from wider social science perspectives has limited utility. In this view the guest-host transaction is essential monetary transaction whereby the host supplies food, drink and/or accommodation for payment in money. This chapter argues that the study of hospitality from these wider perspectives is a worthy exercise in itself, but it can also inform the management of hospitality commercial provision. By considering the nature and quality of the host–guest transaction, commercial hospitality can develop long term relationships with guests and build competitive advantage through the relationship.

Ritzer (2007) suggests that there are powerful drivers in commercial hospitality organizations that will lead hospitality provision becoming 'inhospitable'. Ritzer's comments on McDonaldization suggests that there are corporate drivers to increase

1. efficiency,
2. calculability,
3. predictability and
4. control.

These lead ultimately to the creation of systems which acts as a barrier to frontline performance of hospitality. These McDonaldizing processes inhibit performances which are hospitable and at the same time they generate customer feelings of being undervalued as individuals. These standardizing and systemising processes therefore are a fundamental aspect of the approach to managing hospitality services in bars, restaurants and hotels and effect remove the 'hospitality' from the transaction. In Telfer's (2000) terms the commercial transaction provides an ulterior motive for offering hospitality and therefore prevents genuine hospitality.

Telfer (2000) does suggest that it is not inevitable that commercial hospitality will invariably be a less than authentic version of hospitality in the home. She suggests that it is possible that those who have an interest in, and who value, hospitality will be drawn to work in the commercial hospitality sector. They may run their own hospitality businesses, or choose to work in roles that enable them to be hospitable.

Key point 8.5

There are clearly some tendencies to McDonaldize commercial hospitality and tourism services, however, it is possible that entrepreneurs with a strong personal need to be hospitable may be drawn to opening business which offer guests accommodation, food and drink in a hospitable context.

Work by Lashley *et al.* (2005) on 'memorable meals' suggests that the emotional dimensions of the meal where much more significant than the quality of the food in creating memorable meals. The research asked respondents to provide a written account of their most memorable meal. The texts were subjected to semiotic analysis and a multi-dimensional image of the meal emerged:

- the nature of the occasion of the meal,
- fellow diners who made up the company with whom they dined,
- characteristics that contributed to the atmosphere, food eaten,
- overall setting, and
- the service provided.

The occasion was typically some significant event in which the social dynamic of the meal reinforced the emotional significance of the event. Here the event is made more significant by the hospitality setting. The occasion of the meal or holiday is often a celebration of bonding and togetherness with family and friends. The company of others comes across strongly in these accounts, and although one account involved the company of just one other person, most involved groups of people, and none involved an individual diner on their own. The atmosphere created by the setting, other people and their treatment by hosts provide emotional dimensions to meal occasions which are vital to creating memorable occasions. Interestingly, few of the respondents mentioned the food consumed or quality of dishes as part of their descriptions.

The dominant impression is that these emotional dimensions of hospitality are what make these meal occasions special, and it will be these emotional dimensions of their visit that make for memorable hospitality and tourism events. Interestingly, when asked to recount their most memorable meal experiences about half the respondents quoted occasions which were in domestic settings, whilst the other half occasions were in commercial settings.

Key point 8.6

Commercial hospitality activities provide would be entrepreneurs with business opportunities in which they feel they already possess the key skills or a setting to exercise their hospitality skills a personal need to be hospitable.

ATTRACTIVENESS OF HOSPITALITY ACTIVITIES

The study of hospitality from a wider set of social science perspectives is useful in developing an understanding of entrepreneurship in the provision of accommodation, food and drink products and services.

■ The fact that entrepreneurs regard the provision of these products and service as ones with which they have a developed expertise is directly related to the domestic provision of hospitality.

Would be entrepreneurs, typically, have acted as hosts provided accommodation, food and drink to guest who either visited or stayed in their home. In turn, they themselves will typically have been guests in other people's homes and received these 'hospitality services' from other hosts as friends, relatives or other acquaintances.

■ So for many new entrants to the industry, there is no perceived skill deficit which might hamper their decision to pursue an entrepreneurial decision to buy a guest house, hotel, bed and breakfast, pub, inn, restaurant of café.

Furthermore, individuals with domestic dwellings of the right size, location or structure have been able to consider turning part of their domestic space over to commercial activities.

■ Accommodation services, in particular, lend themselves to this commercialization of the home, or parts of it, to commercial activities.

But there are also examples of individuals using domestic premises to provide food and beverage services through outside catering, banqueting and contract catering in workplaces. Licensing restrictions over the sale of alcohol, will in many countries, limit the conversion of the domestic space to commercials bars and pubs, but many of these licensed premises were originally domestic dwellings.

■ Linkages between gender roles in the home and income generation outside the home typically result in the commercial home providing opportunities for women to become, or remain, economically active without entering the labour market (Lynch and MacWhannell, 2000)

In fact the linkage between the commercial home and economic activity which avoids the labour market is a powerful attraction for many would be entrepreneurs. Research with 'lifestyle style entrepreneurs' (Lashley and Rowson, 2001, 2005, 2007) suggests that there are a number of motives for engaging in commercial activities from a home base.

In the pub sector in the UK, for example, it is possible to take over a pub operation via a tenancy or leasehold arrangement where the 'in-going' is literally a few thousand pounds. One respondent in a major pub company suggested that the pubs with lower sales level would be let as tenancies, typically ranging between £5000 and £7000; whilst pubs with higher sales volumes might be let via leasehold arrangements costing between £40 000 and £50 000 (Lashley and Rowson, 2001). In neither case, are the capital requirements prohibitive for many would be entrepreneurs. In addition, families looking for accommodation and some form of economic income stream are attracted to this sector.

■ Many pub companies looking for tenants or leaseholders who are former service personnel from the armed services or the police because those with long service will come out with a 'lump sum' to pay for the tenancy of lease.

In this latter case, people who have had a career in the service and are now looking for work on 'civvy street' take on a pub because it provides them with a potential business opportunity and income stream as well as domestic dwelling area above the pub. They are in effect avoiding the labour market and gaining access to a 'free house' associated with the business.

■ The fact that 30–40 per cent of these properties can change hands each year is a by-product of the mismatch between the expectations of and the realities of life as an entrepreneur in the pub business (Lashley and Rowson, 2001)

The restaurant and take away meals market are attractive to members of ethnic minorities (Collins, 2000). French, Italian, Greek, Indian sub-continent and Chinese migrants in particular are found in many European, US, and Australian cities. O'Mahony (2007) highlights the important role that Irish migrants played in the development of 'hotels' in Victoria. The Nineteen Century British colonial powers excluded Irish migrants from positions of power and prestige. The Irish migrants found commercial opportunities in the brewing and pub/restaurant sector, often described as 'hotels' (Table 8.1).

Key point 8.7

Low barriers to entry into commercial hospitality businesses means that many potential entrepreneurs running small firms face few restrictions on business start ups.

COMMERCIAL HOMES

The link between commercial hospitality business activities and the home is a complex one, covering varying degrees of business intensity. Lynch (2005) takes more accommodation service model. Table 8.2 replicates his list of categories and types of commercial homes.

TABLE 8.1   Hospitality venues as attractions for would be entrepreneurs

Hospitality establishment type	Attracted groups of would be entrepreneurs
Bed and breakfasts Cultural homestays Farmhouse stays Guest houses Host families Small family run hotels	Married women Married couples Other relationships Redundant workers Semi-retirees Lifestyle changers Those looking for more personal control Those attracted to the area
Pubs Inns Bars	Ex service personnel Former police officers Lifestyle changers Redundant workers Families looking for a 'free house'
Restaurants Cafes Snack bars Take-away restaurants	Migrants Married couples Lifestyle changers Those who enjoy cooking
Contract catering Dinner party catering Office catering	Married women Married couples Collectives of men and women

The commercial home title in the way Lynch employs the term has two dimensions. The first recognises that in many of these establishments guest and host share the same premises with a varying degree of proximity and shared space. Lynch and MacWhannell (2000) suggest that there are several potential levels of interaction between hosts and guests within the premises. The second dimension is that the concept of the home, and homeliness are often implied in the construction of the design of the property and the marketing offer to guests. Often the size of the property is restricted to a small number of rooms more like a private home, or in a location which suggests more historic (and more hospitable?) times. This second dimension brings us back to an earlier point that the word hospitality allows the commercial offer of hospitality to link psychologically to private hospitality.

Lynch and MacWhannell (2000) suggest three levels of interaction between commercial hosts and commercial guest in the home setting. At its most closely linked to notions of private hospitality, commercial guests and their

TABLE 8.2 Commercial hospitality and tourism home types

Categories of commercial homes	Examples of types of commercial homes
Traditional commercial homes	Bed and breakfasts
	Cultural homestays
	Farmhouse stays
	Guest houses
	Host families
	'Monarch of the Glen' properties
	Religious retreats
	Self-catering properties
	Small family run hotels
	Writers retreats
Virtual reality commercial homes	Boutique hotels
	Country house hotels
	Timeshares
	Townhouse hotels
'Backdrop' hotels	Houses used as visitor attractions
	Houses used as film sets

Source: Lynch (2005: 39).

hosts share much of the space of the private dwelling. Bedrooms are similar décor to those used by host family members. Sweeney's work (2008) shows that in this type of establishment many of the guest's rooms are adorned with personal ornaments and photographs from the host family. Indeed being made to feel 'one of the family' is probably an important aspect of this business offer to its clients. So much of the dining space, and living space is shared between hosts and guests. That said, there will be some areas which are held as 'no go areas' for guests. Kitchens and private bathrooms are two common features (Lynch and MacWhannell, 2000).

A second model involves hosts sharing the same premises with commercial guests though there is much more delineation of 'private' 'no go' areas. Typically dining facilities and lounges, as well as bedrooms and bathroom facilities are separated out for commercial guests. Frequently, commercial guest areas are made more 'professional' by making them less personal to the hosts. Often local tourism officials encourage the more anonymous hotel like décor in these premises. Sometimes working counter visitors and strangers to an area who are motivated by the need to stay with a 'real family' (Lynch, 2005).

Self-catering where the owners live away from premises is the third commercial home model identified by Lynch and MacWhannell (2000). Here, the owner lives away form the premises occupied by the commercial guest. They suggest two variants where the property is a 'second home' or an invest-ment property bought specifically for letting. Again, the nature of home and the artefacts with which the property is adorned communicate meaning here.

Whilst Lynch and MacWhannell's (2000) model is related to the accom-modation sector, it does have relevance to the pub and bar, restaurants and contract catering sectors. In the pub sector for example, many properties would fit into the second model where the owner/manager, tenant/leaseholder live on the same premises as the commercial activity, but there are clearly delineated areas which are private to the hosts and family. Commercial guest rarely enter these parts of the property and then only be special invitation of the commercial. Some restaurants, cafes, snack bars and takeaway premises also have private areas which are personal to the hosts and not shared with commercial guests.

Both the pub and bars, and restaurant, café, snack bar and takeaway pre-mises also involve operations where the commercial guests consume hospi-tality goods and services, but where the owner manager does not have a private dwelling on the same premises. Here the arrangement is more a 'lock up' in which the notion of the 'commercial home' still exists but with greater em-phasis on the commercial than the home. That said, many owner managers will regard the commercial aspect as part of their 'home'. It is their property and guests are entering their personal space, even though it is not shared with private domestic hospitality space.

Small firms operating contract catering, workplace catering, business lunches or dinner service out of their domestic dwelling are in yet another relationship with their clients. The private dwelling's kitchen and storage facilities are used to produce hospitality products but the hospitality is con-sumed in the guests' premises or dwelling. The hospitality service provider providing host products and services is at once host and guest (Table 8.3).

Hospitality services offered by small firms cover a wide range of different forms of commercial home. Each represents a different level of interaction between commercial hosts and commercial guests. In the majority of accom-modation service operations commercial hosts and guests share the same premises, though with varying degrees of levels of sharing common areas. There are some, small accommodation premises where hosts live away from the property in which guests are staying. Typically, these might be self-catering operations but there are some small hotels and guests houses where the owner managers do live on the same premises as commercial guests. In other cases, guests and host do not share the same premises, because the commercial operation takes the form of a lock up which is closed to guests when the business is not open for trading, and hosts have their own private dwelling

TABLE 8.3 Levels of interaction between commercial hosts and commercial guests

Levels of interaction	Hospitality types
Hosts and guests share much of the private dwelling space	Bed and breakfasts Cultural homestays Farmhouse stays Guest houses Host families Small family run hotels
Host and guest share the same premises but much private space is off limits to commercial guests	Bed and breakfasts Guest houses Small hotels Inns, pubs and bars Restaurants, cafes, snack bars and takeaways
Owners live away from the premises	Self catering in second home Self catering in an investment property
Owners live away from the premises which take the form of a lock up	Pubs and bars Restaurants, cafes, snack bars and takeaways Some guest houses and small hotels
Hosts use guest premises to service hospitality experiences	Small scale contract catering Workplace catering Business lunch services Domestic dinner services

elsewhere. Finally some small hospitality businesses are run out of private dwellings and the hospitality is consumed out of guest's premises.

Key point 8.8
Commercial homes describes the situation in which many hospitality entrepreneurs operate. To varying degrees the entrepreneur's home is the site of commercial activity.

Sweeney's work (2008) provides some interesting insights into the motives and concerns of those running commercial homes as the venue for hospitality operations. Table 8.4 shows that for most of her interviewees the need to offer hospitality with a commercial context was most important to most of her interviewees in guesthouses, bed and breakfast places and small hotels. Chapter 3 suggested that most of her interviewees could be located on a continuing starting with purely economic motives at one extreme and pure hospitality

TABLE 8.4	Typologies of commercial home owners		
Economic motives	**Economic-hospitable motives**	**Hospitable- economic motives**	**Hospitable motives**
2 respondents	13 respondents	8 respondents	2 respondents

Adapted from: Sweeney (2008: 231).

motives at the other end. Table 8.4 shows the clustering against each of the four positions.

As Table 8.4 confirms the majority of respondents suggest that motives to enter into the accommodation sector have intertwined motives. The need for economic activity but also associated with a need to be hospitable or at least to offer hospitality to others. There are more respondents who see the sector as chiefly about generating economic benefits though a significant majority of these are claiming to do achieve these in the performance of hospitality services.

Sweeney (2008) goes on to provide some insights into the positive and negative discourses in the hosts' perceptions of hosting in a commercial enterprise. Mostly these relate to comments which enable the continuation of domestic roles and relationships but with economic benefits, though recognizing that the underside of the commercial home involves limitations on the freedom to act and do as the family pleases (Table 8.5).

TABLE 8.5	Positive and negative discourses of hosting

Positive	Negative
Own boss	Tied to home
Better lifestyle	On 24 h call
Working from home	Long working hours
Extra income	Family time interrupted
Generate money for children	Very busy
Afford larger property	Little time to themselves
Meeting new people	Missed social occasions
Having time off	Difficult to be spontaneous
Gives status	Summer holidays limited with children
Learning new skills	Not having their home to themselves
Cost effective for home	Inferiority complex about work
Socially desirable	
Increased confidence	

Source: Sweeney (2008: 244).

> **Key point 8.9**
> The hospitality commercial home offers considerable benefits to those entrepreneurs who want an income stream whilst working from a home base. In addition the commercial home brings with it some considerable disadvantages.

The nature of the commercial home and the nature of the business enterprise being pursued by the entrepreneur are likely to influence perceptions of the benefits and limitations of the commercial home. Research on churn in ownership in small hotels (Lashley and Rowson, 2007) and the tenanted and leased pub sector (Lashley and Rowson, 2001) suggests that the change in ownership within the stock of small hotels and tenanted/franchised pubs is in the region of 20–30 per cent per annum.

Any local tourism officer or pub estate manager recognises a cluster of problems of concern by the ease with which it is possible to open hospitality business units. Most countries do have laws relating to the registration of premises providing accommodation, food and/or drink. In many cases, would be entrepreneurs have to be licensed to cover customer safety, in some cases, even to practice hospitality. Mostly, however, the barriers to entry to hospitality business opportunities are relatively low. Many bed and breakfast places, family hotels, guest houses, restaurants, pubs and inns can be bought for the price of medium sized domestic dwelling (Lashley and Rowson, 2001, 2007). Even a McDonald's restaurant franchise in the UK works out at about £250 000 (Lashley, 2000), though there are some considerable barriers to entry for would be franchisees from outside of the company management structure.

Generally, however, the low barriers to entry in hospitality enterprise activities present those concerned with service quality being offered by owner managers of hospitality enterprises with major problems. Local authority tourism officers in Blackpool, for example, are concerned that the low skill levels of people buying small hotels, guest house and bed and breakfast units make difficulties for driving up levels of service quality on the town's accommodation sector (Lashley and Rowson, 2007). Similarly, the pub companies, like the Punch Pub Company are aware that their tenant and leaseholder low skill sets are major inhibitors to business growth and development (Lashley and Lincoln, 2001). To this end the Punch Pub Company now require all new tenants/leaseholders to take a compulsory 10-day training programme prior to their taking over one of the company's pubs (Lashley and Rowson, 2002).

The high levels of churn in business ownership or tenancy/lease arrange in these small businesses also create problems for those concerned with improvements in service quality, improving business productivity, or building competitive advantage against other resorts or firms. In effect there is a considerable portion of the entrepreneurs who are at low levels on the learning curve at anyone time (Lashley and Rowson, 2008).

SUMMARY

This chapter has suggested that the study of hospitality as a human and social phenomenon is helpful in understanding the attractiveness of the sector to many would be entrepreneurs. The fact that hospitality is one of those cultural signifiers by which people attempt to distinguish themselves from other communities or groups suggest that many assume that their community is naturally more hospitable. In addition, the fact that many have been hosts in their own domestic/private setting, and have been guests in the private/domestic settings of others, provides entrepreneurs with a confident evaluation of their skills. Many assume that they have the skills needed to run their own hotel, pub or restaurant (Lashley and Rowson, 2002, 2005, 2007).

The overlap between the commercial home and the hospitality service provision intertwines amongst these entrepreneurs. The commercial home enables entrepreneurs to be economically active whilst at the same time linked to family roles and responsibilities, and maintain social links through hospitality activities. Sweeney's work (2008) shows that many small firm entrepreneurs have aspiration to meet both economic goals and hospitality related social goals. The accommodation sector most clearly provides an exemplar of hosts and guests sharing the same property and in some instances living spaces overlap. That said, the chapter has argued that all small hospitality enterprises involve some aspect of host and guest interactions in shared spaces. In the restaurant, and bar and café/snack bar sectors, for example, it is not unusual for these entrepreneurs to live on the same premises as the business.

Low barriers to entry, in the form of relatively low capital investment requirements and the perceived low skill sets required attract many would entrepreneurs who have limited experience of the commercial hospitality sector, or even of small business ownership for that matter (Lashley and Rowson, 2001, 2006, 2008). As a consequence, there can be problems of service quality management, of limitations on productivity and business growth. Relatively high levels of churn in business ownership increase these problems for interested parties outside of the business, and cause some major difficulties for the would be entrepreneurs themselves.

CHAPTER 9

Preparing a Business Plan

After working through this chapter you should be able to:

■ Understand the need to produce and work to a business plan
■ Gather the information and background detail needed for the plan
■ Write up and present an effective business plan
■ Work to the plan making the necessary adjustments needed.

INTRODUCTION

It is useful to prepare a business plan for your business. For independent business in freehold, tenanted, leased or franchised businesses, a business plan is essential. Even managed units in chain organizations can benefit from producing a business plan. Business plans assist managers to plan the direction of the business, compare performance with the plan, and take corrective action.

■ Preparing a business plan allows you to think about the mission and key objectives of the business, and the actions needed to achieve the objectives.
■ Identify the information needed to understand the customers and competition.
■ Develop a competitive business strategy for the business.
■ Plan all the activities needed to make the strategy work.
■ Forecast the results of the plan to overcome difficulties.
■ Keep track of the business and take corrective action where needed.

Preparing a business plan helps managers to understand the business and the planning process. It is this process that is important to the manger's role as a manager and owner, because the hospitality sector is fast moving and dynamic and a plan provides a sense of direction and purpose. It enables mangers to make changes and amendments as circumstances unfold. The business plan shows how the business will contribute to overall goals and objectives of the organization.

DESCRIBING THE BUSINESS

The business planning process starts with a clear description of the business, the management and team and core business activities.

Mission statement, objectives and actions

The mission statement and objectives are important because they help to give everyone in the business focus and a sense of purpose. Also they help all to consider problems and difficulties to be overcome Figure 9.1.

Mission statements

In large organizations, these will be provided by the organization, managers need to understand the statement and encourage team members to understand their contribution to achieving the mission. A good mission statement provides an organization with focus, and helps to concentrate managers and employees on the key activities, and to avoid trying to do too many things. In particular the mission statement should cover the following points:

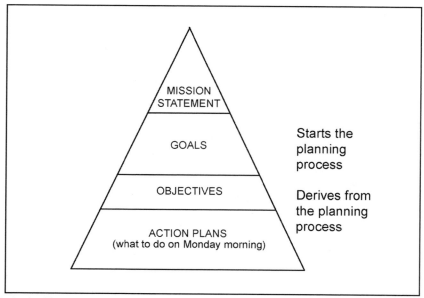

FIGURE 9.1 *The pyramid of goals.*

■ What business is this and what is its purpose?
■ What needs to be achieved over the next 1–3 years?
■ How will this be achieved – what are the core values and standards?

Mission statements should not be too bland, nor should it be so general that is difficult to know what business the organization is in.

Objectives

Objectives are the specific objectives to be achieved over the next 3 years. They have to be written in specific and measurable terms. For example,

1. Increase sales by 20 per cent over three years
2. Reduce employee turnover by 10 per cent each year
3. Increase customer satisfaction scores by 5 per cent within 1 year

By defining the key objectives the plan is providing a set of targets so that are more likely to achieve the overall purpose of the business. They provide a measurable set of pointers that guide actions over the forthcoming period.

Tasks

Tasks are the specific activities that you need to undertake to achieve the objectives set. They are the 'how' statements that will make the objectives happen. For example,

1. Identify complementary customer occasions, so as to attract new customers to the business.
2. Target businesses who might undertake joint products with my products and services.
3. Direct promotional material and special offers to customer who use the business in quiet periods.

Actions

In this case the plan is showing what needs to be done and when, what will happen on Monday morning, thinking ahead to the various actions needed and when. For example,

1. Survey existing customers and potential customers.
2. Visit all competitor units in the area.
3. In August start recruitment and training of staff needed for the Christmas season.

The identification of objectives, tasks and actions are the most important because they are useful in helping to achieve the overall mission as set by the organization.

Key point 9.1

Defining core aims and objectives, tasks to be completed and actions needed to complete them is an essential tool of business planning.

DESCRIPTION OF THE PRODUCTS AND SERVICES

Even in situations where a person is managing a hospitality organization it is worthwhile focusing on one of the key products and services that you are supplying to customers. Hospitality and tourism operations often involve the sale of a mixture of food and beverage items. These need to be analyzed:

- by meal types – say between set meals and snacks,
- between types of drinks – alcoholic and soft drinks,
- through other income streams – say from machines or accommodation, and
- where accommodation is also offered for sale, the analysis should also include room sales and types.

Table 9.1 provides a framework which can be used to note the range of products and services being supplied. It may also be used to identify potential gaps and opportunities that could be added as part of the business development.

Increasingly, the analysis should also consider the primary customer occasions the business is servicing, and identify potential complementary occasions that might be tapped as a source of sales growth.

Customer occasion show that customers come to the business for one of a number of reasons even the same customer may visit the business with different occasions and service needs. Also flowing from this analysis of the customer occasions at the core of the business, it is also necessary to list the key critical success factors which customer regards as core to success. These need to be a key focus of the business because they will impact upon the

TABLE 9.1 Product and service analysis

Product/service	Description	% of sales

customers' evaluation of the success. The business plan helps to focus on these.

- Analysis of product sales mix variations through different parts of the day can be helpful
- Analysis of customer occasions associated with different time periods can also be helpful to identify opportunities

> **Key point 9.2**
> A thorough analysis of products and services supplied in total and in different time periods helps focus the business plan on opportunities and potential actions.

THE MANAGER AND TEAM

A careful consideration of the experience, training and development and skills available within both the management team and the employees is a valuable starting point to considering the skill needs of the unit. Clearly the plan can help you:

- identify potential strengths in the team;
- highlight key skills and experiences that can be used for projects and special initiatives;
- focus on skill shortages and development needs for the future;
- progression plan employees' and mangers' career development.

An organization chart showing both job roles and named job holders clarifies the relationships and identifies potential career progression, and developmental needs. Increasingly, hospitality and tourism businesses are concerned with availability of key staff at all levels. Clearly, the right management team skills and experiences, capable of running and developing a multi-million pound business are vital. In addition, the inability to attract, recruit, and train employees is further compounded in many organizations by high levels of staff turnover that often represents a key weakness and substantial additional cost to the business. A clear commitment to build a strong team and increasing staff retention needs to be a key part of the overall policies and objectives as well as the analysis of the team.

1. Explain the thinking behind the company's mission statement and show how the team will work to achieve the mission.
2. List the objectives for the business:

    (a) long term,
    (b) short term

3. List the tasks and actions needed to take to achieve the objectives.
4. Describe products and service as if to a new employee.
5. How do these goods and services differ from competitors?
6. Are there possible complementary occasions through which it is possible to attract new customers?
7. What relevant skills and talents are available with the team?
8. What are the shortages of skills and talents? How will the team plan to fill the gaps?
9. What are current levels of staff retention and staff turnover?
10. What are the current levels of financial performance – cost levels, sales growth, profit levels, etc., and targets for the future?

Key point 9.3

The team at both frontline and management levels is crucial to business success. Employing the right people, developing their skills, and ensuring motivated performance are all essential.

MARKET RESEARCH

Many branded hospitality and tourism operators commission research on the brand, customers, competitors and markets on national and international levels. Entrepreneurs in large and small firms need to understand these issues as they relate to the particular business and community in which it is located.

An important element of the manager's task, therefore,

- should involve thinking about the core customer needs the business is servicing,
- the types of customer who are attracted to the business,
- the activities of competitors and,
- the general conduct of the market in which the business operates.

An ongoing analysis of these issues helps keep the plan in focus and to react to any changes that come up. Thus the unforeseen opening of a competitor unit or the closure of a major local employer may have adverse impacts to which the business needs to react.

CUSTOMERS

The focus advanced in this text suggests that each business represents a series of tangible and intangible benefits in products and services to customers.

These can be best understood through an analysis of the 'occasions' that customers visit the establishment.

The key starting point of the plan is to consider the various customer needs which are being serviced through the business, and the factors that are critical for success. Furthermore this planning process needs to be further developed by an analysis of the customers themselves Table 9.2.

Reflective practice

1. In a business known to you conduct some research on a sample of customers.
2. Identify the occasions being serviced by the organization at different times.

These matters need careful consideration because over recent decades hospitality and tourism businesses have emerged round changes in the population and their spending power. Here are just a few examples.

- More women working and having careers interrupted by having children, not stopped by them
- More two income households
- More single households.
- More elderly people living longer and with higher incomes
- General increases in people eating out
- More people concerned about healthy eating

TABLE 9.2	Customer segmentation through demographics
Socio-economic group	How do customers comprise the key socio-economic groups? Issues to do with income, status and employment can have important consequences, particularly when building up a picture of key employers for whom the business' customers work.
Life cycle position	A description of the life cycle position(s) of key customer also helps you to analyse the number of potential customers in your locality and their needs and concerns from businesses like yours.
Gender	The mixture of male and female customers has a number of consequences for the product and services you offer. Healthy eating options on the menu, the provision of non-smoking areas, and security are issues that may be important issues where a substantial number of customers are women.
Geographical	What kinds of area do customers mostly live in? What hosing types and locations are there other similar areas that might yield customers? What developments are there in these areas that might impact on your business?
Life style	Are there issues about environmental awareness, health consciousness, or appeals that can be made to those concerned with material rewards? In some units, a series of healthy options might attract customers to use the unit more frequently.
Personality	What personality types mostly dominate the customer base? Are there additional opportunities to attract similar customers or a different sort of customer at different times?

These changes have resulted in some additional opportunities, for example, retired customers can be attracted to use restaurants and bars during the late afternoon and early evening through price offers of special offers. More women with independent income mean that more women are looking to be able to eat and drink on their own, or with other women like themselves. More health consciousness and growth in vegetarianism mean that most menu offers have to include vegetarian and healthy eating options.

Key customer occasions and critical success factors

The following briefly outlines the key customer occasions appropriate to examples of hospitality and tourism operations in general. The list provided was not exhaustive and specific businesses may well be meeting other customer needs that result in them visiting the restaurant, bar or hotel that is not included here.

Employing the concept of customer occasions as a way of thinking about customers and their needs allows a focus which recognises that the same customer may use the same business for different reasons or occasions. Each occasion represents a specific use with different customer expectations of a successful service encounter. There are therefore, different critical success factors which service deliverers need to understand, and deliver, if the customer is to leave in a satisfied state of mind.

The business plan needs to list the core customer occasions and the potential complementary occasions that might *yield more customers.*

Refuel
Can't be bothered to cook
Family outing
Special Meal Out
Out on the Town
Staying Away

In addition, your business plan needs to list the critical success factors that are at the heart of customer expectations of a successful visit to the business.

Key point 9.4

A thorough understanding of customers through demographic analysis and occasionally through different time periods enables the business plan to be focused on customer needs though the identification of potential opportunities.

COMPETITORS

Research on local competitors is an important source of information on which to plan the business activities. Many hospitality and tourism markets are dominated by 'me too brands and businesses'. That is, offers that are aiming at similar market segments and offering to satisfy similar customer needs on similar customer occasions. Business planners need to know their current strengths and weakness so that they can

- learn from their strengths, and
- attack their weaknesses.

Remember, there are both immediate and second order competitors for the customers' spend. Initially, it is important to concentrate on the immediate, first order competitors, but planners need also to think about the other competitors who are also meeting similar customer needs to the same customer base as the business is working with. The business may well have its own features in relation to customers that will add to following list of key concerns. The important point is that the issue under investigation needs to be relevant to the business and the customer needs it is aiming to serve Table 9.3.

When drawing up the business plan planners need to have an honest accurate picture of the strengths and weaknesses of competitors and this should then inform development of the plan. Where is it possible to build genuine competitive advantage? What actions and targets are required to gain the competitive edge needed.

TABLE 9.3 Competitor analysis		
Factor	Competitor	Own unit
Visibility and access		
Menu and range		
Service style		
Additional offers		
Facilities		
Seating		
Opening hours		
Pricing and special offers		
General cleanliness		
Promotional activities		
Estimated sales revenue		
Average check size or transaction value		
Internal competitor audit		

Flowing from the initial research, there is a need to be constantly tracking competitors. Planners must explore issues beyond the immediate customers, goods and services offered. Usually businesses are competing in the same labour markets, and in the same local environment, so there may also be a need to explore wage rates and incomes, and their links with local employers, schools, local government, planning offices, etc.

THE LOCAL ENVIRONMENT

The business plan now must consider the local environment because these provide a context of opportunities and threats that will impact on the business. Contacts with relevant government authorities can help to identify some useful data about the economic, political, social and legal environment. Again these items flow from a thorough marketing analysis, but here are some issues which might be considered:

- Local population demographic profile – trends and changes.
- General level of economic activity – employment – incomes – changes and future trends.
- Local offices or factories – major employers that may impact on the business – either closing or expanding.
- Any planned traffic changes or other planning decisions that might impact.
- The general approach of the planning authorities about this type of business.

The key is scanning the future for potential impacts on the business. Do they potentially generate more customers or fewer? As Wellington once said, 'The value of recognisance is knowing what is over the hill'. In fast moving hospitality and tourism businesses you have to be aware of changes before they occur. By this scanning planners will be in a better situation to benefit from increased customer, or best suited to deal with problems.

1. What is the geographical area from which customers are likely to be drawn? Consider numbers locations, housing stock, etc.
2. What are the customer needs expressed in customer occasions that will be the businesses core customers? Identify potential customer occasions.
3. Consider the critical success factors for each of these customer groups, and differences between groups.
4. Are the markets from which business aims to draw increasing, or declining?

5. Are there potential changes in customer tastes, or habits that might either increase or reduce sales?
6. List the competitors with whom the business will directly compete.
7. List competitor opportunities to satisfy the same customer needs.
8. Highlight the strengths and weaknesses of their approach to serve these customers.
9. Match these with the businesses strengths and weaknesses compare these with customers.
10. Describe the local economic and social context in which the business is located.
11. Identify local firms who might be used to form alliances with the business.
12. Identify the key threats and opportunities posed by the local environment.

Key point 9.5

Effective business plans take account of both competitor activity and environmental factors on local, national and international levels. They shape the environment in which the individual business operators.

COMPETITIVE BUSINESS STRATEGY

Planners are now in a position to formulate a competitive business strategy that will help plan tactics and actions over the short, medium and long term. Planners need to think about the short term as actions within the next year, medium term as over one but under two years and long term as three years plus. In some contexts, the business strategy in terms of the overall direction of the business will be decided and shaped at senior levels. Broadly, there are three types of strategy that organizations follow, these are briefly described below.

Overall cost leadership usually large firms who can take advantage of reduced costs through economies of scale. The size of the business allows the firm to work on reduced costs due to lower production and distribution costs, greater purchasing power with supplier, reduced advertising and selling costs. In addition to provide a Uniformity Dominant service, McDonald's Restaurants also follow a policy that has much in common with price leadership.

Differentiation, through quality, good design and image, that creates brand loyalty and a willingness to pay a price premium. In some cases, the 'label' is the key benefit to the customer. TGI Friday Restaurants are in part attempting to gain competitive advantage in this way.

Focus, here a company focuses a particular market segment on a narrow market segment that is too specialized to attract competitors. By specializing in such a way, the firm makes the market its own. In some cases, being the only supplier of a particular service to a local market can have elements of this, though in many cases the entry barriers for hospitality and tourism firms are too low to make it a realistic national strategy.

The overall business strategy brings together the various elements of the mission and objectives, market research, and marketing strategies, the market place, and the marketing mix leading to an overall plan shown. The service marketing mix needs to be stated in the business plan, and where the appropriate plan needs to give local flavour that will help interpret the action required.

Pricing

As shown earlier in the chapter, pricing is one of the elements of the marketing mix. Here are a few key pointers to pricing.

- The selling price shapes customer perceptions – higher prices can communicate a perception of higher quality.
- Price is associated with concept of value, but customers use the perceptions of the benefits to assess with the price paid represents good value.
- Many competitive markets are price sensitive, and small changes in price can result in large changes in customer demand.
- It is possible to adopt approaches where prices are held constant but bonus offers and the promotional mix increase sales.

The business plan needs a clear statement about the pricing strategy of the brand and how you will use this in local campaigns.

Advertising and promotion

Business planners need to communicate with local market, both customers and would-be customers. Advertising is paid for messages in the form of say local press advertising, whilst promotions are those activities that will help generate sales.

The marketing plan needs to consider how sales will be promoted through an array of different activities. Here are some examples that might be considered.

- Local newspapers and 'free sheets' are often effective that they reach target markets and are increasingly able to tailor their messages to specific localities. These are the most effective when tied to an 'editorial' piece say round a story about the business it is of local interest.

- Leaflets dropped through door ways or sent by post to target post code areas are also useful in that these can direct messages to the people most likely to use the establishment.
- Links with complementary firms – cinemas, theatres and other leisure venues can provide joint offers – say pre-theatre dinners, or price off vouchers to attract them to the business.

The business plan needs to show how planners will promote the business over the period.

- What are the aims and objectives?
- How much is it worth?
- Which methods will be used?
- What benefits are expected?
- How will check the results?

Place

The business plan needs to consider the nature of the premises, these provide sources of tangible and intangible benefits to customers. Issues such as the approach and appearance externally, the signage from various approaches, the cleanliness, visibility to the inside, external décor, the provision of smoking areas, car parking facilities may all be issues that are benefits or limitations.

Internally, the overall atmosphere, cleanliness, décor, music, toilet provision, the availability of children's play areas etc., are also issues that need to be considered, because they may require capital expenditure to meet changed customer expectations.

Often it is said that location is the key to success in hospitality and tourism businesses, but difficulties can be overcome with the right attention to service, customer expectations and promotional activity.

The business plan should include an analysis of the facilities so that these can be analyzed and actions taken relating to the strengths and weaknesses they pose for meeting and exceeding customer expectations.

1. What are the key cost elements that the business has to incur to make an operating profit?
2. What is the overall price strategy?
3. How do prices compare with competitors?
4. Are there differences amongst customers in their price sensitivity?
5. What are your key objectives for advertising and promotional activities?

6. What methods are being used to achieve the objectives and why?
7. How will the results be monitored and evaluated?
8. Are premises adequate for future needs?
9. What development work is needed and why?

Operations

Operations are the name given to the activities required to make the strategy happen. In hospitality and tourism operations, these activities cover the production and service of food and drink, and in some cases accommodation. The business plan needs to show in detail how products are service will be supplied to customers.

1. It is useful to start with an indication of what it is the business is selling in broad terms, though an appendix could include the full product range.
2. From this it is necessary to indicate the opening hours of the business and the sales mix at different times of day.
3. Provide an organizational plan that shows the organization of the business and indicates the key job roles required to produce the goods and services. This will indicate the management posts involved and broad statements of responsibilities. Again, the appendix can be used to provide job descriptions (showing duties and responsibilities) and person specifications (showing skills and qualities) needed for each job title, where these are important for the plan.
4. The plan will also indicate how will the individuals be managed, rewarded and motivated. Issues to do with group and team work in the management of particular customer groups and customer occasions. In other words, how will the critical success factors be managed?
5. Following from this the plan should indicate the businesses approach to customer complaint handling and the responsibilities for dealing with customer satisfaction.
6. The business plan needs to consider the management of materials and cash involved in the operation.
7. In most hospitality and tourism operations there are strict legal responsibilities associated with food hygiene, health and safety, licensing, and other responsibilities to customers and staff. The plan should show how these matters are handled and managed.

The operational plan lays down a blueprint of the key issues that are priorities for the delivery of a successful business which is likely to deliver satisfied customers and employees.

> **Key point 9.6**
> The business plan needs to clearly demonstrate the means by which it will operate and deliver customer satisfaction and achieve the mission.

FORECASTING RESULTS

The business plan was described earlier in the chapter as a map, and the ultimate aim of a business offering hospitality and tourism products is to deliver a profitable operation which will make a positive contribution to the owner's financial performance.

Sales forecasts

The sales forecast is arguably the most important set of figures to arise from the planning process. The sales forecasts help to establish the targets that you will use through the year and establish a set of business profit and loss accounts that will indicate profits or losses.

- Estimates of sales from various income streams – meals – non-alcoholic and alcoholic beverages – machines and accommodation, etc., will need to be, above all else, based on sound reasoning. Previous trading experience will be necessary to build a reasonable estimate of likely sales patterns, even in a new business. In many cases, however, the team will be managing a business that has been trading for some time. The following points provide a check list of issues to bear in mind when calculating and justifying the sales forecasts.
- How big is the market, bearing in mind the customer profile the business will be wanting to attract and the local population within the catchment area. Is the overall market growing or shrinking and at what rate? Avoid unsubstantiated statements - the team need to be convinced that the targets are achievable.
- How many customers are there who are likely to buy from the business and how much do they spend on average per visit? Are there seasonal variations or variations between customer types? Hospitality and tourism traders can get some information about the area, customer types, traffic flows, footfalls, etc from both the local authority and from research organizations.
- The desired income approach is appropriate for these operations and the aim is to achieve the forecast. By a thorough analysis of potential sales there is a chance to make adjustments if sales slip for some reason.

■ Are the product life cycle issues to consider? Some hospitality and tourism businesses, pubs for example, are working in markets where customer visits are in decline, though there are growing opportunities through the provision of restaurant services.

How long a period should your sales forecasts cover? In fast moving retail markets it would be unusual to plan more than three years ahead and most will operate a twelve months cycle.

Operating profit statement

The operating profits statement sets out to match income with expenditure over the appropriate time period of the business plan. It is the way profit and loss can be calculated for the period.

Sales income

This shows the total budget sales income for each month over the year. The figure will include the total income from all the unit's revenue earning activities – sales of meals, snacks, alcoholic and non alcoholic drinks, machines, accommodation etc., by each month as they are likely to occur. That is, the plan must consider potential variations month by month. Traditionally, hospitality and tourism operations in the UK experience low sales in January after peaks in December.

Cost of sales

To show a trading profit is necessary to deduct the costs of the materials purchased to produce the goods sold. Thus the cost of all the food, drinks, and other materials directly used to produce the goods sold are deducted from the sales revenue. The trading profit is the balance after costs of the materials directly used to generate sales revenue have been deducted. Usually these costs could represent an average and be calculated as a percentage, though there may be major differences between the profitability of different income streams and products.

Labour costs

Again these relate to the costs of producing the products and services associated with the sales revenue generated. Thus the total direct labour costs of kitchen, bar, restaurant, and accommodation are calculated as a means of arriving at a gross profits. That is the surplus after the costs directly associated with generating the sales revenue has been taken into account. Again the costs of labour can be calculated as a percentage, though there are differences between departments and section depending on the labour intensity and the use of supplies that require different amounts of handling by staff.

Table 9.4 shows an example from an extract of accounts for hospitality retail operation such as yours.

The gross profit shows how much income will be generated after the immediate costs of producing the products and services sold. However, these are not the only expenses. Managers' salaries and other administration costs, as well as rents, rates, lighting and electricity, unit based advertising, staff uniforms, and other expenses will need to be taken into account to show the profit contribution that your unit makes to the overall business.

Table 9.5 shows an example from the same organization, but shows how the operation profit can be calculated.

Clearly, a branded hospitality and tourism business is different from an independent business because it is unusual for these organizations to produce unit specific balance sheets. However, each business will be considered as a business investment and the return on capital employed might be an issue that company's accounts might want to consider.

Key point 9.6

Forecasts of business outputs and achievements need to be as sensible and realistic as possible. It is important to avoid overly optimistic or overly pessimistic predictions.

TABLE 9.4 Extract from gross profit budget for Mr Bean Restaurant – Chelmsford

YEAR XXX	Chelmsford
Sales (£)	
Food	900 000
Beverages	50 000
	950 000
Cost of sales (£)	
Food	225 000
Beverages	20 000
Total	245 000
Trading profit (£)	705 000
Staff wages (hourly paid) (£)	175 000
Gross profit	530 000

TABLE 9.5 Extract from gross profit budget for Mr Bean Restaurant – Chelmsford

Year	Nottingham
Sales (£)	
Food	900 000
Beverages	50 000
Cost of sales (£)	
Food	225 000
Beverages	20 000
Total	245 000
Trading profit (£)	705 000
Staff wages (hourly paid) (£)	175 000
Gross profit	530 000
Lease and local tax	90 000
Electricity and gas	20 000
Management and admin	54 000
Promotional activity	48 000
Maintenance	36 000
Other consumable	36 000
Depreciation	30 000
Restaurant profit contribution	216 000

WRITING UP, PRESENTING AND WORKING WITH THE BUSINESS PLAN

The business plan is both a document to be presented to colleagues – showing how the team plan to mange the business; it is also a document that the team will use through the year, to work from and to assess progress. The business plan, therefore, needs to be presented in a professional manner, and be capable of easy access.

Presentation of the written document

The business plan needs to conform to professional standards in the way it is written and presented.

■ A simple business folder with a spiral binding will be sufficient.
■ It must be word processed (typed).
■ The layout should be much closer to a report than a memo or essay.
■ The page layout should use wide margins, and be pleasing on the eye, and it should be printed on singles sides of A4 paper.

■ It should paginated.
■ Obviously tables, figures and graphs aid understanding and are a quick way of communicating information, though these should also be explained and discussed in the text.

Remember, the appendix should be used to provide useful background information, all information that is essential to the plan must be included in the main body of the text.

Layout and content

There is no formally accepted business plan format, and a business plan for a unit that is part of a multi-unit organization has to be different from a plan of an independent business. The balance sheet section and the justifications, that an independent business is required to include, are not needed in a document for these purposes.

The front cover of the document should clearly state the name of the business and the date of the business plan. It is important that it is clear that this is the latest version of the plan.

The second sheet behind the front cover should be an executive summary and will include:

1. The current trading position of the restaurant, past successes and the general appraisal of performance over recent years.
2. The products and services currently being sold and the units ranking compared with competitors.
3. The customers and the potential customer base in the area, and the reasons why they use the unit.
4. The unit's aims and objectives, in the short term, and the strategies to be employed in achieving them.
5. A summary of forecasts, sales and profits.

The table of contents

The table of contents are valuable because they help the reader work round the document and focus on the issues of immediate concern. The team will be using this document so they need to be able to turn to the sections that are of interest at a specific time. It is helpful, for example, for the document to be paginated and for the contents page to indicate page numbers where the various headings can be found.

There are a number of ways of numbering pages and sections. It is the most appropriate to use a system that gives every section a new number and subsections are broken down to decimal points.

Though there are likely to be variations between different businesses, the following is an example to work from and that might be useful as basis for designing your own document.

Here's an example

Sample table of contents

Section

Executive summary

The Business and Management

    1.1 History and overview of progress to date

    1.2 Current mission

    1.3 Objectives and actions needed

    1.4 The team

The Products and Services

    2.1 Products and services

    2.2 Current sales mix

Market and Competition

    3.1 Description of customers

    3.2 Customer occasions, needs and benefits

    3.3 Market segments

    3.4 Market size in the area

    3.5 Location of customers and flows

    3.6 Market projects over the period

    3.7 Competition

Competitive Business Strategy

    4.1 Pricing policy

    4.2 Promotional plans

    4.3 Premises

    4.4 Competitor responses

Operations

    5.1 Critical success factors

    5.2 Quality management and control

    5.3 Organization structure

    5.4 Employee management and motivation

Forecasts and results

    6.1 Sales forecasts

    6.2 Operational budget

    6.3 Business objectives and actions plans

The writing of the plan may have to go through several stages, at least a first draft that the team will need to show and discuss with colleagues, and a second draft that will be the final document. It is important that the final draft is clear and well written, free from spelling and grammatical errors. The document has to be both detailed enough to show that you have though through the issues and records your thinking at the time, but the document must not be overly long. So part of the editing process is to ensure that the information that is needed is in the document and that you have not over written parts.

WORKING WITH THE BUSINESS PLAN

The business plan should be used throughout the year to monitor and keep track of progress. The assumptions and calculations built into the plan should make sense to the team of the time so they need to think critically about the how they will use the plan to guide trading performance.

Sales analysis – hourly, daily, weekly and monthly sales audits can keep track of issues such as the sales mix, sales of most profitable lines, average transaction values, numbers of transactions, party sizes, irregular flows in the times customer use the business, etc.

Promotional plans and activities – impacts of particular offers, bonuses, national and local initiatives that were more, or less, successful.

Customers – who are regular users and what is the level of customer retention; their location and reasons for coming to the business; demographic profiles; complaints and comments of satisfaction, customer focus groups, mystery customer reports.

Employees – staff retention and labour turnover, staff satisfaction surveys, costs of training, benefits from training and developments, sales analysis and up-selling opportunities, labour costs and investment in human capital.

Competitor activities – making records of their initiatives that impact negatively on sales, and how they respond to the team's initiatives.

Cost control and profitability – ensuring that the team keep control of the costs of the materials and labour need for the production of goods and services, is essential in developing the basis for profitable performance.

CONCLUSION

The business plan provides the team with a detailed map of how the business will develop and will undertake its activities. It is essentially a tactical account of the business and the issues that need to be managed for it to meet the business commitment to customer satisfaction, sales and profitability growth, continued success in the community in which it is located.

Though there are no hard and fast rules about how this type of business plan should be presented it is important that the team undertake the research necessary and undertake the activities suggested in this chapter in as thorough a manner as possible. The more the team invests in making rational decisions based on a sound understanding of the most relevant information the more likely that the plan will form a sound basis for arriving at the desired objectives.

The business plan, is above all else a working document designed to assist the team to plan with sense and realism, and through which to monitor performance against desired objectives. Regular use of the document and comparing performance against predicted performance is an essential feature of how the document should be used. In some cases, adjustments to the plan need to be made to the plan in the light of events which have happened.

CHAPTER 10

Leadership and the Entrepreneur: ''I'm right Behind You Leading the Way''

INTRODUCTION AND DEFINITIONS

Entrepreneurial success can be attributed to a number of factors including expert knowledge of a technical field together with a sound understanding of markets and the behaviour of competitors. Good fortune is also something which differentiates mediocre enterprises from their successful counterparts (see Chapter 11 for a discussion). However, capitalizing on this knowledge, cognisance and luck requires a long-term entrepreneurial perspective and a recognition that consistent high performance depends on a collective effort rather than that of a single 'heroic' founder. In other words, successful small to medium-sized hospitality enterprises must have effective leadership. Interestingly despite the hyperbole surrounding such entrepreneurs as Richard Branson, Anita Roddick, Donald Trump and others, the role of entrepreneur and leader are not always synonymous. History attests to a number of failures which could be attributed to poor leadership skills. Making the transition from an insular creator or innovator to an inspirational and consistent motivator of people is a challenge which some fail to manage.

As small hospitality firms grow, the role of the founder needs to develop accordingly. No longer can the entrepreneur rely on an intuitive or even haphazard style of management that may well have been appropriate in the early stages when the organization was small and had few staff. Most growth models (Greiner, 1972; Churchill and Lewis, 1983; Scott and Bruce, 198) acknowledge that the role of the founder needs to change as the business develops and grows. For example, Churchill and Lewis group these changes into founder's goals, management and strategic and operational ability. The emphasis of each depends on the entrepreneur's attributes and the developmental stage or size of the firm. To lead a growing hospitality firm effectively the founder must now begin to consider their role as one of facilitator and team leader rather than an entrepreneurial 'hero'.

According to Burns (2001) leaders should have the ability to establish a vision and generate ideas so followers understand the firm's challenges, its values and where it needs to be within a certain time frame. They are responsible for ensuring their firms work as a unified whole in pursuit of a common goal by providing appropriate guidance to followers who are motivated in their place of work (Yukl, 2006). Leaders must also be able to undertake long-term strategic planning so that the firm can achieve its aims or satisfy its vision. Strategies may be planned or emergent. If the latter, leaders must be able to spot the successful ones and exploit them.

Several definitions of leadership exist but that cited by Daft (2005) serves the purpose of this book adequately as it helps to clarify of what leadership is comprised:

> "*Leadership is an influence relationship amongst leaders [entrepreneurs] and followers who intend real changes and outcomes that reflect their shared purpose*" (p. 5).

This contemporary idea of leadership is something quite different to earlier versions which considered it to be a one-way power and control relationship between superiors and subordinates. 'New' leadership actively seeks and embraces change rather than one person maintaining a *status quo* in order to keep their position of power. Moreover, change is viewed as something constructive and a reflection of the shared purpose of all involved irrespective of organizational position; with the purpose aimed at sharing a vision created by the leader (and in some cases the followers). Ultimately we can see that entrepreneurial leadership has a strong visionary dimension with a significant people or 'follower' focus.

Key point 10.1

To lead a growing hospitality firm effectively the founder must consider their role as one of facilitator and team leader rather than an individual entrepreneurial 'hero'.

This chapter explores the concept of leadership by introducing some key historical and contemporary developments in the field. It continues by outlining the transition from founder to leader whilst the firm is growing with a focus on 'people' and team leadership skills. Here, we are less concerned with how this happens, as this is discussed elsewhere in the book, but what the founder needs to do in order to lead the growth effectively. Finally, organizational culture is discussed in an attempt to highlight its overarching influence and importance to the area of leadership in small to medium-sized hospitality organizations.

Making a racket
by Colin Morris

David Lloyd, as they say, knows his own mind. Indeed, he is on intimate terms with it. He thinks The City is ''full of crooks'', Hull's sports fans don't know what's good for them and the All England Lawn Tennis and Croquet Club should tear up its hallowed turf in favour of a more modern surface or risk becoming irrelevant on the world tennis stage and he's not shy about sharing such wisdom. So much so, that the Guardian recently quipped: ''A legend in his own change of ends, Lloyd should do British tennis a favour and keep it buttoned.''

Having spent an afternoon with the man I can tell the Guardian, and anyone else who cares- that this is as likely as unearthing a multi-grand slam winner who is British.

I met Lloyd in his uber-posh Wisley Golf and Country Club near Waking, where the suburbs of south London give way to the green rolling hills of Surrey. It is impressive. Words like rarefied, stunning and immaculate come to mind- and that's just the gravel on the drive leading up to the clubhouse.

Once inside, a front-office employee with cut-glass accent directs me to the lounge where I may await Mr Lloyd's arrival. In front of me lies the splendour of the club's superb 18th green – inside is the kind of drinking establishment you would expect to find in a middle England inspired heaven. But the conversation in the room isn't about birdies and bogeys but about David Lloyd's involvement in the troubled Clubhaus venture, a golf course chain that he studiously backed away from that is now facing the scrutiny of the DTI – with Lloyd crying foul from the sidelines.

My eavesdropping is interrupted by the man himself. All smiles, a quick handshake and then a brisk walk to an empty conference room for a more 'private conversation'. Despite a pronounced limp, Lloyd walks way too fast. The obvious starting point is David Lloyd Leisure – the fitness chain he created 20 years ago, spread throughout England with great success and sold on to brewer Whitbread. He continued to work in partnership with the brewer for a while, but eventually the relationship turned sour. Indeed, it doesn't take long for the legendary Lloyd pugnatiousness to surface and, as if on cue, he delivers a scathing assessment of corporate Britain: ''Big companies are all the same – they make sure all the directors have a chauffeur driven car – but that's not in the shareholders' interest.''

The former British tennis number one rates Whitbread's handling of David Lloyd Leisure as sub-par. He wasn't happy with the way Whitbread handled its staff, treating them as ''numbers instead of people'' and was even more displeased with what the brewer saw as an acceptable bottom line. ''They (Whitbread) were happy with an 11 per cent return on the business (when I ran it) we wouldn't get out of bed for less than 15. I told Whitbread 'You've got this great business – why don't you step back and let me make you money'?''.

Lloyd finally sold out to the brewer in 1995 to go his own way. ''I used to enjoy going to work but when I went to work (after Whitbread came in) I hated it. They were destroying a great business and I couldn't stand it.'' So much for pulling your punches. Lloyd may have left his leisure business behind, and his name with it a situation that he admits ''bothers me sometimes'' – but he wasn't about to sit around his country club hideaway and sulk. He hung on to his tennis school along with a variety of interests managed under the umbrella of David Lloyd Associates and remained a central figure in British tennis.

Tim Henman was an early protégé and Lloyd led both him and Greg Rusedski when he was captain of England's Davis Cup team. It didn't work out particularly well and Lloyd was replaced with Roger Taylor last year. Outside tennis, Lloyd kept himself busy with a variety of ventures, most notably his involvement in Clubhaus which has turned messy – and a dabble in pro sports that doesn't involve fuzzy balls when he strode into Hull and snapped up the city's professional sports trinity of Hull City Football Club along with Rugby Leaguers Hull Kingston Rovers and Hull FC The Hull dream was typical of efforts to wring money from lower echelon football clubs in the late 90's – but with some twists only David Lloyd could provide. He scooped up Hull City Football Club and its Boothferry Park ground with the team on the brink of financial ruin, along with the city's two bitterly divided rugby clubs.

The plan was deceptively simple, instead of three clubs playing from three different run-down grounds Lloyd would build one modern stadium where the gate receipts from all three teams would keep the clubs and stadium humming, while the various real estate deals around the grounds would line Lloyd pockets. The x-factor, the one thing Lloyd hadn't figured into to his equation, was the intractable nature of the average English sports fan. In Hull, Lloyd finally bumped heads with a constituency as stubborn, headstrong and opinionated as himself. ''It seemed really simple and logical,'' reflects Lloyd. ''Trouble is, between the two different sides (Hull RFC and Hull KR) there is war. Fans wouldn't cross to the other side of the city to watch their team. They would rather stay in a leaking stadium with asbestos in the roof and no hot food than cross to the other side of town (and into enemy territory) to a nice new stadium.''

Unable to link the three teams under a rainbow of harmony, Lloyd was eventually forced to sell his stake in 1998 – with Hull City on the brink of Football League elimination. Ironically, Hull City Football Club and rugby leaguers Hull FC will share a stadium from 2003 after all. Atypical to the end, Lloyd put in almost £1 million of his own cash to leave Hull City debt free. But it hasn't been all bad news for Lloyd – in fact even the bad news has been good. Lloyd was involved with the golf and country club chain Clubhaus in its infancy and was excited about the prospects of the business. But when it came time to stump up his own cash Lloyd performed due diligence and didn't like what he saw when the company opened up its books.

''An entrepreneur is not a gambler. He'll put his cash and his head on the line but you have to put controls in as well because, after all, it's a dream. They (Clubhaus) had a good idea but they tried to make everything too big, too fast with lots of paper and no cash.''

Months after Lloyd backed away from the company, Clubhaus is labouring under debts of £105 million and is facing an inquiry by the DTI into its bookkeeping. In a bid to stay afloat Clubhaus, a publicly traded company, has swapped outstanding bonds for equity in the company – effectively waylaying its shareholders. The move incensed many who owned shares, including Lloyd and Eddie Shah, the former newspaper tycoon who is reported to be writing a novel about the debacle.

While Lloyd holds no grudges with management at Clubhaus, ''They were nice guys'', he was outraged by the equity-for-bonds swap and is even more furious that investigating bodies don't want to look at the due diligence he performed on the company long before its troubles came to light. ''The City is a rip-off in a lot of ways, which is sad. There's punters out there who don't know what's going on and auditors need to be taken to task. We are talking about people's life savings in some cases.'' Perhaps- but not in the case of David Lloyd himself, who's exposure to Clubhaus was minimal.

Lloyd has kept his powder dry for another venture into, you guessed it, the leisure centre business. Next Generation, which has seen Lloyd teaming up with his son Scott, was launched three years ago but is currently in the throes of a significant rollout. The venture has seen Lloyd move away from the mass market to concentrate on the more discerning customer. Clubs are often built in the exclusive suburbs where land is more expensive, are more spacious and contain unusual features such as children's gyms, cinemas, homework rooms and creches. Indeed, Lloyd is planning to spend £50 million on just four clubs this year at London's Maida Vale, Bristol, York and Dartford. With a further ten clubs planned for the next three years, this is quite a hefty initial outlay, but he has managed to secure backing for the venture from the Bank of Scotland, Royal Bank of Scotland and a number of private investors. Understandably, he hasn't sought to raise any funds through the City.

Questions

1. What leadership characteristics does this entrepreneur display?
2. What style (s) of leadership does this entrepreneur display?
3. Discuss what impact his early sporting career is likely to have had on his business perspectives.
4. Identify and discuss issues of organizational culture amongst the companies mentioned in this article.
5. Identify and comment on some of the business decisions made by this entrepreneur.

Reproduced with permission, Hospitality, July/August, 2002, pp. 38–40.

LEADERSHIP THINKING

The emergence of leadership theories could hardly be described as proactive. In a business sense they have evolved due to shifts in the socio-economic climate in which they were positioned originally. Daft (2005) summarises the major approaches as Great Man, Trait, Behavioural, Individualized, Contingency, Influence and Relational. A discussion of each appears below.

Great man theories (early 1900s – 1950s)

Leaders are always male heros and born with universal natural leadership qualities which inspire and influence others to obey unquestioningly. Many hundreds of traits have been identified such as creativity, self-confidence, risk-taking propensity, intelligence, drive and so on. Despite a consensus that traits and leadership effectiveness are difficult to predict in all situations, traits remain popular with some being identified as powerful predictors of leadership behaviour (Bass and Stogdill, 1990).

Trait theories (1940s to present)

Rooted in the above theory whereby early researchers sought to identify specific traits which would predispose individuals to become great leaders. Some traits are now recognised as having a role in predicting whether someone is likely to be an effective leader but a robust and reliable list of such traits is yet to be identified.

Behaviour theories (1940s and 1950s to present)

Research here focuses on what an individual does rather than who they are by dint of traits. Similar to trait theory effective and ineffective leadership is defined by behavioural differences between these two extremes. This school coined the terms 'autocratic' and 'democratic'. Essentially, the autocrat prefers centralized power being derived from position, controlling rewards and coercion. The equal and opposite is the democrat who prefers to delegate authority, encourages others to participate and relies on followers' knowledge. A significant contribution to the field was that of Tannenbaum and Schmidt (1958) who recognised that leadership style is dynamic and exists at any point along the autocratic (or 'boss-centred') and democratic (or 'subordinate-centred') leadership scale. The extreme points of the continuum are characterized by managers making decisions and announcing them with no consultation to one where managers encourage followers to work with a degree of autonomy within defined limits.

Other seminal studies on leadership behaviour include the 'Ohio State Studies' from where the exclusive terms 'Consideration' and 'Initiating Structure' styles emerged. The former concerns the sensitivity with which the leader treats followers, for example, are their ideas and feelings respected? The initiating structure style focuses more on the work task and the extent to which the leader directs followers toward a designated objective. Other related studies were conducted at the University of Michigan with similar outcomes. On this occasion, leadership behaviour was classified as 'Employee-centred' or 'Job-centred'. These studies differed from the Ohio-based research in that both behaviours could be adopted by leaders simultaneously.

Another behavioural contribution adding to that of the former two studies was that of Blake and Mouton (1978). Their Leadership Grid shown in Figure 10.1 summarizes the tenets of their leadership theory.

Like the Ohio and Michigan State studies, the grid features two continua with concern for people and concern for results as their focus. Research suggests that entrepreneurs may be both people and results oriented simultaneously. Five leadership styles are shown in the figure with the universal 'high high' or 'team management' being the preferred approach in most situations. However, the assumption here is that leaders use the same leadership style with all followers.

Reflective practice

1. In your opinion, is it possible for leaders to have high concern for results and for people?
2. Which of the above five styles of leadership would be most appropriate for:

   ■ A fast-food restaurant
   ■ A fine dining restaurant
   ■ A motel
   ■ A busy small city hotel
   ■ A busy small resort hotel

Individualized Leadership

Yammarinow and Danserau (2002) contend that an individualized leadership style is more effective whereby the leader strikes a different relationship with each individual in the firm. Daft (2005) considers this to be based on 'Dyadic theory' or two-person exchanges where each party give and receives from the other. Leaders are said to provide a sense of self-worth for the follower (amongst other things) and the follower offers a commitment to the job and the firm. Ultimately this individualized exchange can be extrapolated more broadly to build cross company networks. However, this style of leadership ultimately results in the creation of two overall groups of followers; an 'in' and an 'out' group. Much like the existence of a two tier hospitality labour force

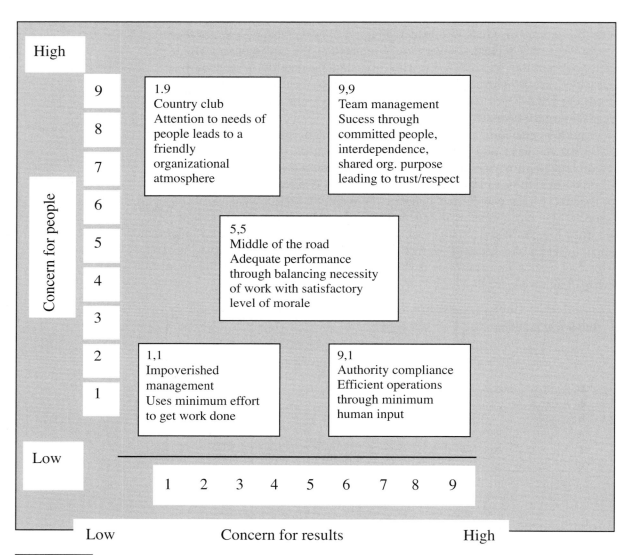

FIGURE 10.1 *The leadership grid.*
Adapted from: Blake and Mouton (1978).

(year-round and seasonal workers), the in groups enjoys preferential treatment and quality exchanges with their leader whereas the out group do not. Instead the pattern of exchanges is more likely to be based on coercion and formal authority.

Contingency theories (late 1950s to present)

Given the equivocal nature of results from the above constructs, situations and contexts were then identified as variables most likely to impact on leadership behaviour. Simply, researchers proposed that situations can be effectively managed by analysis and a subsequent change in leadership behaviour to match the requirements of the context. Contextual variables may be grouped into categories of:

- The work environment;
- The external environment; and
- The characteristics and tasks of followers.

Contingency theories hold that effective leadership styles depend on their fit with the context or the situation and the requirements of the followers. In short, there is no universal optimum way to lead, it very much depends on other issues. The basic assumption here is that leaders have the ability to diagnose situations and behave accordingly. Based on the trait theorists notion of concern for task and concern for people, a leader who has a high concern for tasks will focus on short-term planning, task clarification and monitoring. Alternatively, a focus on people or relationship behaviours will optimise behaviours including support provision, recognition for work done well, empowerment and so on. Several contingency models exist with some differences between them however, they all agree that appropriate leadership depends on situational characteristics. The main contributors to this field are Fiedler, Hersey and Blanchard, House (Path-goal theory) and Vroom-Jago.

According to Fiedler (1954) situations are characterized by three elements:

- Quality of leader – follower relations – working atmosphere (trust, respect, confidence in leader);
- Task structure – extent of definition, clear goals and instructions; and
- Position power – over followers, planning, directing, rewarding, punishing.

The possible configurations of situations using these three criteria vary from 'favourable' where leader–member relations are healthy, leader position power is strong and task structure is high to 'unfavourable' situations where relations are poor, position power is weak and task structure is low. For this approach to be successful, the leader must first understand where they fit along the relationship/task scale and then see whether the situational elements (relations, position power and task structure) are favourable or unfavourable. There are various instruments available to diagnose leadership style. One example linked to Fiedler's theory is known as the Least Preferred Co-worker scale (LPC). The scale used is a form of semantic differential with adjectives including efficient vs. inefficient; open vs. guarded; gloomy vs. cheerful and so on. If the entrepreneur uses positive words to describe the least preferred co-worker she is a 'relationship-oriented' leader. If negatives are used then the entrepreneur is deemed 'task-oriented'. Like most instruments, the LPC has its critics.

Hersey and Blanchard's (1982) model focuses on the characteristics of followers as the main situational elements. Essentially, an effective leadership style must consider the nature and state or prior development of followers. Follower development is divided into four overall characteristics shown in Figure 10.2.

The model suggests that when workers are at a low state of readiness as they have poor ability and skills (or may even be unwilling to take responsibility), a telling style of leadership works best. This would be where the hospitality entrepreneur has codified a set of instructions for a food server in the delivery of say a Cappuccino coffee. At the other extreme, where followers are well educated and are willing to accept responsibility for their own behaviour, a delegating style of leadership is most appropriate. This model is simpler than Fiedler's as one only has to consider followers rather than other situational variables.

Key point 10.2

Effective leadership depends on a diagnosis of followers' state of readiness and instigation of the appropriate style.

Other contingency constructs include Path-Goal Theory (PGT) (House, 1971) where it is incumbent on the leader to increase follower

Follower characteristics	Leadership style
Low state of readiness	Telling (high task-low relationship)
Moderate state of readiness	Selling (high task-high relationship)
High state of readiness	Participating (low task-high relationship)
Very high state of readiness	Delegating (low task-low relationship)

FIGURE 10.2 *A situational theory of leadership.*
Adapted from: Daft (2005, p. 91).

motivation by clarifying what they must do in order to receive rewards. She is also responsible for increasing meaningful rewards for followers. The main difference between this contingency theory and that of Fiedler is that PGT suggests leaders change their behaviour to match the situation. These behaviours are classified as supportive, directive, achievement-oriented and participative. Situational contingencies here are follower characteristics (similar to those of Hersey and Blanchard) and the work environment which is classified according to the presence of task structure, nature of formal authority system and the follower work-group characteristics (education and quality of relationships) (Daft, 2005, pp. 93–100).

Essentially, all contingency theories consider how the situation impacts on leadership behaviour. Being able to identify and understand how tasks, followers and other contextual variables interact, allows the hospitality entrepreneur to adopt an appropriate leadership style.

Influence theories (1960s to present)

These constructs explore the two-way process of 'influence' between leaders and followers. Charisma and visionary leadership fall into this category whereby an individual emerges as a leader based on their behaviour (rooted in personality). These inquiries attempt to identify charismatic behaviour and the context giving rise to the phenomenon. This approach has much in common with the earlier 'Great Man' theories of leadership.

Relational theories (1960s to present)

These models look at how leaders and followers interact and influence each other (not to be confused with Influence theories). This perspective regards leadership as a shared process whereby followers become engaged meaningfully in the process, highlighting the key role played by interpersonal relationships. These tenets are enshrined in both 'Transformational' and 'Servant' leadership theories. The former is alleged to develop followers in to leaders. The second considers the leader as the servant of others rather than the controller or directors of followers.

Adapted from: Daft (2005, pp. 23–25).

Reflective practice

1. Think of an entrepreneur known to you and consider how useful the above theories are in explaining their behaviour.
2. 1 How would you measure the success of an entrepreneur in the hospitality industry?.

FOUNDER TO LEADER

The following questions and answers were abstracted from three interviews conducted with hospitality leaders in the UK.

Stan Counsell – Consultant to the hospitality industry and owner of an environmental certification business –UK

What's the best aspect of your work?

Helping others to achieve their objectives

What's the biggest lesson you've learned in business?

Tenacity will usually overcome adversity

What do you think makes a good manager?

An ability to get the job done, while paying attention to the needs of the team as well as individuals. Being able to plan for the expected and cope with the unexpected

Joanna Chugh – Cluster finance director Marriot Hotels – UK

Name three qualities that define a good manager?

Leadership, discipline and drive

What's the best aspect of your job?

Watching people I've recruited and trained do well for themselves. I am delighted to see my team move on to bigger and better positions

How would you describe your management style?

I enjoy training and coaching and always try to be non-prescriptive. I want to give the team around me the opportunity to step up to the challenge and make decisions for themselves. Decision-making is a skill that all future managers need to sharpen and practice. I try and instil in my team to bring me their solution, along with their problem and we can talk about it.

Andrew McKenzie – Managing Director – Donnington Valley Hotel and Spa.

Name three qualities that define a good manager?

Fairness, openness, clarity and humour.

What's the best aspect of your job?

Being amazed by most of the great young people who work with me.

How would you describe your management style?

Open, fair, clear and happy.

Adapted from: *Hospitality*, February 2004, p. 25, Dec, 2007, p. 70, March, 2008, p. 70.

Whilst the thrust of questions is management focused, the answers from the three leaders reveal their main approaches to leadership. All would appear to be based on a modern style which values empowerment, equity and a delight in the success of followers.

The modern view of leadership results from 'enlightened' thinking, a greater understanding of what motivates people and an acknowledgement that one should do what is morally and ethically appropriate when dealing with people; it is also rooted in plain good business sense. There is little doubt that the world is now in a constant state of ever increasing change. Indeed, Daft (2005) considers that predictability is a thing of the past. Instead it has been replaced by random events much espoused by chaos theorists (for example, see Gleick, 1987). It is therefore in the best interest of entrepreneurs to take note that such significant events require a new leadership approach. Table 10.1 shows a summary of responses to these circumstances.

In the current environment hospitality entrepreneurs must either use or develop personal skills and qualities to establish a compelling and shared vision or direction for the business. They must be able to motivate and inspire all employees to embrace external or internally generated change and establish a culture of integrity (Daft, 2005). This is different to the entrepreneur as a manager where concern is targeted at administrative and procedural efficiency and effectiveness through organizing, planning, directing, controlling and so on. Obviously both are important roles and in small hospitality firms the founder will be expected to occupy them both to a lesser or greater degree depending on context. Indeed it is difficult to imagine a situation where they do not coexist. However during later stages of growth, sound team leadership is essential if the firm is to succeed.

Stages of growth have already been discussed elsewhere in this book and so we will not be discussing them at length here. However, the transition of a business founder to team leader (and player) is an essential part of this process and the entrepreneur must be able to behave in an appropriate manner according to the stage of growth the firm is experiencing. For example, as an hospitality firm matures the founder should begin to think as a team leader rather than a lonely 'crisis manager' and seek to employ individuals with sound team management skills despite the contextual difficulties inherent in the

TABLE 10.1 A new reality for entrepreneurs

Old reality	New reality
Control and directing subordinates	Empowerment of followers
Competition between individuals, departments and other firms	Appropriate collaboration between all stakeholders
Uniformity of employees	Diversity of followers – new ideas and innovations
Self-interest	Higher purpose – accountability, integrity and responsibility
Hero – celebrity-type status, self-promoting	Humble and hard-working behind scenes, promoting and developing others

Adapted from: Daft (2005, p. 8).

TABLE 10.2	Guiding management styles for growing hospitality firms

Style	Details
Craftsman	■ One person does everything ■ Focus on quality ■ Minimal operating expenses ■ Limitations on growth unless others are employed
Classic	■ Other employees involved to exploit opportunities ■ Delegation limited ■ Tight control regime operated by founder
Entrepreneur-plus-employee	■ Shift from entrepreneur only to team working with significant delegation of responsibilities to trusted others ■ Team members must be ready for this change and to accept extra responsibilities
Partnership	■ Sharing responsibilities with new partners or shareholders ■ Skills must be complimentary ■ Increased potential for disagreements between main players

Adapted from: Zimmerer and Scarborough (2002, pp. 502–503).

industry.[1] Zimmerer and Scarborough (2002) offer some guidance by discussing management styles and matching them with organizational growth. Table 10.2 suggests that team leadership skills become increasingly important through growth and especially during the 'Entrepreneur-to-employee's stage.

Similarly, Frederick, Kuratko, and Hodgetts (2007) discuss the changing role of the founder during the firm's growth stages through the decision-making process. They explain that entrepreneurs typically face certain risks depending on which stage of growth the firm has reached. These stages are matched by a certain 'type' of entrepreneur:

I. Entrepreneurial genius – new company, enthusiastic founder with little interest in anything other than the firm's success;
II. Benevolent dictator – founders act as parents surrendering no autonomy to followers;
III. Dissociated director – founders may feel alienated as they begin to realize that followers do not want to depend on them to make all

---

[1] In the SME sector of the hospitality industry this is easier said than done for a number of reasons including the job insecurity seasonality bestows. Another key challenge is a lack of career structure within independent hotels. A reasonable strategy would be to offer incentives linked to the continuing success of the entrepreneurial hotel. What could be offered really depends on the context, stage of growth of the firm, whether the individual hotel is linked with others informally or in the form of a joint venture and so on.

decisions, however, many will still work at an operational hands on level despite this. At this point, a key decision must be made whether to grow further or remain the same. A decision to grow will necessarily mean that founders must operate more strategically and delegate responsibilities to others; and

IV. Visionary leader – leadership used to position hospitality firm strategically for sustainable growth. Founders at this level tend to be removed from day-to-day operations, communicate openly with followers and adopt a more transformational style of leadership.

Adapted from: Frederick *et al.* (2007, p. 458).

Once again the founder as leader becomes important during a latter stage of organizational development.

Key point 10.3

Leaders now operate in a 'new reality' characterized by empowerment, leaders and followers rather than control and direction of subordinates.

ENTREPRENEURIAL LEADERS

According to Frederick *et al.* (2007), entrepreneurial leadership is the most important factor in managing high growth ventures successfully. Drawing on the work of Ireland and Hitt (1999) they also hold that 'strategic leadership' is most effective for fast growing entrepreneurial organizations. Using Ireland, Hitt and Hoskisson (2001) they choose to define entrepreneurial leadership as:

> "... *the entrepreneur's ability to anticipate, envision, maintain flexibility, think strategically and work with others to initiate changes that will create a viable future for the organization*" *(p. 468).*

Given the near celebrity status of often cited entrepreneurs such as Conrad Hilton and Lord Forte and the mythology surrounding their successes, it is often assumed that they are also effective leaders; this is not necessarily the case. Whilst some evidence suggests that entrepreneurs and leaders have many characteristics in common (see Dubrin and Dalglish, 2003) there are some differences. For example, Dalglish and Evans (2000) consider a key difference to be the way leaders deal with interpersonal relationships. A common reason for many individuals to opt for an entrepreneurial lifestyle is because of their dislike of working closely with and taking orders from others. This is not an ideal characteristic on which to base effective leadership. On the other hand, the hospitality industry is awash with small or lifestyle firms employing only one or two family members. In this instance, dealing with others and delegating responsibility may not be an imperative. These small organizations tend to rely on the entrepreneur replicating their family leadership role as partner or parent which is often autocratic.

However, in a growing hospitality firm entrepreneurs must overcome their communication shortfalls because the role of leader relies on the ability to motivate and inspire followers toward a well-communicated and shared vision. Moreover, if the small hospitality business is to grow significantly, the entrepreneur's ability to apply these skills externally through networking, seeking alliances, partnerships and joint ventures is also crucial.

Notwithstanding the various contributions made to the field of leadership by competing theories, there exist several desirable behaviours about which commentators agree. Zimmerer and Scarborough (2002) note that today's workforce is altogether more knowledgeable and sophisticated than at any other time in history. their expectations are therefore similarly urbane. Figure 10.3 provides a summary of these desirable behaviours.

Burns' (2001) perspective of behaviours common to both leaders and entrepreneurs is not dissimilar to the above and includes:

- Stamina;
- Commitment and dedication;
- Opportunism;
- Ability to bounce back;
- Motivation to excel; and
- Tolerance of risk, ambiguity and uncertainty.

Do these behavioural tendencies then give rise to an identifiable leadership style amongst hospitality entrepreneurs? The question is difficult to answer. In practice it is difficult to be overly prescriptive because small business owners and contexts differ wildly. Leadership styles are wide and varied even outside the entrepreneurial context. Instead, it would be fair to say that styles of leadership are driven by a combination of contextual and personal factors (this is the major tenet of the contingency theorists). Typically, the hospitality entrepreneur is viewed as single-minded, driven, hard-working (and expects the same of others) and, to some extent, charismatic (Dubrin and Dalglish, 2003). Whilst charisma is difficult to categorize exactly, it is rooted in an array of variables including personality traits, culture, contextual variables and situations.

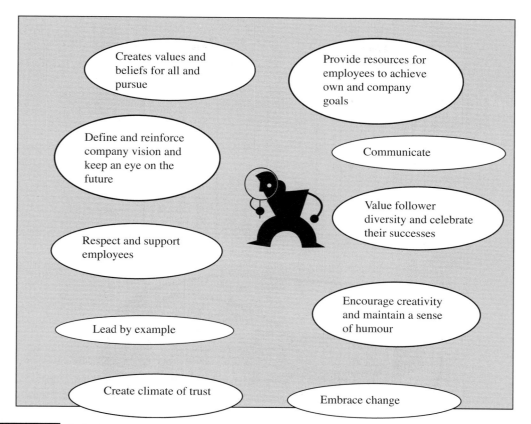

FIGURE 10.3   *Behaviours for effective leadership.*
Adapted from: Zimmerer and Scarborough (2002, pp. 485–487).

Reflective practice

1   Consider three leaders that have been described as charismatic. To what extent were their personal circumstances and/or world events responsible for their leadership style?

According to these authors entrepreneurial leadership style emerges from various configurations of the characteristics shown in Figure 10.4.

Once again we see recognizable behavioural characteristics in common between the perspectives of Zimmerer and Scarborough (2002), Burns (2001) and the above authors. For example all contain characteristics or equivalent of achievement, commitment, enthusiasm and so on.

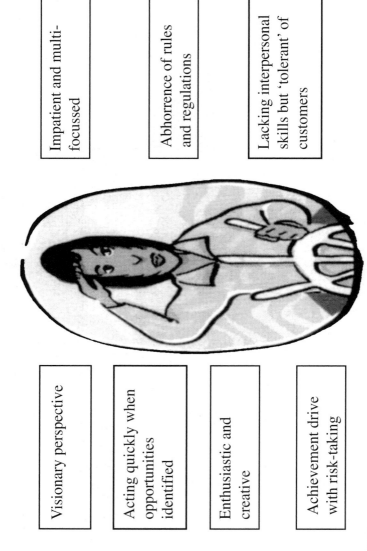

FIGURE 10.4   *Behavioural attributes of entrepreneurial leadership style.*
Adapted from: Bubrin and Daglish (2003, pp. 316–318).

However, we can also see some typical behavioural weaknesses amongst entrepreneurs.

Key point 10.4
Entrepreneurial leadership is the most important factor in managing high growth ventures successfully.

If the founder is not skilled in such areas these abilities must be acquired otherwise the firm may either become unsuccessful or enjoy only limited growth. An area entrepreneurs typically have difficulty with is developing interpersonal empathy and communication. It is also the case that as firms grow management becomes difficult so the founder must also consider delegating responsibility to other capable people. The adage that to be successful means surrounding oneself with a talented team of people could not be truer than when the lifestyle firm moves into rapid growth phase. So what can the hospitality entrepreneur do to improve their ability as leader? The obvious answer of 'skills acquisition' is rather glib but, resources permitting, this is exactly what must be done. However, these skills may be 'borrowed or 'purchased' by recruiting individuals who already possess the desired behavioural attributes. It is therefore vital that the hospitality entrepreneur creates an appropriate framework for this to take place. Second, an organizational culture should be established which will reinforce and maintain these behaviours. As firms grow there is a consensus that entrepreneurs should adopt a team leadership approach and the following section introduces the idea of teams in the small hospitality firm.

Reflective practice

1. Think of an entrepreneur known to you. How would you describe their behavioural characteristics.
2. A successful entrepreneur may not necessarily be an effective leader. Why do you believe this to be the case?

TEAMS

There is much discourse in the literature concerning teams and groups, that is, what are they; are they the same; if not, how are they different? In short, teams and groups differ according to the degree of interdependence individual members enjoy when engaged in work. Group members tend to work independently of each other whereas teams rely heavily on members integrated outputs in order to complete the overall task successfully. Jobs can be designed with groups or teams in mind. For example traditionally, restaurant kitchens used a team of chefs each having a part to play in the production of a menu item. In the small hospitality firm these individual tasks are often combined and undertaken by a single person for reasons of cost saving (amongst others). In any event, whether the entrepreneur chooses to classify employees as a team or a close working group makes little difference in terms of providing effective leadership.

Clegg, Kornberger and Pitsis (2008) define a team as:

"Two or more people psychologically contracted together to achieve a common organizational goal in which all individuals involved share at least some level of responsibility and accountability for the outcome" (p. 92).

Essentially, a team leader needs to achieve inter-member harmony and cohesion whilst optimizing productivity. In service industries, productivity is difficult to define but essentially concerns transferring inputs into outputs at the lowest possible cost (Robbins, 2005, p. 27). This is no easy task and is doomed to failure if the members are haphazardly assembled. All other things being equal, members of the management team need to have complimentary rather than competing skills. They also need to be heterogeneous to capitalize on their differing perspectives but not so different that they have absolutely nothing in common.

After reviewing the evidence, Robbins (2005) concludes that team effectiveness depends on a number of factors. They are summarised below in Figure 10.5.

To build an effective team, entrepreneurial leaders should consider:

- Communicating clear performance standards, setting the tone for such early on such as at the first meeting;
- Creating a compelling context;
- Setting clear rules for team member behaviour and abide by them yourself;
- Ensuring team is supplied with appropriate information about the task in hand;
- Giving feedback regularly both formal and informal;
- Making sure members have complimentary skills and abilities;
- Ensuring team's activities resonate with the overall strategy of the hospitality firm;

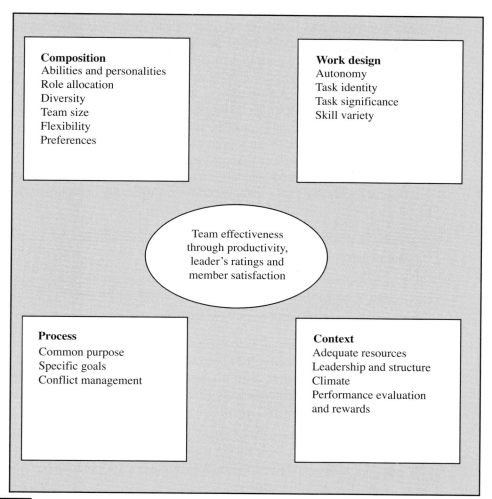

Composition
Abilities and personalities
Role allocation
Diversity
Team size
Flexibility
Preferences

Work design
Autonomy
Task identity
Task significance
Skill variety

Team effectiveness
through productivity,
leader's ratings and
member satisfaction

Process
Common purpose
Specific goals
Conflict management

Context
Adequate resources
Leadership and structure
Climate
Performance evaluation
and rewards

FIGURE 10.5 *A model of team effectiveness.*
Adapted from: Robbins (2005, p. 278).

■ Being able to identify conflict and the emergence of political behaviour within the team and dealing with the situations promptly; and

■ Encouraging creativity and risk-taking.

Adapted from Katzenbach and Smith (1993); and Hultman (1998).

Obviously the degree to which each of these actions is pursued depends on the contextual specifics of each situation. Clearly structural issues of context process and work design have a key role in the effectiveness of hospitality management teams (although work design variables seem more appropriate for operational activities). Scant attention to any of them could result in disaster but if a management team has an inappropriate composition, no amount of content, structure or process will remedy the situation. There has been much research attention on the composition of teams (for example, see Margerison and McCann, 1990; Stevens and Campion, 199). All authorities agree that individuals should be selected carefully to obtain the optimum mix of skills and abilities. In a practical sense, management team members almost always occupy more than one role. This is especially the case in small hospitality firms where the management team may only number between two to four individuals. These managers have the difficulty of occupying multiple roles.

Reflective practice

1. Team working is often held as an effective way of operating an hospitality business. Can you give some examples when this may not necessarily be the case?

The pioneering work of Belbin (1981) helps to identify and explain what these roles are. There has been subsequent research but much still retains the tenets of the earlier author's work. Belbin identifies nine key roles played by members of management teams. In no particular order they are classified as:

- The plant – creative and solves challenging problems but tends to get too absorbed in their role to communicate effectively;
- The shaper – thrives on pressure and has a strong drive but may be tactless and provocative;
- The team-worker – cooperative and diplomatic but may be prone to indecisiveness;
- The implementer – reliable, conservative and practical but may resist change;
- The resource investigator – explores opportunities and develops contacts but quick to lose interest in an idea;
- The co-ordinator – clarifies the teams goals and delegates effectively but may be seen as offloading too much of their own work;
- The monitor evaluator – judges accurately and has a strategic focus but may not inspire others;
- The specialist – self-motivated and provides rare skills but has ability to focus too much on minutiae; and

■ The completer finisher – conscientious and delivers on time but may worry unnecessarily and be reluctant to delegate.

Adapted from Belbin (1981).

Reflective practice

1. Consider a small hospitality firm employing only four people including the owner. Which of Belbin's team roles would you consider essential for such an operation?

As discussed previously in this chapter team working is the ideal approach for hospitality firms when growing and developing. However, even with the best intention, teams will have difficulty prevailing when they are not supported by an appropriate organizational culture. Culture has been described as the 'social glue' which holds organizational practices together. The following section discusses what it is, how it is established and applies to hospitality firms.

CULTURE

Organisational culture may be viewed from two perspectives (Legge, 1995). That is, organizations either 'have' it or organisations actually 'are' it. The former is a structural view and the second holds that culture is separate from any framework imposed by management and is best described as a root system of meanings (Gregory, 1983). One can see immediately that if culture is 'objective' or a summary of organisational values it is manageable. Conversely if we adopt the second perspective, culture is now an outcome of social interaction. As such, it may only be possible to describe or interpret it. This is not to say that management has no impact on organisational culture, just that all members of the organisation have their own constructions of reality. In practice, both espoused and spontaneous cultures exist alongside each other so managers should have an understanding of how the latter impacts on the former.

Reflective practice

1. Think of two dissimilar small or medium-sized hospitality business known to you or that you have identified through a literature/desk search. Describe the culture that each appears to have and how you came to that decision.
2. What impact has the founder had on the organizational culture?

If the entrepreneurial leader fails to establish an appropriate culture, followers will begin to form one of their own. Situations like these are all too common in the hospitality industry, particularly in the unaffiliated sector where some entrepreneurs fail to identify, create and reinforce a common set of values for followers. This may not be so important where the firm is small employing only a handful of people as its culture often tends to be an extension of the founders beliefs and attitudes. Such a small group of followers may not always need a formal and organized set of core values but employers will nonetheless have expectations of behaviour. Moreover, communicating these may not be overly difficult as the channels are likely to be short and direct. Usually, they are encapsulated in items like job descriptions, recruitment and selection protocols and by virtue of being in close proximity to the founder for most of the time. However, as the organization grows, communication channels become more complex and there is an increased chance of 'drop out' and misunderstanding. In other words, the effective proliferation of these values to others becomes more difficult. The hospitality entrepreneur must not assume that all followers will share her values, beliefs and attitudes.

Indeed, the nature of the hospitality labour market and characteristics of the industry present extra challenges for the entrepreneur. Any attempt to create an organizational culture must account for the fact that much hospitality work is unskilled, temporary, seasonal or part-time with reduced benefits and working conditions. Levels of labour turnover are extremely high in some sectors and 'tipping' is still an accepted way for some employers to justify low pay. Traditionally, management is autocratic and despotic and union membership is low. There is also a mindset shared by some employees in the seasonal tourist sector that hospitality employment is not a 'serious' job only to be tolerated until something better turns up. Finally, some workers view hospitality jobs as little more than an opportunity to enjoy a paid holiday. These are significant contextual factors which if ignored will seriously undermine any attempt to create a positive organizational culture.

ORGANIZATIONAL CULTURE: WHY BOTHER?

Why is the establishment of an organizational culture so important? Some argue that a strong culture is a replacement for company policies and procedures. Peters and Waterman (1982) claim that culture replaces the need for formal protocol because everyone knows exactly what needs to be done.

Robbins (2001) defines organisational culture as:

"*A common perception held by the organisation's members; a system of shared meaning*" (p. 510).

In an organizational sense, culture is tricky to define because it is comprised of so many things but is often described as a code of conduct which governs the way people act and think in the work place. In service industries and particularly in small hospitality firms, culture can have a significant impact on success or failure. The most effective entrepreneurs recognize the role played by workers in service delivery and the potential impact that they have every time they interact with customers. A leader's ability to create and maintain (and change if necessary) an appropriate service-oriented culture for their business is therefore important.

According to Robbins (2001) organizational cultures are based on several characteristics shown in Figure 10.6.

The position of individual firms along the 'low'/'high' scale for each characteristic has driven others to create cultural typologies. For example, Handy (1990) conceptualises four different, but not exclusive, types of 'power', 'role', 'task' and 'person'. The power culture is often found in small firms where much is based on trust, empathy and personal communication. The role culture tends to be present in larger firms and where there are strict controls, bureaucracy and a strong sense of positional power. Leaders, by definition, have authority within hospitality organizations. Their authority can be either conferred by dint of their official role and status or emergent from the degree of respect they receive from followers. French and Raven (1960) classify five sources of power into:

- Legitimate – authority granted by individual's position within the firm where followers simply accept the formal authority of that person;
- Reward – authority to bestow; and
- Coercive – authority to withhold or punish.

These are conferred by position power defined by the firm's policies and procedures. The remaining two sources of power are 'Expert' and 'Referent' power and are based on the entrepreneur's special knowledge and or their personal characteristics. Ideally, the leader's sources should be expert and referent as they stem from followers' respect and admiration. The positional sources of power tend to be less about effective leadership but more about an individual's role within the firm. Founders should bear in mind that the accomplishment of the organization's goals requires more that leadership based on positional power. Handy's task culture characterises firms who are project or matrix oriented and the person culture has a focus on the person where autonomy is enjoyed where control is agreed by mutual consent.

Founders should be aware that if left unchecked their firms may begin with a task culture but end up with a power culture especially if the entrepreneur

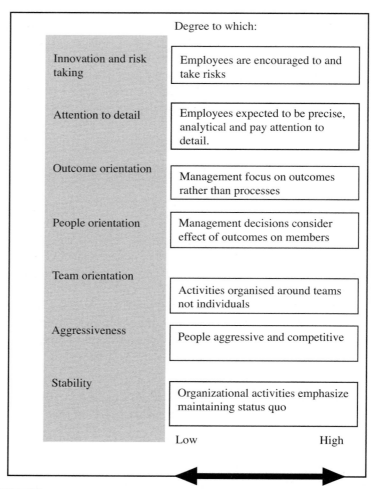

FIGURE 10.6 *Primary characteristics of organisational culture. Adapted from: Robbins (2001, pp. 510–511).*

has difficulty delegating. In turn, this culture may morph into a role culture where job titles become more important that the job itself.

Other typologies also exist but all basically tell a similar story, for example, Deal and Kennedy (1982) refer to cultures of:

- Macho;
- Work hard/play hard;
- Bet-your-company; and
- Process.

Armed with the knowledge that all organizational cultures are subject to key influences and that all can be described along continua defined by basic characteristics we can begin to think about what makes for a successful culture. After reviewing the evidence, Zimmerer and Scarborough (2002) argue that entrepreneurial firms need to focus on the following principles:

■ Respect for work life balance through flexible scheduling, job sharing, part-time work, on site day care and so on;
■ A sense of purpose through defining the hospitality firm's vision and communicating it clearly to everyone;
■ Promoting a sense of fun in the workplace;
■ Valuing and pursuing diversity in the work place to build strength through use of different skills, talents and abilities of followers;
■ Promoting a high sense of ethical and moral responsibility in the work place;
■ Use of participative management styles consistent with new transformational leadership approaches; and
■ Retain a life long learning environment in order to attract, motivate and retain followers.

Key point 10.5

The elements affecting the formation of organisational culture are philosophy of founders, selection criteria and socialisation to founders' mindset.

Similarly based on the earlier work of Timmons (1999), Burns (2001) considers that a desirable entrepreneurial organizational culture is based on six dimensions:

■ Extent to which employee's are committed to organizational goals;
■ Extent to which they feel recognized and rewarded for good performance;
■ Degree to which org goals, policies and procedures and understood;
■ Degree to which high standards are expected;
■ Extent to which employees feel responsible for goal achievement without excessive monitoring; and
■ Extent to which a sense of team cohesion is present.

How do we know what kind of culture an hospitality organization has? Cultural artefacts are relatively easy to identify in a firm and may include dress code, use of 'company language'[2] and the physical appearance of a building such as that used by various fast-food restaurants internationally. Other facets of culture are more subtle and therefore less easily observed. Schein (1985) explains the differences between the observable and non-observable factors through levels of culture. For example, dress code exists at level one (artefacts and creations) whereas values and basic assumptions are 'invisible' or 'taken for granted'. An example of Schein's level two (values) would be why work groups behave as they do, for example, is it permissible to call the employer or managers by first name? The extent to which members hold these behavioural values and norms as unquestionable determines whether the organisational culture is 'strong' or 'weak'. Level three concerns basic and tacit assumptions that determine how members perceive, think, and feel. This stage represents that which is taken for granted by the group or that which is so deeply rooted it enters the unconscious. If a strong team culture is to be established and sustained successfully by the founder, this is the level at which training and socialisation procedures should focus.

So how does the hospitality entrepreneur establish and sustain an appropriate organizational culture? Robbins (2001) considers the following to be important (Figure 10.7):

- ■ Philosophy of founders – early culture formation when firm first established; founder's vision easily imparted to all members; for example, original Forte and Marriott groups union-busting and paternalistic culture is a philosophy of both Charles Forte and Bill Marriott; founders able to influence 'espoused' or formal culture but not actual/informal or 'culture-in-practice';
- ■ Selection criteria – staff hired in founders' image; other human resource practices such as training and reward systems linked similarly;
- ■ Top management – behave in a manner which supports original philosophy; rituals and physical symbols which reinforce key values, norms and goals; and
- ■ Socialization – to founders' mindset, success perceived as linked directly with founding philosophy; self–perpetuating, sustained by legends of how firm began which justifies present behaviour or culture in the past, for example Conrad Hilton, Richard Branson; use of

---

[2] The Disney corporation is a prime example where staff are referred to as 'cast members' and jobs become 'performances' (Zimmerer and Scarborough, 2002).

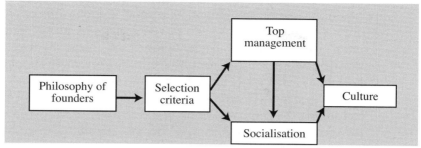

FIGURE 10.7 *Key elements affecting the formation of organisational culture. Adapted from: Robbins (2001, p. 523).*

company 'language', for example in many hotels staff from different departments are often referred to by use of acronyms or other terms (KPs – kitchen porters or stewards; food service staff may be labelled, rather disparagingly, as 'plate carriers' by chefs).

Adapted from Lashley and Lee-Ross (2003).

SUMMARY

There is a tendency to believe that successful entrepreneurs make good leaders. Whilst there are individuals who excel in both roles there are also others for whom leadership is something more of a challenge. Effective leadership requires certain abilities and skills, for example, does the entrepreneur have the capacity to analyse and diagnose work contexts and situations before behaving in the capacity of leader?

Many theories exist all having their own perspective on the best way to lead organizations. In the main they are complimentary with the possible exception of the newer postmodern constructs which regard leaders as stewards and servants. In short the leadership role here becomes inverted to the extent that followers become leaders and *vice versa*. Nonetheless, founders of small and growing hospitality firms need to grasp and use this knowledge and that afforded them by experience and good fortune if they are to be both notable entrepreneurs and leaders.

Whilst firms stay small (and many do in the hospitality industry) the requirement for the business founder to grow and develop into an effective leader is of lesser importance than when firms move from the lifestyle type into the entrepreneurial firm. During the transition, there are a number of behavioural characteristics which are essential for robust leadership. These include respecting and supporting employees, embracing change, leading by example, creating an appropriate culture, communicating effectively and so on. However, evidence suggests that entrepreneurs are not particularly adept at interpersonal relations and communication. These are two key areas which must be addressed as firms grow and employ more people otherwise the hospitality business is likely to be compromised. Indeed, as the firm grows most commentators agree that the entrepreneur must adopt a team approach to running the company. To do this well requires the establishment of good interpersonal relationships and effective communication amongst and between the team.

Thus, the founder must have a basic understanding of organizational culture and the levels at which it manifests itself and how to affect and maintain core values through:

- establishing and perpetuating through selection criteria;
- embodiment through the management team; and
- socialization.

She must also be aware of some important environmental and labour market characteristics likely to influence organizational culture such as 'tipping', temporary, casual and part-time working, attitudes of some hospitality workers and so on. Finally, the founder must be clear that if little attempt is made to espouse an official culture another version will surely fill the void. In many instances this 'culture in practice' will impact negatively on the organization.

Case: Simon Says. . ..

By Michael Fahy

It wasn't really surprising to learn that Simon Woodroffe had once been a stage designer for Rod Stewart and The Moody Blues. After all with his cultivated sideburns and trademark yellow suede boots, the 50 year old entrepreneur looks as if he has just walked in from the latest Spinal Tap video. To describe Woodroffe as flamboyant would be an understatement, but the founder and chairman of YO! Sushi argues that business needs a dash of colour. He thinks we should all dream a little more too, so long as we have the courage of our convictions and follow them.

I've yet to meet the person who, even at the risk of their own financial security, went out to do what they dreamed of and regretted it, regardless of success or failure. It has certainly worked for him. After leaving school with only three 'O' levels he became a roadie and eventually found himself sitting in the same rooms as Stevie Wonder, the Rolling Stones and others. Seizing the opportunity, he set about convincing them that their stage shows needed fireworks, trapeze wires and other cunning stunts. He then established a company to deliver his service. After playing his part in Live Aid, he went off to set up a TV company securing the rights to live concerts and selling them to broadcasters around the world.

After turning 40 he decided his potential had not yet been realized and so decided to start a retail business so he could be at the 'sharp end'. He considered a number of ideas but none really grabbed him. A Japanese friend suggested he should open a conveyor belt shushi bar with food served by girls in black PVC. He immediately began researching the prospect and was initially disappointed to find the idea was not totally original. ''Then I opened another magazine and at the top of the page it said 'How to open your own conveyor belt sushi bar'. I thought this is too good to be true. Three months later he had a business plan, knew a huge amount about sushi and had outline sketches of the YO! logo. His problem, however, was a lack of cash. He says he wasn't interested in building a conventional restaurant and wanted YO! Sushi to be a kind of Planet Hollywood for the 1990s – a chain that would grow remarkably quickly. Yet apart from his own £150 000, the money was hardly flowing in. He had dismissed the idea of venture capital as ''too scary'', but had managed to land £100 000 through the Government Loan Guarantee scheme. He also borrowed £50 000 from a childhood friend and £50 000 ''from a bloke I met off the street in Paris''.

Moreover, the launch of his first restaurant was delayed by around a year as the property company with whom he was signing a deal sold its entire portfolio. With hindsight, he argues this was the best thing that could have happened, as he ditched many parts of a blander concept for something much more radical. For instance, he introduced huge plate glass windows so people could see the food moving around on the conveyor from outside. He also blagged some satellite equipment and TVs from Sony, so he could beam in Japanese TV. The piece de resistance, though, was the robots. He had approached an industrial manufacturer about building robots that could dispense drinks to diners but was quoted the rather ridiculous price of £700 000 more than the combined budget for his first two restaurants. Eventually, he was put in touch with a man who designed robotic systems for wheelchairs through Edinburgh University's robotics department who said he could build the first two for less than £50 000. Each robot followed a wire circuit which was placed underneath restaurant floors. They also had individual voices and characteristics. Four weeks before the first YO! Sushi was due to open on London's Poland Street, a prototype was brought onto the site for a trial and everyone downed tools to watch it. ''I remember thinking ''That is the making of this place people are going to come in at least to have a look at that. Especially when it spoke!''

He had also attracted two corporate 'sponsors' – Sony had provided him with the TVs and Nippon Air had given him a couple of flight upgrades. Then Honda provided him with a six month loan of a 'Girocycle.' I wrote back to them saying that I was so pleased I'd decided to make them an official sponsor, and if I didn't hear from them within seven days I'd assume they'd agreed. Of course, I knew big companies were incapable of responding quickly, so I had my third sponsor.'' This turned out to be more useful than he'd imagined. Once the restaurant was open, the customers had started to flock in and he started thinking that he could continue without any external funding. He'd contacted his biggest creditor (who he owed £250 000), showed him around the booming restaurant and asked for a minimum of six months' grace on payment. ''I heard later they'd had this big meeting at which one of the senior guys said 'let's give the guy a chance – it's probably going to work but if it does all go wrong those Japanese giants who are behind it will cough up the money'.''

Woodroffe made sure that it didn't and set about expanding YO! Sushi while thinking up ideas for other ventures and becoming the new Virgin around the world. Unsurprisingly, he says he is a big fan of Richard Branson and is a firm believer in building a series of businesses around the one brand, saying that the instant recognition given to a new business far outweighs bad publicity affecting another part ''Why build a mountain twice?'' he asks. ''If you look around the world, nobody does these brand extensions. I've heard people talking about Virgin, Stelios and YO! in the same breath, but we're a tiny, tiny company compared to the others.'' He currently has 16 YO! Sushi restaurants, spread mainly across London but an Edinburgh unit opened last August and one is planned for the food hall of Manchester Selfridges by September. There has also been a number of spin-offs from the restaurants including events Catering, food delivery and YO! Branded Sushi for Sainsbury's. He has also opened three basement bars underneath restaurants known as YO!-Below which have self-service beer taps and smoke-extracting ashtrays on each table. Staff have also been trained in giving out massages to stressed customers. He says the next business to be launched will be YO!tel, which is described as a cross between a Japanese capsule hotel and British Airways First Class. He admits that he has been talking about this for years, but feels it is important that he gets it right. ''If we are successful with YO!tel, then it will follow very quickly that we can go into all sorts of different areas,'' he says ''I sometimes think we're like a pop group,'' he says, ''We've had our first album, we've done lots of spin offs from the first album, but I don't think until we've had a second album that we can seriously call ourselves a big band.''

Questions

1. What leadership characteristics does this entrepreneur display?
2. How would you describe his leadership style?
3. What impact would his early life as a roadie have had on his entrepreneurial style?
4. Has this entrepreneur made the transition from founder to leader?
5. If so, estimate the point at which the change was made.
6. What role has dedicated 'business' education played in this entrepreneur's success?

Reproduced with permission, *Hospitality*, July/August, 2002, pp. 38–40.

CHAPTER 11

Growth: the Harder I Work the Luckier I Get

After working through this chapter you should be able to:

- Discuss the growth of small hospitality firms as it applies to entrepreneurial and lifestyle firms;
- Understand the strengths and weaknesses of 'growth' models;
- Discuss the major components of growth strategies for small; hospitality firms and the role good fortune plays in their success; and
- Outline the major challenges the entrepreneur faces during the growth of firms.

INTRODUCTION

Take 10 budding entrepreneurs, furnish with a certain sum of money and instructions to start, grow and sustain a successful small hospitality business; some would succeed, some would fail and others simply 'tread water'. Obviously, exact amounts of financing, time frames and so on would need to be established for everyone to compete equally but there would still be different outcomes for these firms. The key questions would be 'why' and 'what' caused them?

To understand why firms grow (or not) requires knowledge and acquired experience of economic conditions, markets, individual capabilities, strategic competence, an awareness of company strengths/weaknesses and so on. Furthermore, it is one thing simply ticking off these boxes but quite another to understand how all of this knowledge works holistically to bring about firm growth. Indeed, a single configuration of these factors would most certainly not be appropriate for all business development. There is yet another conundrum; what role does good fortune play in the successful growth of the small hospitality firm?

Dictionary.com, defines the word 'growth' in several ways:

- to increase by natural development as any living organism;
- to form and increase in size by an inorganic process;
- to arise or issue as a natural development from an original happening, circumstance, or source.

Reflective practice

1. How would you define the organic and inorganic growth of small hospitality firms?

In an entrepreneurship context, commentators often divide organisations into growth or entrepreneurial and 'lifestyle' firms (see Chapter 5). The intent of the former is to achieve sustained growth through market expansion and increasing profitability, that is, through economic growth. These firms play a major role in wealth creation and yet only represent a minority of small hospitality firms. For example using aggregated data, Deakins and Freel (2006) assert "...out of every 100 small firms, four will provide around 50 per cent of all employment over a given time period" (p. 159). On the other hand, lifestyle firms are more concerned with survival by generating enough income to sustain a given living standard for the owner(s). Here, economic growth is part of a more holistic strategic aim but remains consistent with the above definitions. Thus, even though the hospitality industry is dominated by small and micro lifestyle businesses we can still assert that they are concerned with growing and developing albeit differently to truly entrepreneurial firms. This perspective broadly concurs with that of Schaper and Volery (2004) who make a similar case on the basis that all firms share at least one of three goals; all of which pertain to growth. These are:

- Survival; and
- Consolidation and continued success; and/or
- To expand or grow.

The following case is a typical example of a small hospitality lifestyle firm

---

Changing the Harrogate Model: Alison's 'Spur of the Moment' lifestyle business.

Notes from a meeting with Alison Evans, co-owner and operator of Westlands House Bed and Breakfast, Buxton, 22nd May 2007

Alison has recently resigned a teaching position with the University of Derby Buxton to work full-time on a three room bed and breakfast business established in February 2005. Alison, and her husband Alex, own the business, which was purchased in December 2004. Alison is now in her forties, the couple have no children and were wondering what the future would hold for them. They would often drive into the country at weekends just for something different to do; they were easily bored. Alison is a Derbyshire lass and her husband was brought up in Devon and Yorkshire. Now they run a thriving and attractive bed and breakfast business from their own home. Alison has been recently inspected and given a four star and silver award for her efforts.

The property is a well maintained late Victorian (circa 1901) stone house, semi-detached with a front and back garden and on-site parking for cars. Alison said that she and Alex more or less spontaneously bought the property with the intention of running a business. They have a mortgage on the property but were able to extend themselves financially by selling a previously owned freehold property elsewhere.

The house extends over four levels. There is a cellar which the couple eventually may convert into further living space. The ground floor has an elegant living room with deeply upholstered furniture, a sunny dining room, entrance lobby and kitchen–all used by guests. The first floor has three well-appointed guest rooms–doubles or twins with en-suite bathrooms. One room has a particularly large bathroom and a magnificent view from the bedroom to the rear of the property over the spectacular and rugged Derbyshire moors. The road frontage is very neat and well maintained and, at time of interview, leafy and verdant whilst being easily accessible (5 minutes by car) to downtown Buxton with its Opera House and Georgian and Edwardian terraces.

Buxton is a pretty elevated spa town, at 300 m, almost at the head of the River Wye in the High Peak Borough of the Peak District. There are just over 20 000 residents in the town and excellent rail and road links with Cheshire, Manchester and Sheffield. In any year in excess of 25 million visitors, predominantly from the domestic United Kingdom market, visit Buxton and environs. Most visitors are keen to see the natural scenery and enjoy short and long walks and hiking. A significant proportion of Alison's guests come for two major events in the town itself each season—the Gilbert and Sullivan Opera season and the Buxton Festival in July. In addition there are a number of smaller venues dotted around the town that are used for events such as Antique Fairs. One could assume that Alison made a wise choice in investing in property for her business based largely on Buxton's centrality in the United Kingdom and proximity to the former grimy industrial metropolitan areas of the Midlands and North. However, Alison is a Buxtonian by birth so in many ways she has made a commitment to her town in this business.

In the first 2 years of operation Alison, and to a lesser degree Alex, worked exceedingly hard to make Westlands a successful bed and breakfast business. Alison rose each morning by 7 am to prepare for a day of cooked English breakfast (eggs, bacon, black pudding, oatcakes, sausage and rounds of toast) and, having farewelled her guests, would make her way into the University campus to work full-time as an early childhood lecturer. At night she would return to Westlands, clear up after departed guests, make beds and wash and iron bed linen to the point of exhaustion. Alex had, and still has, a full time job outside of the bed and breakfast. His role has been accounts, finances and general support. Alex does not cook or clean or do maintenance; those roles are filled by Alison. The telephone is answered by whoever is available. Alison and Alex have an answering machine and can access incoming calls away from the business as required. Alison is the prime contact and host for the business and, for 2 years, managed the business whilst holding down a full-time job. To understand the operating success of the business one must acknowledge the role of technology. Alison claims to have received most reservations through her website. It cost her £800 to set-up but this is money well spent. The second technological asset is the credit card processor. Now all bookings are taken with a deposit against a credit card, effectively minimising the risk of no-shows. Alison understands that for major events bookings are made up to 6 months in advance. Even late bookings are usually made a week prior. Alison is therefore seldom dependent on cold callers and last minute clients. She receives referrals from the neighbouring establishment which acts as a top-up. Alison estimates 20 per cent of her business is derived from repeat customers and referrals and the balance is from the Buxton Tourism Information Centre. Adding value by offering evening meals is considered unnecessary. Alison knows that there are many restaurants with a variety of cuisine and at a range of grades within easy walking distance. Shrewdly she worked out that clients expect fine dining experiences but are not prepared to pay for that standard of service under her own roof. Understanding the market needs and preferences and expectations is an important part of this case study.

Alison is fortunate in having a local network of bed and breakfast owners. Her neighbour, Hillary, runs a successful and slightly larger business (5 rooms and 5 stars) and has provided Alison with a lot of information to help her understand the customers' needs and, more importantly referral business when her accommodation is full. The adjoining house, on the other side of the property, has recently been sold and may revert to a bed and breakfast business which will mean three sets of accommodation businesses in a row. Alison is not anxious about this; she sees that there is sufficient demand for accommodation to make this an asset to her own operation. She assumes that the standards required of a bed and breakfast business would raise the tone of the street and she would welcome professional neighbours rather than a noisy family with teenagers.

In future Alison may consider expanding her business by converting the cellar and using existing second floor rooms that are currently occupied by Alison, for further guest accommodation. Alison and Alex could use the cellar for their own quarters.

Alison is a person of neat and tidy appearance and by her own account, a people person. This couple have a defined division of labour and responsibilities. Alison is the operational partner and Alex is in charge of finances. Alex is somewhat risk-averse, what Alison calls cautious, and an important check on Alison's tendency to impulsiveness. Alison recognises that the challenge to a successful, quality product delivered to the clients is her outgoing nature coupled to her ability to operate with networks of useful people for both her business and for herself. Alison and Alex have become shrewd judges of people and behaviour. Despite the characteristics described, Alison admits to originally having fears about having guests in her home. I suspect that after 2 years she has been able to overcome this trepidation and she admits that she can get a good night's rest now.

Many of the factors which impact this business depend on good judgement and prior knowledge. Insurance as appropriate, redecoration as required and to an expected level of quality, minimised risk, partnerships, networks, and understanding the impacts that running a bed and breakfast has on one's lifestyle are all considered relevant in this case study. Alison and Alex can manage 2 weeks in each year to take a break from the business. This is partially due to being able to judge the peak demand periods surrounding events in Buxton (Opera, festivals and weddings) and partly to developing some skills in judging booking patterns and trends. Although this is the first year that Alison has committed totally to the bed and breakfast it is apparent that this decision was properly considered and relevant factors weighed up. Alison admits to the learning curve having been steep but reflects on support and advice from friends and being smart about decisions and the market.

It is apparent that a good understanding of the market and supply in Buxton was central to Alison's decision to focus on this lifestyle business.

Source: Wiltshier (2007).

Clearly, both lifestyle and entrepreneurial perspectives are important so a discussion of growth must consider both. The main aim for this chapter is therefore to identify key factors responsible for the sustainable growth of hospitality organisations. It does this by first reviewing two important 'growth' models to clarify the stages through which firms progress when developing together with a discussion of some challenges faced by the entrepreneur at these times. Second, the chapter discusses several strategic growth perspectives addressing whether growth should be pursued in the first instance and then identifies key elements of each approach including the key enablers, dimensions and interrelatedness. The role of Ansoff's (1968) product/service/market matrix in decision-making is also introduced. The chapter continues by considering some important barriers to the growth of small hospitality firms.

Key point 11.1

A comprehensive discussion of growth must include both entrepreneurial and lifestyle firms.

GROWTH MODELS

There have been several attempts to conceptualise the manner in which firms grow and some of the challenges that will be encountered along the way. The best known of these include Greiner (1972) and Churchill and Lewis (1983). Scott and Bruce (1987) and Burns (1996) used the Churchill and Lewis construct as a basis for their adaptations and additions.

Greiner's model essentially maps five stages of growth each characterized by a period of crisis which must be managed by shifting leadership style and

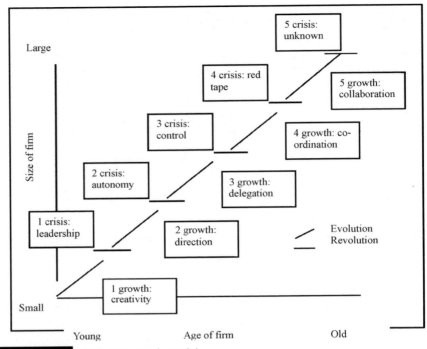

FIGURE 11.1 *Greiner's growth model.*
Source: Greiner (1972).

practices and procedures in order to progress to the next stage of the model. The model is shown in Figure 11.1.

In short, each stage of the above model is defined by a particular entrepreneurial behaviour. For example, creativity characterizes stage 1, whereas collaboration defines stage 5. As the organisation grows within a stage it reaches a crisis point, that is, the point at which behaviour becomes inappropriate if it is to develop. In stage 1, 'random' creativity becomes difficult to harness productively unless the business establishes clear leadership and vision for all stakeholders. Stage 4 is characterised by a more managerial 'coordination' approach with clarity of goals and control procedures. The firm is now far too complex for only one entrepreneur to manage and thus begins to lose its original character. The standard policies and procedures are now likely to cause excessive bureaucratic 'red tape'. The model advocates a move toward collaboration between employees with a focus on 'mission' rather than slavishly adhering to standard practice. This perennial problem for all growth firms is a significant challenge. The entrepreneur must try and capture the original spirit of the small firm by establishing an appropriate business culture.

TABLE 11.1	Greiner's model of firm growth				
Attribute	**Stage 1 Creativity**	**Stage 2 Direction**	**Stage 3 Delegation**	**Stage 4 Co-ordination**	**Stage 5 Collaboration**
Management	Produce and sell	Operational efficiency	Market expansion	Organizational consolidation	Problem-solving and innovation
Organization structure	Informal	Centralized and functional	Decentralized and geographical	Line staff and product groups	Matrix
Top management style	Individualistic	Directive	Delegation	Watchdog	Participative
Control system	Market results	Standards and cost centres	Reports and profit centres	Plans and investment centres	Mutual goal setting
Management reward emphasis	Ownership	Salary and performance-based	Individual bonuses	Profit sharing and stock options	Team bonus
Crises	Leadership	Autonomy	Control	Red tape	Unknown

Adapted from: Deakins and Freel (2006: p. 163).

Greiner's construct may also be expressed in a tabular format as shown Table 11.1.

The Churchill and Lewis' (1983) model similarly follows the five-stage life-cycle pattern of Greiner (1972) but is more general and has no crises which precipitate the movement from one stage to the next. The stages are:

- ■ I Existence;
- ■ II Survival;
- ■ III Success;
- ■ IV Take-off; and
- ■ V Maturity.

Reflective practice

1. Through an internet search or through a small hospitality organization know to your consider whether either of the growth models in this chapter accurately reflect its growth and development?

Essentially, both constructs map the growth of firms from a relatively simple beginning where most things are fuzzy or difficult to define through to a highly formal bureaucratic structure which then has to be reconceptualised. Flexibility and qualities of the early simple structure must be reintroduced and retained through advanced leadership and management techniques. Another difference between the two models is that Churchill

TABLE 11.2	Critique of growth models—some factors

- Most firms do not grow and therefore fail to reach the second or third stages.
- Growth experienced may not follow the prescribed pattern.
- Firms will plateau at particular stages and not progress further.
- The sequence of factors inherent in the models is not supported, for example many firms lurch from crisis to crisis in an unprescribed manner whilst other may have a relatively uniform unhindered progression.

Adapted from: Burns (2001) and Deakins and Freel (2006).

and Lewis differentiate between lifestyle and growth firms. During the third stage (success) there are two options. The first is 'disengagement' whereby the entrepreneur can choose to exploit an emerging niche and go no further. The second is the growth option where the entrepreneur chooses to establish a vision, strategy and clear objectives for continued expansion. However, like most models, both are simple representations of reality and should only be used heuristically. Burns (2001) and Deakins and Freel (2006) provide an adequate critique shown in Table 11.2.

Key point 11.2

Growth models help map the progress and development of firms but often do not reflect the reality of all growth situations. As such they should be only used for guidance, orientation and to aid decision-making for hospitality firms as much depends on context and situational specifics.

The following case illustrates a lifestyle-type firm where the entrepreneurs have managed to successfully integrate their business and way of life.

Lifestyle Tourism Entrepreneurship in a South Australia wine Region

Is it possible to combine your entrepreneurial pursuits with your lifestyle? Ben and Lisa Thompson believe that it is not only possible, but essential to their full enjoyment of life to conceive of their livelihood synonymously with their personal lifestyle. They are people who have sought and found a happy balance between comfort and necessity. They are also examples of what Richards and Wilson (2006), called 'prosumers', people engaged in a mixture of skilled production and consumption. Richards and Wilson cited lifestyle entrepreneurs as examples of this, such as the avid surfer who opens a surf-related business as a means of supporting a lifestyle preference. The Thompsons, both in their 60s, have realized this combination in a tourism context through the establishment and operation of a vineyard, accommodation and restaurant complex in McLaren Vale, South Australia.

McLaren Vale is located in the Fleurieu Peninsula, one of the state of South Australia's 12 tourism regions. The region attracts more domestic same day visits than any other SA region (2.1 million) except the capital city of Adelaide (SATC, 2007). The Fleurieu Peninsula is positioned as the Water, Wine and Wildlife Region, and McLaren Vale is the region's dominant wine destination with approximately 50 cellar doors, and is joining the select group of areas that can claim to be part of the 'cradle of the Australian wine industry' (Faulkner, Oppermann and Fredline, 1999). Recent developments in McLaren Vale's marketing and management have raised the destination's profile, such as the construction of a gateway Visitor Information Centre, the integration of neighbouring wine producers with the local destination management organisation, and an active events agenda that emphasises the combination of food and wine, such as the annual *Sea and Vines Festival*, and *Meet your Maker* events when tourists spend a weekend with McLaren Vale winemakers.

Ben (a former government official) and Lisa (a former corporate executive) traded their city life in Adelaide for a more rural existence in McLaren Vale. Long-time self-described 'wine romantics' and lovers of country living, they saw the potential in a block of land with one residential building on it to establish a vineyard and hospitality operation that would allow them to pursue their love of wine. They began the project in 1998, and by 2007 had established a viable restaurant, catering and accommodation business, and had harvested and bottled a modest amount of their first grape crop. As Ben said, 'We took this three bedroom, three bathroom house which was entirely the wrong design and the wrong shape and colour and wrong everything else but in the most wonderful location. We decided we wanted to turn it into something that fitted the location on our terms. And we knew we were going to end up with some money at the end of it.'

While they feel that the change has been overwhelmingly positive, in many ways they have traded some constraints for others. As Lisa explains, 'in the office you're within the office system discipline. Here it's my own discipline, well not quite because it's also the discipline imposed by the vineyard, the guestrooms, and the food and beverage operations.'

Additionally, vineyard and hospitality work is physically demanding, and can take a heavy toll, particularly on a body that is wearing out. The biggest trade-off has been financial, as the returns generated in their new venture have fallen below their combined earning capacity in their former careers. However, the Thompsons feel that this has been more than offset by the psychic gains that they have realized in terms of greater happiness and satisfaction.

References

Faulkner, B., Oppermann, M., and Fredline, E. (1999) Destination competitiveness: an exploratory examination of South Australia's core attractions. *Journal of Vacation Marketing* **5**(2):125–139.

Richards, G., and Wilson, J. (2006) *Developing creativity in tourist experiences: a solution to the serial reproduction of culture? Tourism Management* **27**(6):1209–1223.

South Australian Tourism Commission (SATC), (2007) Fleurieu Peninsula regional tourism profile, June, Adelaide, pp 1–4 www.tourism.sa.gov.au/publications.

Source: Gross (2007).

CHALLENGES FOR THE ENTREPRENEUR

Burns' (1996, pp. 241–242) notion of an entrepreneurial organization helps to explain the shift of procedural and behavioural emphasis as firms grow. He notes that on start up the entrepreneur sits at the centre of the firm with all reporting to her and operations are characterized by:

- An informal management style with all business decisions being similarly predisposed;
- Informal staff employer relationships;
- Hands-on training;
- Influencing structures rather than rigid control;
- Personal relationship-building; and
- Job flexibility.

It is also important to note that small entrepreneurial firms are by no means problem-free, especially if the entrepreneur has little or no experience of employing people. For example, where employees are not provided with clear guidelines, roles and responsibilities, communication can often become unclear between entrepreneur, employee and vice versa. In these situations employer/employee psychological contracts can become confused with misunderstandings becoming common. Ultimately this leads to unrest, dissatisfaction and can often lead to high levels of labour turnover. These situations may be particularly acute in small businesses where the entrepreneur employs family and friends. The negative fall-out is not only bad for business but also compromises former friendships and family relationships. The adage of actors never working with children or animals is appropriate here, that is, never work with family or friends!

Notwithstanding the problems that may occur resulting from communication breakdown and misunderstandings, Burns' idea of the small entrepreneurial firm structure can work well with only a few employees but once staff numbers begin increasing a different and more formal approach is warranted. Once the organization reaches this point a more formal design and clear structure become key. The negative side of formal reporting structures and hierarchies are well documented elsewhere (e.g., see Robbins, 2007, etc.) but, all things being equal, to operate efficiently and effectively, firms must adopt a structure which is appropriate to their size. Clearly, one cannot be too prescriptive here as even large and hierarchical organizations often establish smaller more organic internal structures for the purpose of intrapreneurship. However at a pinch, simple standardized jobs are more suited to hierarchies and where the trading environment is undynamic and predictable; complex/creative jobs and a dynamic environment require flatter and more flexible organization design.

Of course technically the above prescriptions seem reasonable, however, people (including entrepreneurs) have a number of attitudes and behaviours which may actually detract from this logic. The small entrepreneurial firm is organic and some commentators note that it is simply an extension of the entrepreneur's personality and idiosyncracies. Du Toit (1980) takes this further by arguing that entrepreneurs were formerly difficult employees. Whilst this may be the case for some, there is general agreement that a key entrepreneurial trait is locus of control (Rotter, 1966; Cromie, 2000) where the individual attributes success to their own input rather than the impact of other variables. Indeed, an opportunity to gain control over one's destiny is one of the four most common reasons given by entrepreneurs for starting their own business (Zimmerer and Scarborough, 1996). Some cruelly refer to individuals with this characteristic as 'control freaks'!

The potential problem with an overly controlling and inexperienced founder is that they are likely to 'meddle' or micro-manage in the belief that only they can achieve the optimum outcome for their business even after stage one of Greiner's (1972) model has been surpassed. Kirby (2003) refers to this as 'founder's disease' (p. 287) which can cause an inordinate amount of problems in all areas of the business including role ambiguity for managers, informal reporting structures, staff alienation through reduced job tasks and autonomy and so on. To avoid these negative outcomes Kirby (2003, p. 287) notes that entrepreneurs must appreciate that:

- As firms grow they become more complex;
- They cannot make all of the decisions;
- Science cannot clone the founder; and
- Their authority will never equal the degree of responsibility.

In short, as firms grow so too must the entrepreneur by learning new skills. They must avoid the hands on approach in favour of a more strategic, monitoring and decision-making role. This can be difficult, at start-up founders typically spend almost 90 per cent of their effort 'doing' and 10 per cent 'thinking'. Clearly, delegation is important here so the firm will need to have a more formal structure including new control systems and team-working rather than relying on informal relationships and ill-defined operating procedures of the past.

A firm deciding to grow rather than remaining in lifestyle mode faces a number of challenges and choices. Growth models are reasonable in expressing the various stages through which the firm passes (notwithstanding the weaknesses identified earlier) but they do not make clear those issues responsible for success. These matters are vital and entrepreneurs must reflect and understand them if growth is to be sustainable.

Key point 11.3

The successful growth of hospitality firms depends not only issues of context but also the ability of the founder to become less 'hands on' and to develop a number of management competencies.

Reflective practice

1. Interview an entrepreneur known to you. Investigate what major challenges they faced during the growth of their hospitality firms and how they were dealt with.

A SECRET FORMULA FOR SUCCESSFUL GROWTH?

We have already established that a key trait of entrepreneurs is a strong sense of locus of control. It is therefore unsurprising that many successful ones attribute their success to personal efforts and competencies rather than anything else. A few may acknowledge that luck or chance played a role but many others do not. Research has identified a number of key enablers but not necessarily a winning formula. Good fortune is difficult to rationalise and is downplayed in much the same way as some chief executive officers overstate how their strategy, vision and insightfulness were responsible for record windfall profits, turnover, reduced costs and so on. Similarly, when national rates of interest and inflation are low governments are quick to point out the sage-like nature of their fiscal and monetary policies in bringing about such a state of affairs. In fact, many argue that these issues are more to do with global booms and recessions. The question becomes, was a particular government successful economically because it was riding an international period of good fortune? The answer is probably yes, although economic and societal issues can be exacerbated at a nation state level by government policy.

Ultimately entrepreneurs are human beings (believe it or not!) and invest significant amounts of time and effort into their projects. When asking them the $64,000 'luck' question many would probably answer, 'The harder I work, the luckier I get' and in a sense this is understandable given the sacrifices they have made and the amount of personal ego involved.

Obviously, arguing that all one needs to be a successful entrepreneur in the hospitality industry is good fortune would be something of an oversimplification. Whilst high early business failure rates might suggest that a reliance on chance alone is a factor, one must have the certain skills and abilities in order to capitalize on luck or chance if it is encountered. This is the essential difference between highly successful firms and those which become compromised and a number of researchers consider good fortune to be the differentiating factor (e.g., Reid and Jacobsen, 1988; Nelson and Winter, 1978). Indeed, the often quoted and perhaps mythological 'location, location, location' by Conrad Hilton is a tacit acknowledgement of good fortune. It certainly would be for budding entrepreneurs who happen to reside in a popular tourist destination prior to start-up and who want to convert their existing premises into a Bed and Breakfast or something similar. The same could not be said of entrepreneurs living elsewhere but relocating after identifying opportunities in primary tourist areas. Burns agrees (2001) noting that the distinguishing feature of successful entrepreneurs is recognising an opportunity and acting on it.

So what actually is a growth strategy and of what is it comprised? There is no shortage of available constructs and they are all quite similar. The only real differences between them are the focus and perspectives adopted. However first, Barringer and Ireland (2006) point out that developing a growth strategy will depend on whether the small hospitality firm can realistically take advantage of the following:

■ Economies of scale–where increasing production lowers the average cost of each unit (bed night, restaurant meal, etc.). In the hospitality industry, economies of scale achieved through bulk purchase (in an attempt to minimize variable costs) are insignificant compared to other sectors but other economies may be realized through a sound knowledge of the product. For example, hotels have a limited amount of bedrooms to sell at a particular time. There is also the linked matter of 'perishability' where sales failure results in a missed revenue generating opportunity forever due to its intangibility and dimensionless nature. This defining characteristic is usually dealt with by careful manipulation of room rates and yield management procedures. This is a common tactic used in other service industries (transport, entertainment, etc.) where fixed costs are similarly high.

■ A scalable business model–where increased revenues will cost less to deliver than current revenues. This is clearly the case in the hospitality sector when all variable costs are covered and significant contributions are made to fixed costs and also helps to explain why hotels can offer such vast accommodation price reductions; profits increase as sales escalate. Clearly their is a fixity of supply issue here which limits actual growth unless the entrepreneur decides to acquire another property by various means including outright purchase, lease, amalgamating with another company, joint venture of partnership. However, before taking such a step the entrepreneur must be convinced that demand will increase.

■ Influence and power–closely linked with market leadership through setting industry standards, enhanced access to major customers and suppliers and prestige. It also augments the firm's resilience and ability to recover from bad publicity. For example, neither of the above cases had any lasting negative effect on either company. Additionally, risk management becomes more effective with more expertise on which to draw from an inflated pool of employees and managers. Thus, better risk-management occurs through an ability to attract and retain good workers.

Top 100 Hotel Companies:
Is Bigger Better?
Chart: Top 100 Hotel Companies
By M.A. Baumann H&MM Contributing Editor
Is bigger better? Do bulging portfolios, brand segmentation, globalization and unprecedented growth give some companies a distinct advantage over others? Critics claim that size affects quality and consistency. They believe midtier firms actually can outperform the megacompanies by using a more-focused approach. Super-players say it isn't so, arguing that combined resources, brand identity and sheer magnitude give them stronger hands in shaping the industry's future and creating a healthier bottom line.
Mark Mutkoski, industry analyst for BT Alex.Brown in New York, explained the 'bigger is better' argument.
'There are a lot of advantages to being bigger' he said. 'It's more efficient to have more assets and brands. You also have a greater revenue base over which to spread costs. Particularly in franchising, you have to have critical mass before you can generate invested returns on capital. If you're large, typically you have a greater asset base and have more opportunity to go in and focus efforts internally and focus on return.'
Large companies also have better access to capital, more-liquid stocks, and can borrow unsecured debt at attractive prices, which provides a huge advantage over smaller outfits, Mutkoski said.

Source: http://www.hotel-online.com/News/PressReleases1998_4th/Oct98_BiggerBetter.html, accessed January 2008.

■ Firms may seek growth due to significant increased demand from individual and other key customers. Failure to do so might risk loss of business.

■ Market leadership–where the firm is usually number one or two in a particular niche. Being a market leader has particular advantages not only for securing extra business but also in terms of becoming a preferred employer and likely future business partner with former competitors. However, along with certain benefits come a number of disadvantages including increased public scrutiny through inflated stakeholder expectations of fairness and justice. The case below is some years old, however, the issue raised is perennial.

Adapted from Barringer and Ireland (2006: pp. 311–312).

Reflective practice

Profit **Nike Accused of 'Slave' Child Labor by Andreas Harsono**

(AR) JAKARTA–**An Indonesian** labor advocate said that American shoe maker Nike Inc. is employing Indonesian children under 16 years old to produce their athletic sneakers, confirming an earlier report by an American lobbying group that the children work in sweatshops like 'slaves.'

Indera Nababan of the non-profit Yakoma PGI labor advocacy organization said on Monday that the employees are paid the official minimum wage of 5 200 Indonesian rupiah (US $2.17) per day, which is 'just enough to survive to the following day to work again.'

'How can you live with [$2.17] in an expensive metropolis like Jakarta' asked Nababan, adding that Nike Inc. has more than a dozen subcontractors in Indonesia, one of which, PT Nikomas Gemilang, based about 100 km west of Jakarta in Serang, employs child workers, he said.

'**We are subsidizing, encouraging and failing to criticize the enslavement of young people in the Third World**.'

Source: Albion Monitor *June 30, 1996* (http://www.monitor.net/monitor).

Similarly, McDonald's is open to constant scrutiny for its business practices including employee working conditions, employment policies and ethical use of food products as the case below attests.

Fat flap at McDonald's
May 3, 2001: 4:01 p.m. ET

McDonald's refutes class action suit alleging deceptive use of beef flavouring

'While we are not familiar with the details of the litigation filed in Seattle, we have never made any vegetarian claims about our French fries or any other product', McDonald's said in a statement.

The statement is in response to Seattle attorney Harish Bharti's decision to sue Oak Brook, Ill.-based McDonald's after reading an e-mail from the company to a California man acknowledging its suppliers use tiny amounts of beef flavouring to flavour its fries. Bharti, who filed the suit on behalf of all vegetarians, said the e-mail contradicts previous claims McDonald's has made assuring customers it uses 100 per cent vegetable oil for its fries.

'This is an outrage. This is the height of corporate greed', Bharti told CNNfn.com. 'How can you be so insensitive? This is something that is ingested. You can't take it back'.

In its statement, McDonald's said beef flavouring is added during potato processing at the plant, and is standard in making French fries. McDonald's Corp. said it 'has always used' beef flavouring in its French fries, refuting allegations made in a class action lawsuit brought against it by a vegetarian lawyer.

'The natural flavouring consists of a minuscule amount of beef extract', the company said. 'These fries are then shipped to our restaurants. Our French fries are cooked in vegetable oil at our restaurants'.

Source: http://money.cnn.com/2001/05/03/news/mcdonalds/accessed January 2008.

Presuming that one or more of the above criteria can be realized by the business a decision may then be made to proceed in developing the small hospitality firm.

Storey (1994) divides the key enablers of small firm growth into three overall areas, each having a number of components shown in Table 11.3.

Schaper and Volery (2004) agree but use a different perspective where business growth is viewed from three perspectives of financial, strategic and organizational. The first concerns performance and how well the firm serves its markets through conversion of resources it is allocated into assets. Growth here provides the means for acquisition of further resources which stimulates strategic growth. Financial growth is also aided by sound strategy which contributes to further asset growth within a broader and growing organisational design or structure. These relationships are shown in Figure 11.2.

Not too dissimilarly, Burns (2001: p. 272–273) agrees and considers four important elements for successful growth, these are entrepreneurial character

TABLE 11.3	Key enablers for small firm growth	
Entrepreneur	**Organization**	**Strategy**
Education	Location	Market positioning – niche with focus on quality (in short-term)
Management experience	Size and age – bigger firms are more likely to survive due to accumulated resources although new firms tend to grow faster than old ones	Innovation
Motivation	Niche – some will be more attractive than others	Effective management recruitment as firms become increasing complex to manage by founder
Ability to build teams	Ownership – of other businesses	External equity where possible will contribute to growth
Age as a proxy for accumulated experience and wealth		

Adapted from: Deakins and Freel (2003).

(comprised of key characteristics including risk-taking, desire for achievement, locus of control etc.); business culture (including overall ambition to grow); company strengths (including effective management team, financial control and comprehensive understanding of the market); and making good business decisions including:

- Using quality rather than price;
- Domination of a niche;
- Ongoing innovation; and
- Exploiting company areas of strength to compete.

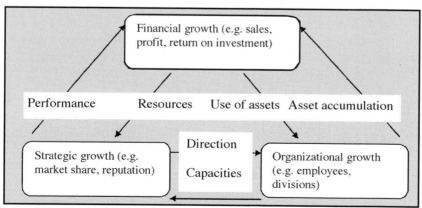

FIGURE 11.2   *Dimensions and interrelatedness of growth dimensions. Adapted from Schaper and Volery (2004: p. 342).*

In order to maximise the potency of each area, Burns (2001) recommends a re-engagement with the original pre start-up SWOT analyses to identify the strengths and weaknesses of current performance; conditions and situations will have undoubtedly changed since start-up. He then advocates developing a market strategy for the service being offered in terms of what would be appropriate generically; the stage in its life cycle; and how it fits with other hospitality services offered.

Key point 11.4

Whilst we can be reasonably confident about the essential ingredients for small hospitality firm growth, the 'recipe' or configuration of these inputs is less clear.

Additionally, Burns (2001) adopts Ansoff's (1968) product/market matrix model to help the conceptual phase of this planning process and is shown in Figure 11.3. This permits a systematic appraisal so risks and opportunities can be identified for each of the four quadrants.

When considering these, the entrepreneur needs to ask a series of questions before making a final decision:

- Existing service/existing market
  - Withdrawal
    - Is industry consolidating?
    - Have you achieved good growth so far?
    - Can you adapt to changing conditions to grow business?
  - Consolidation (same service different operating procedures)
    - Is market growing or declining?
    - Is market mature?
  - Penetration (selling more of same to existing and new customers)
    - Do you understand your customers fully and their buying behaviour?
    - Is market static, declining or growing?
- New service/existing market
  - Service development
    - Any market opportunities?
    - Replacing old service or selling alongside?
    - Small or large differences between old and new services?
    - Can you copy a competitor or will you need to a better service?
    - Growth or mature phase for service?
    - Are your customers loyal and growing?

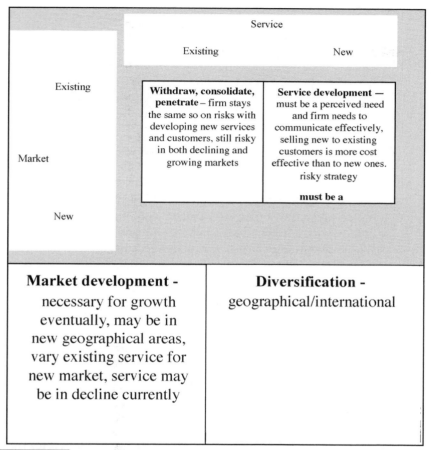

FIGURE 11.3 The service/market matrix.
Adapted from Burns (2001).

- ■ Do you have a strong customer focus?
- ■ Do they 'trust' you?
- ■ Existing service/new market
- o Market development
  - ■ Are economies of scale important to your firm?
  - ■ Is your service nearing decline?
  - ■ Barriers to entry and exit: high or low?
- ■ New service/new market
- o Diversification
  - ■ Both are location based and each has challenges. However, international growth in the micro and small-firm sector of the

hospitality industry is insignificant (with some exceptions) and so will not be discussed here. Small-scale geographical expansion can be seen in many resort regions whereby the successful entrepreneur may own a small hotel along the busy coastal strip and another establishment in the hinterland. Such examples are common and one advantage of this kind of growth is the inherent risk-spreading through cross-subsidization of one organization by the other.

■ Especially important where seasonality impacts on trade. For example, Great Yarmouth in the UK is a typical sea-side 'bucket and spade' resort attracting many low to medium spend tourists from June to September. Only a few miles inland, the Norfolk Broads attracts a somewhat different and more sophisticated market with a higher disposable income and expectations. Whilst this market is also seasonal, a reasonable year-round trade is enjoyed by boat-hire companies, pubs and hotels alike. Recognizing this opportunity, several local entrepreneurs have grown geographically from the seaside location to the hinterland.

■ Clearly, one cannot expect the same style of hospitality enterprise to thrive in both locations but provided market expectations are satisfied in both and the service offered reflects this, this type of growth can be successful.

This is an example of related diversification where the service remains in the same industry but outside its present market and service style or complexity. For example, accommodation and menu choice might be limited for the seaside location but considerably more complicated or 'customized' for the Broadland market having higher expectations. The three types of related diversification are shown in Table 11.4.

TABLE 11.4 Related diversification

Horizontal integration	Activities are complimentary with firm's current ones (see above example)
Forward vertical integration	Firm establishes a presence 'nearer' customer. Hotels may only integrate horizontally or backward vertically as they are directly at the client interface.
Backward vertical integration	Firm becomes own supplier. Hotels may diversify into travel agencies, transport, raw materials, linen supply, etc. The rationale here, amongst other things, is to control quality and reduce competition by establishing a direct chain from customer and supplier to hotel.

In short a key question for the hospitality entrepreneur is how risky are these options? According to Burns (2001) the lowest risk lies in market penetration, followed by service development with diversification (particularly into unrelated industries) as the least risk averse option. However, Ansoff's (1968) model is a simple guide and no more. Nonetheless it does allow a less subjective assessment of entrepreneurial options and pathways for growth. Most small hospitality firms, like others in different sectors, tend to grow internally by increment offering their existing product to the same and new markets or new services to existing customers (Burns, 1994). The following case is an example of both locational good fortune and risk management in terms of potential growth opportunities.

Marketing Wine and Wine Tourism in the 'Fortunate Islands'.

*Source: Alonso, Sherridan and Scherrer (2007).*For many decades the Canary Islands have been a synonym of sunshine, package holidays and mass tourism, and a very popular destination for many travellers that mainly come from the U.K., Germany, Scandinavia and mainland Spain. Because of their mild climate and natural beauty, these islands are dubbed 'fortunate'. Not surprisingly, the number of tourists visiting the Spanish archipelago in recent years has reached the 10 million mark, more than six times the total number of its local residents.

Unknown to many tourists is the fact that the Canary Islands have produced wine for centuries, and some of the varieties are only produced in selected areas of the islands, and nowhere else in the world. However, for a long time the local wine industry went through a phase of decline, and eventually wine became a product for local consumption, with little or no impact outside the archipelago. This situation progressively changed in the early 1990s as regional local wine denominations of origin were created, in part as a European Union (EU) initiative to preserve traditional foods, local culture and local landscapes (Sainz, 2002).

Today, the Canary Islands not only continue to produce many unique varieties of wines, but the quality of the local wines has also increased, earning them international recognition. The vast majority of the islands' wineries are small and medium in size and family owned, and many are open to the public, for the most part offering tasting rooms, and cellar door sales. However, the recent re-development of the Canary wine industry also includes a blend of hospitality and wine with the opening of some restaurants, space for conferences on some winery grounds, and promotion of wine trails to visitors (Tacoronte-Acentejo, 2006).

With sunshine, beaches, and landscape being among tourists' top reasons to visit the islands, other potential attractions, including the local wine industry, have been relegated to a secondary role. In fact, while currently efforts to promote and market the islands' wine regions are being undertaken, still very little is known about the local wine, wine tourism and wineries.

To investigate this relatively unknown industry, a study was conducted among wineries from the islands of Tenerife and La Palma. A total of 61 businesses were approached in both islands and their owners/managers invited for an interview; 23 wineries accepted the invitation to participate in the study, a 37.6 per cent response rate.

The winery owners and managers felt that there was considerable potential for wine tourism in the Canary Islands but this was often undermined by factors outside of their control. Stricter drink-drive laws, for example, had reduced visits to wineries and less participation in wine tasting, a crucial tool in the cellar door sales process. International terrorism sparked new aviation laws limiting the quantity of liquids permitted in in-cabin luggage. This reduced cellar door sales as tourists could not carry wine on board, as it exceeded the volume limits, and they did not feel comfortable with placing wine in their checked luggage in case it spilled or spoiled. Some winery owners even felt that the traditional tourism industry was sabotaging their local wine tourism efforts by importing cheap local wines rather than serving local Canary Island wines at hotels and restaurants. Package deal tourism to the Canary Islands encouraged tourism enclaves rather than the exploration of the Canary Islands which could foster a rich culture of local wine production.

At the end of the day, winery owners wanted to build stronger associations with tourism but only in scenarios where there would be a genuine, quality, wine tourism experience. Their goal was to build relationships with the tourists and convert them into customers but also achieve important long term goals such as building brand recognition and positive world of mouth experiences of wine in the Canary Islands.

Questions

1 Using Ansoff's product/service/market matrix identify the strategy chosen by winery owners for future development of their industry and comment on the riskiness of this option?
2 Identify strategies that could help local wineries link their product to the tourism market?
3 Discuss potential difficulties wineries may face in the process of marketing their wines to tourists.

Key point 11.5

Accepted wisdom concludes that an effective strategy for small business growth is to focus on quality rather than price; dominate a particular niche; innovate continually; exploit company areas of strength.

Reflective practice

1. Interview a successful entrepreneur known to you. Find out what role opportunity and good fortune played in the development of their hospitality firm.
2. What other issues do they think are responsible for their success.
3. Were there any skills and competencies they had to acquire in order to become successful business founders?

INTRINSIC AND EXTRINSIC GROWTH

Barringer and Ireland (2006) take a slightly different perspective of small firm development using the lens of intrinsic or internal and extrinsic or external growth. This focuses on matters intrinsic to firms such as whether to introduce, improve or enhance existing products. This internal growth may also be achieved by reconfiguring marketing strategies and expansion into other geographical areas including the international arena. In other words, development is a function of in-house skills and competencies; Mcdonald's is an example of a firm that has expanded internally. The other means of growth is through extrinsic or external means. Simply, this means using third parties in the form of mergers, alliances, joint ventures and so on. The use of a third party is not limited to physical 'bricks and mortar'. Recent evidence suggests that from almost 20,000 small UK businesses a key mode of external expansion in the Hotels & Restaurants' sector is through e-commerce, notably through own web sites and those of third parties (Carter and Mason, 2006). Another important mode of external expansion for hotels remains the 'franchise' and Ibis, Comfort Inn, Mercure and Courtyard are examples of this approach. Additionally, many smaller hotels use the affiliated network model typified by Best Western.

Both types of growth have associated advantages and disadvantages. The main advantages of growing internally are based on incremental advances. A measured uniform growth strategy helps to ensure development is managed effectively requiring few significant changes. Additionally, the firm can exercise more control over quality standards and maintain its organisational culture. Moreover, a strategy of internal growth is more likely to foster innovation and intrapreneurship as long as appropriate rewards are bestowed on employees such as bonuses and accelerated promotion. Conversely, internal growth may be too slow-paced to achieve significant economies, market penetration and competitive advantage in particular geographical areas. This is typical in the hospitality industry where acquisitions and mergers are commonplace. Innovative service package ideas will almost certainly require input from organizations elsewhere in the service chain. Such new ideas would be difficult to offer by only one firm. Additionally, a basic issue is that of capacity and the effect of over supply. Too many new organizations providing the same product in a particular tourist location, be it accommodation or food and beverage provision, will ultimately force prices down and thus reduce overall profitability.

External growth may also be an option for expansion as acquisition of other firms effectively reduces competition, allows access to older establish brands and may lead to increased economies of scale. Additionally, expansion permits sharing of expertise and helps to diversify risk. On the other hand, external growth has some challenges which are similar to those experienced by firms growing internally although more extreme in nature. Essentially these fall into categories of organizational culture and operating procedure differences. For example, styles of service delivery and quality management philosophy and practice may differ between firms. These may be exacerbated if a firm chooses to expand internationally. Indeed, legal differences in employment law and antitrust regulations may prove significant for example.

However a small hospitality firm chooses to grow it is necessary to consider whether to develop new products (if entrepreneurs can identify a need to satisfy), to provide products that add value, to strike an appropriate balance between quality and price, to identify and exploit a niche, and to make sure the feasibility analysis is iterative. Firms will also increase their chances of sustainable growth (to a point) if they consider issues of service improvement, extension and differentiation. For example, the notorious Club 18–30 club was an ingenious marketing ruse by the Horizon Travel to fill unused seats on night flights to tourist destinations in continental Europe. Whilst the brand has been bought and sold by a number of companies the concept is still popular despite (or perhaps because of) some negative publicity about the antics of customers and the occasional risqué slogan such as 'One Swallow Doesn't Make a Summer'!

Club 18–30's controversial past

By Clare Matheson

BBC News Online business reporter

The antics of Club 18–30 reps in Greece have earned the company another bout of negative publicity. BBC News Online goes behind the headlines to look at a company that has dominated the youth holiday market for years.

Despite being for 18–30 year olds the brand is now 38 years old

Club 18–30 began life in 1965 when it took 580 yuppies to the Costa Brava, an event that the tour operator claims 'made history'. But Club 18–30 really came into its own in the 1970s and 1980s under the wing of ILG group, entering into common parlance as the generic name for youth holidays.

All change

Even though ILG later collapsed in 1991, Club 18–30 survived, and was rescued by a management buy-out and re-launched as 'The Club.'

In 1994 it reverted to its old name, but by 1999 it was all change again after Thomas Cook Group bought the brand. The group says it now owns 65 per cent of the youth holiday market and takes more than 110,000 guests away each year–most expecting a break filled with sun, sea, sex and sangria. And the formula seems to work. In the financial year of 2001–2002, Club 18–30 racked up sales worth £48 million, and 'still managed to achieve a good profit' despite only partly achieving its targets.

Sun, sea and sex

Club 18–30 prides itself on the belief: 'Nothing is sacred, if it's going to be a good laugh then we're in'.

That marketing has pulled in millions of holidaymakers, keen to align themselves with the party-loving attitude it promotes.

But that 'in your face' label has attracted plenty of controversy.

In 1995, its tongue-in-cheek adverts earned it a place in the Advertising Standards Authority's Hall of Shame–it was the second most complained about firm that year.

'Irresponsible'

The Saatchi & Saatchi ads generated 490 complaints centred on posters featuring the taglines 'Beaver Espana' and 'It's not all sex, sex, sex. There's a bit of sun and sea as well.' Even today, Club 18–30 cannot steer clear of controversy. Three of its reps have just been acquitted of organising bar crawls in Faliriki, despite a ban brought in last week after a man killed a tourist. And last month, five of the firm's reps quit after allegedly taking part in 'live sex acts' on a beach in the Greek resort of Kavos.

Future controversy

But will the latest upsets affect the firm? Spokesman David Smithson said that 'from past experience' the current controversy was unlikely to affect business.

'It's a product that's aimed at a very specific target audience who are not discouraged by publicity', he added A case in point, he described the raunchy 1990s advertising campaign as 'successful' and achieving 'its objective.'

'It's a younger audience that tends to recognise these incidents are blown out of proportion by the media', Mr Smithson added. 'But that's not to say we like or seek negative publicity'.

Questions

1 Discuss whether Club 18–30 is an example of internal, external or a combination of both kinds of growth.
2 Identify the extent to which Club 18–30 is an example of service improvement, extension or differentiation.

*Source:*http://news.bbc.co.uk/1/hi/business/3163077.stm, accessed January 2007.

BARRIERS TO GROWTH

It is one thing to advance notions of growth enabling factors and another to identify those which act as barriers to growth. Data aggregated by the Cranfield School of Management holds six primary culprits:

- A lack of planning–over two-thirds of owner-managed firms studied with a turnover of £10 million did not have any;
- A lack of market focus–many small firms diversify too early and lack market focus;
- A lack of effective leadership during times of change–most founders run their growing businesses as they did in start-up;
- Inappropriate objectives–sales growth is the sole and primary target, set without regard to others including gross margin, profit and cash generation;
- Failure to work 'smartly' and inability to delegate – too many owner-managers spend time interfering and overseeing work which others are employed to undertake. The most key activity for the owner-manager is focusing on future business strategy for the business; and
- Lacking a financial strategy and poor accountability–a majority of entrepreneurial firms in the UK use overdrafts as a long-term means of finance. This is due to ignorance of alternative sources, the ease with which overdrafts may be obtained and a result of having no business plans.

Adapted from CUSM (2007).

Key point 11.6

Barriers to enter the hospitality industry are relatively low. Despite this, the rate of business failure is high. However, it is possible to mitigate the effect of each above barrier by careful research and planning. Therefore, the success or failure of the small hospitality firm depends on the extent to which the founder works 'smarter' rather than harder.

An earlier 1997 study by the ESRC Centre for Business Research found that increased competition, availability and cost of finance for expansion and marketing and sales skills were the most important barriers to small firm growth (Burns, 2001).

Based on the earlier work of Penrose (1959), Barringer and Ireland (2006) note that in addition to entrepreneurship, 'managerial capacity' is essential to administer opportunities as they are spotted. They consider this to be high on the list of those factors which challenge the growth of firms and use the terms 'Adverse selection...' (p. 315) and 'Moral hazard...' (p. 315) to explain the dilemma. Essentially, the former describes a situation where increased demand for labour creates a situation where the firm may not be able to achieve good 'job fit'. Moral hazard is similarly unfortunate situation where new workers fail to share the aims and objectives of the founder. In short, there is no consistent organizational culture. The entrepreneur may hire managers to ensure this does not happen but this often results in a hierarchical structure with a pool of isolated and sometimes estranged managers. Clearly, growth becomes a challenge in itself and managers must be selected carefully with the knowledge that they will need to be trained, socialized and motivated in order to minimise problems as the firm grows.

Reflective practice

1. Interview a successful hospitality entrepreneur known to you. Ask if there were any significant obstacles to overcome prior to start-up. If so, how were they overcome?

SUMMARY

The term 'growth' is often only applied to the truly entrepreneurial firm as opposed to the 'lifestyle' organisation. This chapter contends that the process of growth needs to be understood in a more holistic way and as such is a pertinent topic for discussion irrespective of firm type. For example, all firms grow in one way or another as they are concerned with survival and/or consolidation and continued success and/or expansion. Moreover, they both make significant societal and economic contributions.

A firm's development may be conceptualised in a number of ways, this chapter discussed the 'growth' model approach as, for the sake of simplicity, divides progress into five stages. Each of these stages is characterized by a particular set of activities and leadership/management styles. For the sake of efficiency and effectiveness, with growth comes a need to make management and operational changes to cope with the new working environment. Some firms choose deliberate growth and will continue through all stages explicit in growth models but most hospitality firms rarely progress beyond the second or third stages. These constructs are useful for 'journey' mapping and insight but they do not address the inherent challenges of the growing firm in any detail.

Along with entrepreneurial success through growth comes the requirement for skill development and new competencies. This includes an acute need for delegation as once firms reach a certain size it becomes impossible for the founder to do everything. This problem is sometimes known as 'founders disease' where the entrepreneur 'meddles' in the work of her employees.

Ultimately this can cause a number of problems if left unchecked including high labour turnover, role conflict and poor morale.

It is difficult to be prescriptive about enablers of successful growth but number of approaches are relevant here. They are similar in nature and content but often frame essential inputs differently for example Deakins and Freel (2003) divide them into three generic areas of entrepreneur, organization and strategy, Shaper and Volery (2004) focus on dimensions of finance, strategy and organization and their interrelationships. Burns (2001) prefers to use a frame which assess growth options in terms of the market and how risky they might be. However, before adopting any of them, the entrepreneur must answer an number of key questions, for example would growth allow the firm to take advantage of economies of scale. The hospitality industry differs from other industries including retail and manufacturing as the product is intangible and economies from suppliers of raw materials are not significant relatively speaking nor are they significantly different between competitors irrespective of firm size (within reason). Once this and other questions have been answered to the satisfaction of the founder, a decision may be made to grow and develop the hospitality firm.

Accepted wisdom concludes that an effective strategy for small business growth is to focus on quality rather than price; dominate a particular niche; innovate continually; exploit company areas of strength. The strategic framework to achieve this differs between commentators but all agree that the basic elements must include:

- An entrepreneur of appropriate character having traits including risk-taking, locus of control, desire for achievement, etc;
- A positive business culture including and overall ambition to grow;
- A company possessing certain strengths including an effective management team, good financial control and a comprehensive understanding of its market; and
- An ability to make good business decisions.

However, there are a number of barriers to growth of which founders must be aware including a lack of planning, market focus and effective leadership. Others include having inappropriate objectives, impoverished knowledge of sources of finance and an inability to delegate. Clearly, these obstacles are not inherent or systemic in the hospitality industry. Indeed, the sector has low barriers to entry which in some ways may prove disadvantageous to some operators due to the sheer volume of competition. However, these challenges can be overcome by the entrepreneur so long as they are prepared to focus more attention on strategic matters rather than continuing to operate technically.

In short, the fate of small businesses is less to do with working harder but rather, working smarter.

CASE

Riu Hotels: From a Small Family Business to an International Company

September 25, 2001–Riu Hotels: from a small family business to an international company came into being in 1953 with a small hotel in Majorca, and now has 96 establishments with 12,000 employees and is present in 10 countries.

A total of 96 holiday hotels with categories ranging from three to five stars in Spain, Portugal, the Caribbean, the United States, North Africa and the eastern Mediterranean, offering globally 25,960 rooms and just over 50,000 beds, with 1.5 million customers and 12,000 employees, united by one motto: give the guest service with heart. These figures sum up the RIU Group's (www.riu.com) current situation. This small family business was created in 1953 in Playa de Palma (Majorca), with the purchase of the small 80-bed hotel San Francisco, and has now become the 31st biggest hotel chain in the world, specialising in sun and beach holidays, with guests mainly of central European origin but also an incipient American clientele (from the United States, Canada and Argentina) as well as Spanish guests.

The chain had a turnover of 105,000 million Pesetas (567 million dollars) in the year 2000 and foresees 120,000 million (14.3 per cent more) for the year 2001. This data consolidates RIU as the second largest chain in Spain in terms of turnover.

RIU's establishments are located in the Balearic Islands (16), the Canary Islands (36), Portugal (2), Baleares España Andalusia (7), Gerona (1), the Dominican Republic (7) Cuba (2), Florida (2), Mexico (4), Jamaica (1), Tunisia (11), Bulgaria (5), Cyprus (1) and Madeira (1).

RIU Hotels head office has been in the Riu Centre, in Playa de Palma, since 1982. One hundred fifty metres from the Riu Centre, on the beach front, is the Riu San Francisco, the chain's very first establishment, where the family business was started up in 1953 by Mr. Juan Riu and his son, Mr. Luis Riu Bertrán, both natives of the La Garrocha region of Gerona in Catalonia.

Luis Riu Bertrán was chief executive of the chain until his death, at the age of 65, on 7th April 1998. Since then the company has been directed by the second generation, in the form of Mr. Riu Beltrán's two children: Carmen Riu Güell (a specialist in administration and finance) and Luis Riu Güell (in charge of expansion). Both born in Palma, they share the post of chief executive.

All the hotels in the chain are managed by Riusa-II, a company created in 1993 for the running of hotels, 50 per cent of which belongs to the Riu family, with the other 50 per cent being held by the German tour operator TUI, RIU's traditional partner and number one tour operator in Europe.

Riusa-II and some shareholder-type companies together make up the RIU Hotels & Resorts Group.

For its part, TUI (www.tui.com), a member of the HTU (Hapag Turistik Union) tourism consortium, renamed the TUI Group on January 1st 200, constitutes the tourism division of the industrial group PREUSSAG (www.preussag.de), the 21st biggest company in Germany in 1999. PREUSSAG purchased TUI in 1998 as part of its strategy to transfer investments to the tourism sector.

As from August 23rd 2001 the tourism consortium adopted the new name of 'World of TUI.' (www.the-world-of-tui.com)

Since its creation RIU Hotels has never shared out profits. They are reinvested in full in the creation of new hotels, the renovation of those already in existence or the purchase of other establishments. Like the 11 Iberotel hotels acquired in 1993 and the nine hotels bought from the British Belhaven chain. In this way the company has basically self-financed its growth and its current level of debt is low.

After the creation of the family business in the 1950s, the company grew in the '60s due to the opening up of Spain to Europe and the consequent in rush of European holiday tourists to Spanish beaches. After increasing its number of hotels in Majorca and consolidating itself as a company, in the '80s RIU expanded its activity in the Canary Islands, an archipelago which, added to the attraction of its beaches, is also a non-seasonal destination due to its mild climate, allowing hotels to remain open all year round.

Due to the importance of the turnover contributed to the chain by the Canaries (approximately half), RIU established part of its head offices in Playa del Inglés in Gran Canaria, amongst them the Human Resources Department and the Staff Training Centre, devoted to the retraining of the chain's professionals. After its solid expansion in the Canary Islands (where it is now the leader in the supply of accommodation), Riu Hotels began its internationalisation in the '90s, with the inauguration of the hotel Riu Taíno in Punta Cana (Dominican Republic). From this island, the beaches of which are amongst the most beautiful in the world, the chain has expanded to Cuba, Florida, Mexico, Jamaica and the Portuguese island of Madeira.

In November of 1997 RIU acquired the emblematic hotel Maspalomas Oasis in Gran Canaria, one of the best holiday establishments in Europe, and since then the chain's flagship in Spain.

At the beginning of 1998 the chain opened a Contracting and Sales Office in Madrid with the aim of opening up to the Spanish outward bound market, and struck up agreements with Spain's most important wholesalers. In mid-1999 RIU took over the management of 12 hotels in the Iberotel chain in Tunisia (8), Morocco (One hotel, later dissociated from the chain), Bulgaria (2) and Cyprus (1). Thus, the chain began its expansion in North Africa and the Eastern Mediterranean.

In the case of Morocco and Bulgaria this was RIU's debut of the franchise formula, with which the chain hopes to incorporate more new hotels over the coming years, preferably in Andalusia, the Algarve (Portugal) and the Canary Islands.

In October of 1999, 31 RIU hotels ranked amongst the 100 best hotels in the world in the holiday sector, according to the votes of TUI customers, for which the TUI-Holly prizes are awarded. And furthermore four RIU hotels were amongst the top 10, with the Riu Palace Maspalomas in first place for the second time in just 10 years of its existence. On 15th November 1999 the Riu Palace Mexico, a luxury five-star hotel, was opened. This establishment is buried deep in the Mayan Riviera and is the chain's new flagship outside of Spain.

High quality of service and personalised treatment of guests constitute the cornerstone of RIU's philosophy, a philosophy which has allowed a modest family business with 80 beds to be turned into an international hotel chain with over 50,000 in four decades. A chain which is still expanding, exclusively in sun and beach holiday destinations, without abandoning the values on which its success is founded, and which foresees an increase in its accommodation capacity in the first years of the 21st century with new hotels in the Canary Islands, Andalusia, Tunisia, Bulgaria, the Caribbean, the United States and Africa.

Questions

1. Map the development of Riu Hotels using the growth theories in this chapter. Discuss the strategy followed, the challenges faced and how they were managed as the firm grew?

Source: http://www.hotel-online.com/News/PR2001_3rd/Sept01_RIU.html, accessed January 2008.

Case authors

Dr Abel D Alonso
Edith Cowan University
School of Marketing, Tourism and Leisure
Australia

Dr Michael J. Gross
School of Management
University of South Australia
Australia

Dr Lynnaire Sheridan
Edith Cowan University
School of Marketing, Tourism and Leisure
Australia

Dr Pascal Scherrer
Edith Cowan University
School of Marketing, Tourism and Leisure
Australia

Peter Wiltshier
School of Culture and Lifestyle
University of Derby
UK

References

1. ABS. (2004) Australian Bureau of Statistics, 8127.0 Characteristics of Small Business, Australia (Reissue), http://www.abs.gov.au/Ausstats/abs@.nsf/lookupMF/E49E3B4DC3595C92CA2568A900139377, 2007.
2. Acs, Z., Arenius, P., Hay, M., and Minniti, M. (2005) *2004 Global Entrepreneurship Monitor*. London Business School and Babson College, Babson Park, MA/London, UK.
3. Allen, K. R. (1999) *Launching New Ventures and Entrepreneurial Approach*, 2nd ed., Houghton Mifflin Company, New York.
4. Amabile, T., Conti, R., and Coon, H. (1996) Assessing the work environment for creativity. *Academy of Management Journal* **39**(5): 1154–1184.
5. Anderson, R. B. (1999) *Economic Development Among the Aboriginal Peoples of Canada: Hope for the Future*. Captus University Press, Toronto.
6. Anderson, R. (2002) Entrepreneurship and aboriginal Canadians: a case study in economic development. *Journal of Developmental Entrepreneurship* **7**(1): 45–66.
7. Anderson, R. B., and Gilbertson, R. (2004) Aboriginal entrepreneurship and economic development in Canada: thoughts on current theory and practice. In: Stiles, C., and Galbraith, C. (Eds.), *Ethnic Entrepreneurship: Structure and Process*. Elsevier Science, Amsterdam, pp. 141–170.
8. Andrews et al., (2000).
9. Anon. (2007) Retrieved March 2007 from http://www.mercasa.es/es/publicaciones/Dyc/sum64/pdf/alimentos.pdf.
10. 0/4c2567ef00247c6a4c2567fc0010f4b8/$FILE/alltabls.xls.
11. http://dictionary.reference.com/browse/grow.
12. http://www.albionmonitor.com/9606a/nikelabor.html.
13. pasfull/pasfull.nsf/0/4c2567ef00247c6acc2570bd000fb351/$FILE/alltabls.xls.
14. Anon. (1999) Schumpeterian competition, *Bell Journal of Economics* **9**: 524–548.
15. Ashforth, B. E. (2000) All in a day's work. *Academy of Management Review* **25**(3): 472–491.
16. Audretsch, D. (1995) Innovation, growth and survival. *International Journal of Industrial Organization* **13**: 441–457.
17. Augustyn, M. (2004) Coping with resource scarcity: the experience of UK tourism SMEs, In: Thomas, R. (Ed.), *Small Firms in Tourism: International Perspectives*, pp. 257–275.
18. Babl, R. (1994) All in the family, *Business News*, Winter, pp. 9–11.
19. Barringer, B. R., and Ireland, R. D. (2006) *Entrepreneurship: Successfully Launching New Ventures*. Pearson Prentice Hall, Upper Saddle River, New Jersey.
20. Barrow, C., Barrow, P., and Brown, B. (1998) *The Business Plan Workbook*. Kogan Page, London.
21. Bass, B., and Stogdill, R. M. (1990) *Handbook of Leadership: Theory, Research and Managerial Applications*, 3rd ed., The Free Press, NY.

22. Basu, A., and Goswami, A. (1999) South Asian entrepreneurship in Great Britain: factors influencing growth. *International Journal of Entrepreneurial Behaviour & Research* **5**(5): 251–275.

23. Beaver, G., and Lashley, C. (1998) Barriers to management development in small hospitality firms. *Strategic Change* **4**: 4.

24. Beaver, G., Lashley, C., and Stewart, J. (1998) Management Development. In: Thomas, R. editor. *The Management of Small Tourism and Hospitality Firms.* Cassell, London.

25. Belbin, R. M. (1981) *Management Teams: Why they Succeed and Fail.* Heinemann Professional Publishing, London.

26. Berglund, K., Dahlin, M., and Johansson, A. W. (2007) Walking a tightrope between artistry and entrepreneurship: the stories of the Hotel Woodpecker, Otter Inn and Luna Resort. *Journal of Enterprising Communities: People and Places in the Global Economy* **1**(3): 268–284.

27. Bhide, A. V. (2000) *The Origin and Evolution of New Businesses.* Oxford University Press.

28. Blake, R., and Mouton, J. (1978) *The New Management Grid.* Gulf, London.

29. Bolton, J. E. (1971) *Report of the Committee of Inquiry on Small Firms*, Cmnd. 4811, London, HMSO.

30. Bolton, B., and Thompson, J. (2000) *Entrepreneurs: Talent, Temperament, Technique.* Butterworth Heinemann, Oxford.

31. Burns, P. (1994) *Winners and Losers in the 1990s,* 3i European Enterprise Centre, Report No. 12, April.

32. Burns, P. (1996) Growth. In: Burns, P., and Dewhurst, J. (Eds.), *Small Business and Entrepreneurship.* Macmillan, London.

33. Burns, P. (2001) *Entrepreneurship and Small Business.* Palgrave, Basingstoke.

34. Canada Business Network. (2007) Retrieved November 2007, http://www.infoentrepreneurs.org/servlet/ContentServer?pagename=CBSC_QC%2Fdisplay&lang=en&cid=1081945275631&c=GuideFactSheet.

35. Carree, M., van Stel, A., Thurik, R., and Wennekers, S. (2002) Economic development and business ownership: an analysis using data of 23 OECD countries in the period 1976–1996. *Small Business Economics* **19**(3): 271–290.

36. Carter, S., and Mason, C. (2006) *Lifting the Barriers to Growth in UK Small Businesses: The FSB Biennial Membership Survey 2006, Report to the Federation of Small Businesses*, FSB, UK.

37. Chandrasekhar, S. (2001) Shakespeare, Newton, and Beethoven, or Patterns of Creativity, South Asian Women's Forum, February, http://www.sawf.org/Newedit/edit02192001/musicarts.asp, Retrieved, May 2008.

38. Chapman, P. (1998) *Pat Chapman's Balti Bible.* Hodder and Stoughton, London.

39. Chin, K. H. (1988) Chinese in Modern Australia. In: Jupp, J. editor. *The Australian People: An Encyclopaedia of the Nation, Its People and Their Origins.* Angus & Robertson, Sydney, pp. 317–323.

40. Churchill, N., and Hatten, K. (1987) Non-market transfers of wealth and power: a research framework for family business. *American Journal of Small Business* Winter.

41. Churchill, N. C., and Lewis, V. L. (1983) The five stages of business growth. *Harvard Business Review*, May–June.

42. Clegg, B., and Birch, P. (2008) *Instant Creativity,* Publisher unknown.

43. Clegg, S., Kornberger, M., and Pitsis, T. (2008) *Managing and Organizations*. Singapore, Sage.
44. Collins, J. (1991) *Immigrant Hands in a Distant Land: Australia's Post-war Immigration*, 2nd ed., Pluto Press, Sydney and London.
45. Collins. (1993) *Softback English Dictionary*. Harper Collins, Glasgow.
46. Collins. (2002) Chinese entrepreneurs: the Chines diaspora in Australia. *International Journal of Entrepreneurship Behaviour and Research* **8**(1–2)**:** 112–133.
47. Collins, J. (2007) *Cosmopolitan Capitalists: Immigrant Entrepreneurs in Australia*, submitted for publication.
48. Collins, J., and Castillo, A. (1998) *Cosmopolitan Sydney: Exploring the World in One City*. Pluto Press, Sydney.
49. Collins, J. C., and William, C. I. (1995) *Managing the Small to Mid-Sized Company – Concepts and Costs*. Irwin, Chicago.
50. Collins, J., Gibson, K., Alcorso, C., Tait, D., and Castles, S. (1995) *A Shop Full of Dreams: Ethnic Small Businesses in Australia*. Pluto Press, Sydney and London.
51. Collins, J., Sim, C.-L., Dhungel, B., Zabbal, N., and Nole, G. (1997) *Training for Ethnic Small Business*. University of Technology Sydney (UTS), Sydney.
52. Commonwealth of Australia(1992) *Aboriginal Deaths in Custody: Overview of the Response by Governments to the Royal Commission*. Australian Government Publishing Service, Canberra ACT.
53. Contribution to the U.S. Economy – a framework for assessing family business statistics, *Family Business Review,***9**: 2, pp. 107–119.
54. Coulter, M. (2001) *Entrepreneurship in Action*. Prentice Hall, Upper Saddle River, NJ.
55. Cromie, S. (2000) Assessing entrepreneurial implications: Some personal characteristics. *Journal of Organizational Behaviour* **4**: 317–324.
56. Crosland, K. (2007) We're here to help you drive out drugs. *Caterer & Hotelkeeper*, June 21.
57. CUSM. (2007) 6 Classic Barriers to Growth and How to Overcome Them, Cranfield Management Development Limited, www.cranfield.ac.uk/somwww. som.cranfield.ac.uk/som/groups/enterprise/credo/downloads/Barriers.pdf, accessed January 2008.
58. Daft, R. (2005) *The Leadership Experience*, 3rd ed., Thomson South-Western, Canada.
59. Dalglish, C., and Evans, P. (2000) *Entrepreneurship vs Leadership*, ICSB Conference, June 2000, Brisbane.
60. Davila, T., Epstein, M. J., and Shelton, R. (2006) *Making Innovation Work: How to Manage It, Measure It, and Profit from It*. Wharton School Publishing, Upper Saddle River.
61. De Bono, E. (1971) *Lateral Thinking for Management: A Handbook*. McGraw-Hill, London.
62. De Bono, E. (1994) *Parallel Thinking – From Socratic to de Bono*. Penguin, London.
63. Deakins, D. (1996) *Entrepreneurship and Small Firms*. McGraw-Hill, London.
64. Deakins, D., and Freel, M. (2006) *Entrepreneurship and Small Firms*, 4th ed., McGraw-Hill, London.
65. Deal, T. E., and Kennedy, A. (1982) *Corporate Cultures*. Addison–Wesley, Reading Massachusetts.

66. Derrida, J. (2002) *Acts of Religion*. Routledge, New York.
67. Donaldson, A. (2004) How I got started. *Caterer and Hotelkeeper*, September 2, p. 105.
68. Drucker, P. (1985) *Innovation and Entrepreneurship*. Heinemann, London.
69. DTI. (2006) *News Release National Statistics*. Department of Trade and Industry, UK Government.
70. Du Toit, D. E. (1980) Confessions of a successful entrepreneur, *Harvard Business Review*, November/December.
71. Dubrin, A. J., and Dalglish, C. (2003) *Leadership: An Australian Focus*. John Wiley and Sons, Sydney.
72. Economist intelligence Unit(2005) Continuing concerns over European R&D: ongoing decline in R&D investment could seriously affect Europe's manufacturing future. *Strategic Direction* **21**(4): 33–35.
73. Edgar, D. A., and Nisbet, L. (1996) Strategy in small business – a case of sheer chaos!, proceedings of the IAHMS Spring Symposium, *Issues Relating to Small Businesses in the Hospitality and Tourism Industries*, Leeds Metropolitan University, pp. 197–205.
74. *Equivalent Persons Engaged. By ANZSIC, February 1999*. Retrieved May 20, 2006 from http://www2.stats.govt.nz/domino/external/pasfull/pasfull.nsf/.
75. Fiedler, F. E. (1954) Assumed similarity measures as predictors of effectiveness. *Journal of Abnormal and Social Psychology* **49**: 381–388.
76. Foley, D. (2003) An examination of Indigenous Australian Entrepreneurs. *Journal of Developmental Entrepreneurship* **8**: 133–152.
77. Fontela, E., Guzman, J., Perez, M., and Santos, F. J. (2006) The art of entrepreneurial foresight. *Foresight* **8**(6): 3–13.
78. Frederick, H. H., Kuratko, D. F., and Hodgetts, R. M. (2007) *Entrepreneurship, Theory, Process, Practice*. Thomson, Victoria, Australia.
79. French, R. P., and Raven, B. (1960) The bases of social power. In: Cartwright, D., and Zander, A.F. (Eds.), *Group Dynamics*. Row Peterson, Evanston Illinois.
80. Fuller, D., Dansie, P., Jones, M., and Holmes, S. (1999) Indigenous Australians and Self-Employment. *Small Enterprise Research: The Journal of SEAANZ* **7**(2): 5–28.
81. Galbraith, C., and Stiles, C. (2003) Expectations of Indian reservation gaming: entrepreneurial activity within a context of traditional land tenure and wealth acquisition. *Journal of Developmental Entrepreneurship* **8**(2): 93–112.
82. Getz, D., Carlsen, J., and Morrison, A. (2004) *Family Businesses in Hospitality and Tourism*. CABI Publishing, Wallsingham.
83. Gleick, J. (1987) *Chaos - Making a New Science*. Penguin Books Ltd, Harmondsworth, Middlesex.
84. Global Entrepreneurship Monitor. (2005) Executive Report, Babson College, Babson Park, MA, US, London Business School, London, UK.
85. Goodman, C. (1997) Sparking Your Imagination. *Entrepreneur*, September, p. 32.
86. Greiner, L. E. (1972) Evolution and revolution as organizations grow. *Harvard Business Review*, July/August.
87. Haber, S. (2005) Small business entrepreneurship. In: Pizam, A. (Chief editor), *International Encyclopedia of Hospitality Management*. Elsevier, Sydney, p. 582.
88. Handy, C. (1990) *The Age of Unreason*. Random Century, London.

89. Harris, J., Saltstone, R., and Fraboni, M. (1999) An evaluation of the job stress questionnaire with a sample of entrepreneurs. *Journal of Business and Psychology* **13**(3): 447–455.

90. Heal, F. (1990) *Hospitality in Early Modern England*. Oxford University Press, Oxford.

91. Herrmann, N. (1996) *The Whole Brain Business Book*. McGraw-Hill, NY.

92. Hersey, P., and Blanchard, K. H. (1982) *Management of Organizational Behaviour: Utilizing Human Resources*, 4th ed., Prentice Hall, Englewood Cliffs, NJ.

93. Hindle, K., and Lansdowne, M. (2005) Brave spirits on new paths: toward a globally relevant paradigm of indigenous entrepreneurship research. *Journal of Small Business and Entrepreneurship* **18**(2 (Spring)): 131–141.

94. Hofstede, G. (1980) *Culture's Consequences*. Sage, Beverly Hills, CA.

95. Hofstede, G. (1994) *Culture and Organizations: Software of the Mind: Intercultural*. Harper Collins, London.

96. Hofstede, G. (2001) *Cultural Consequences: Comparing Values, Behaviors, Institutions and Organizations Across Nations*, 2nd ed., Sage Publications, London.

97. Holt, D. H. (1992) *Entrepreneurship: New Venture Creation*. Prentice Hall, Englewood Cliffs, New Jersey.

98. Holt, D., and Keats, D. (1992) Work cognition's in multicultural interaction. *Journal of Cross-Cultural Psychology* **23**(1): 151–159.

99. House, R. J. (1971) A path-goal theory of leadership effectiveness. *Administrative Science Quarterly* **16**: 321–338.

100. Hultman, K. E. (1998) The ten commandments of team leadership. *Training and Development* **52**(2): 12.

101. Inkeles, A., and Smith, D. H. (1974) *Becoming Modern: Individual Change in Six Developing Countries*. Harvard University Press, Cambridge, Mass.

102. Ireland, R. D., and Hitt, M. A. (1999) Achieving and maintaining strategic competitiveness in the 21st century: the role of strategic leadership. *Academy of Management Executive* **13**(1): 43–57.

103. Ireland, R. D., Hitt, M. A., and Hoskisson, R. E. (2001) *Strategic Management: Competitiveness and Globalisation*, 4th ed., South-Western Thomson Learning, Ohio.

104. Jones, P. (2004) Finding the hospitality industry? Or finding hospitality schools of thought? *Journal of Hospitality, Leisure, Sport and Tourism Education* **3**(1): 33–45.

105. Katzenbach, J. R., and Smith, D. K. (1993) The discipline of teams. *Harvard Business Review*, March/April, pp. 118–119.

106. Kirby, D. (2003) *Entrepreneurship*. McGraw-Hill, Maidenhead.

107. Klitgaard, R. E. (1990) *Tropical Gangsters*. Basic Books, New York.

108. Kolb, D. (1984) *Experiential Learning Experience as the Source of Learning and Development*. Prentice-Hall, Engelwood Cliffs, New Jersey.

109. Kottler, P. (2003) *Marketing Insights from A to Z*. John Wiley and Sons, New York.

110. Kuratko, D., and Hodgetts, R. (1998) *Entrepreneurship: A Contemporary Approach*. New York, Dryden Press.

111. Kuznets, S. (1971) *Economic Growth of Nations, Total Output and Production Structure*. Harvard University press/Belknap Press, Cambridge, MA.

112. Lambing, P. A., and Kuehl, C. R. (2007) *Entrepreneurship*. Pearson Prentice Hall, Upper Saddle River, New Jersey.

113. Lashley, C. (2000) Towards a Theoretical Understanding. In: Lashley, C., and Morrison, A. (Eds.), *In Search of Hospitality: Theoretical Perspectives and Debates*. Butterworth-Heinemann, Oxford.

114. Lashley, C. (2001) *Empowerment: HR Strategies for Service Excellence*. Butterworth-Heinemann, Oxford.

115. Lashley, C. (2008) Studying hospitality: insights from social sciences. *Scandinavian Journal of Hospitality and Tourism* **12**(3).

116. Lashley, C., and Lee-Ross. (2003) *Organization Behaviour for Leisure Service*. Butterworth-Heinemann, Oxford.

117. Lashley, C., and Morrison, A. (2000) *In Search of Hospitality: Theoretical Perspectives and Debates*. Butterworth-Heinemann, Oxford.

118. Lashley, C., and Rowson, B. (2001) 'Wasted Millions: Staff turnover in Licensed Retail Organisations' Proceedings Hospitality Research Conference, University of Huddersfield.

119. Lashley, C., and Rowson, B. (2003) 'Divided by a common business? Franchisor and franchisee relations in the pub sector', *Strategic Change* (with Rowson) **12**: 3.

120. Lashley, C., and Rowson, B. (2005) *Developing Management Skills In Blackpool's Small Hotel Sector: A Research Report for England's North West Tourism Skills Network*. Nottingham, Nottingham Trent University.

121. Lashley, C., and Rowson, B. (2006) The Trails and Tribulations of Hotel Ownership in Blackpool: Highlighting the skill gaps of owner managers, *CHME Research Conference Proceedings*, Nottingham Trent University.

122. Lashley, C., and Rowson, B. (2007) The trials and tribulations of hotel ownership in blackpool: highlighting the skills gaps of owner-managers. *Tourism and Hospitality Research: the Surrey Quarterly* **7**(2).

123. Lashley, C., Lynch, P., and Morrison, A. (2007) *Hospitality: A Social Lens*. Elsevier, Oxford.

124. Lashley, C., Morrison, A., and Randall, S. (2005) 'More than a service encounter? Insights into the emotions of hospitality through special meal occasions' *Journal of Hospitality and Tourism Management* **12**(1): 80–92.

125. Lashley, C., and Rowson, B. (2008) Life Style Businesses: Insights from the Hotel Sector, 18th Conference Proceedings – Conference of Australian Tourism and Hospitality Educators, The Gold Coast, Australia.

126. Leach, P. (1996) *The BDO Stoy Howard Guide to the Family Business*. Kogan Page, London.

127. Lee-Ross, D. (1998) Comment: Australia and the small to medium-sized hotel sector. *International Journal of Contemporary Hospitality Management* **10**(5): 177–179.

128. Lee-Ross, D. (1999) *HRM in Tourism and Hospitality: International Perspectives on Small to Medium-sized Enterprises*. Cassell, London.

129. Lee-Ross, D., and Mitchell, B. (2007) Doing business in the Torres Straits: a study of the relationship between culture and the nature of indigenous entrepreneurs. *Journal of Developmental Entrepreneurship* **12**(2): 1–18.

130. Legge, J., and Hindle, M. (2004) *Entrepreneurship: Context, Vision and Planning*. Palgrave Macmillan, Basingstoke.

131. Legge, K. (1995) *Human Resource Management: Rhetorics and Realities*. MacMillan Business, London.

132. Lever-Tracy, C., Ip, D., Kitay, J., Phillips, I., and Tracy, N. (1991) *Asian Entrepreneurs in Australia*. Australian Government Publishing Service, Canberra.

133. Lewis, R. C., and Chambers, R. E. (2000) *Marketing Leadership in Hospitality: Foundations and Practices*, 3rd ed., Wiley, Brisbane.

134. Lindsay, N. J. (2005) Towards a cultural model of Indigenous entrepreneurial attitude, *Academy of Maketing Science Review* (Online), Vol. 5: www.amsreview.org/articles/lindsay05-2005.pdf, accessed 2007.

135. Litz, R. A. (1995) The family business: Toward definitional clarity. *Family Business Review* **8**(2): 71–81.

136. Litz, R. A. (1997) The family firms exclusion from business school research; explaining the void; addressing the opportunity. *Entrepreneurship: Theory and Practice* **21**(3): 55–72.

137. Lockyer, C., and Morrison, A. (1999) *Scottish Tourism Market Structure, Characteristics and Performance*. Scottish Tourism Research Unit, Fraser of Alander Institute, University of Strathclyde University, Glasgow.

138. Lomaine, A. (2005) In: Walton, editor. *Histories of Tourism*. Channel View Publications, Clevedon.

139. Lynch, P. A. (2005) The commercial home enterprise and host: a United Kingdom perspective. *Hospitality Management* **24**: 533–553.

140. Lynch, P., and MacWhannell, D. (2000) Home and commercialized hospitality. In: Lashley, C., and Morrison, A. (Eds.), *In Search of Hospitality: Theoretical Perspectives and Debates*. Butterworth-Heinemann, Oxford.

141. Manikutty, S. (2004) *Success and Succession in Family Firms: An Investigation into Changes in Managerial Practices with Generations*, presented at the Annual Meeting of the Academy of Management at New Orleans, August 8, 2004.

142. Mapunda, G. (2005) Traditional societies and entrepreneurship: an analysis of Australian and Tanzanian Businesses. *Journal of Asia Entrepreneurship and Sustainability* **1**(2): 1–23.

143. Margerison, C., and McCann, D. (1990) *Team Management: Practical New Approaches*. Mercury Books, London.

144. Mars, G., and Ward, R. (1984) Ethnic business development in Brita. In: opportunities, resources, In: Ward, R., and Jenkins, R. (Eds.), *Ethnic Communities in Business: Strategies for Economic Survival*. Cambridge University press, Cambridge.

145. Martin, C., Martin, L., and Mabbert, A. (2002) *SME Ownership Succession*. Small Business Service, Sheffield.

146. McGrath, R. G., MacMillan, I. C., and Scheinberg, S. (1992) Elitists, risk-takers and rugged individualists? An exploratory analysis of cultural differences between entrepreneurs and non-entrepreneurs *Journal of Business Venturing* **7**: 441–458.

147. Mead, L. (2000) Welfare reform and the family: lessons from America. In: Saunders, P. editor. *Reforming the Australian Welfare State*. Australian Institute for Family Studies, Melbourne.

148. Merriam-Webster Online Dictionary (2008) retrieved May 9, 2008, from http://www.merriam-webster.com/dictionary/create.

149. Minniti, M., Bygrave, W. D., and Autio, E. (2006) *Global Entrepreneurship Monitor: 2005 Executive Report*, Babson College, Babson Park, MA, US, London Business School, London, UK.

150. Moen, P., and Yu, Y. (2000) Effective work-life strategies: Working couples, work conditions, gender and life quality. *Social Problems* **47**(3): 291–327.
151. Molz, J. G., and Gibson, S. (2007) *Mobilizing Hospitality: The Ethics of Social Relations in a Mobile World*. Ashgate Publishing, Aldershot.
152. Morisson, A. (1998) Small firm co-operative marketing in a peripheral tourism region. *International Journal of Contemporary Hospitality Management*.
153. Morris, G. G. (1996) *Psychology: An Introduction*, 9th ed., Prentice Hall, Upper Saddle River, NJ.
154. Morris, M. H., Williams, R. O., Jeffrey, A., and Avila, R. A. (1997) Correlates of success in family business transitions. *Journal of Business Venturing* **12:** 385–401.
155. Morrison (2002).
156. Morrison, A. (2000) Entrepreneurship: what jiggers it? *International Journal of Entrepreneurial Behaviour and Research* **6**(2): 59–71.
157. Morrison, A. (2001) Small hospitality business: emerging or endangered? *The Journal of Hospitality and Tourism Management* **9:** 1–11.
158. Morrison, A., Rimmington, M., and Williams, C. (1999) *Entrepreneurship in the Hospitality, Tourism and Leisure Industries*. Butterworth Heinemann, Oxford.
159. Morrison, A., Rimmington, M., and Williams, C. (1999) *Entrepreneurship in the Hospitallity, Tourism and Leisure Industries*. Butterwort-Heinemann, Oxford.
160. Moutray, C. (2006) *The Small Business Economy for Date Year 2005: A Report to the President*, SBA Office of Advocacy, p.v.
161. MSI. (1996) *MSI data brief hotels: UK*. MSI, London.
162. Mueller, S. L., and Thomas, A. S. (2001) Culture and entrepreneurship potential: a nine country study of locus of control and innovativeness. *Journal of Business Venturing* **16:** 51–75.
163. Neblett, J., and Green, M. B. (2005) Linking development, indigenous entrepreneurship and tourism, with special reference to Barbados, http://www.siue.edu?GEOGRAPHY/ONLINE/neblett.htm, accessed 2007.
164. Nelson, R., and Winter, S. (1978) Forces generating and liberating concentration under Penrose, T. (1959) *The Theory of the Growth of the Firm*.
165. Nouwen, H. (1975) *Reaching Out: The Three Movements of the Spiritual Life*. Doubleday & Co, New York.
166. O'Brien, K. (1998) How to succeed in business, *American Printer*, April, No. 60.
167. O'Gorman, K. D. (2007) Dimensions of hospitality: exploring ancient and classical origins. In: Lashley, C., Lynch, P., and Morrison, A. (Eds.), *Hospitality: A Social Lens*. Elsevier, Oxford.
168. O'Mahony, B. (2003) 'Social and domestic forces in commercial hospitality provision: a view from Australia'. *Hospitality Review* **5**(4): 37–41.
169. O'Mahony. (2007) The role of the hospitality industry in cultural assimilation: a case study from colonial Australia. In: Lashley, C., Lynch, P., and Morrison, A. (Eds.), *Hospitality: A Social Lens*. Elsevier, Oxford.
170. Ornstein, R. (1975) *The Psychology of Consciousness*. H. Freeman, San Fransisco.
171. Pearson, N. (1999) Positive and negative welfare and Australia's indigenous communities, *Family Matters***54**, Spring/Summer, Australian Institute of Family Studies.

172. Peredo, A. M. (2001) *Communal Enterprises, Sustainable Development and the Alleviation of Poverty in Rural Andean Communities*, PhD Thesis, University of Calgary.

173. Peredo, A. M., Anderson, R. B., Galbraith, C. G., Honig, B., and Dana, L. P. (2004) Towards a theory of Indigenous entrepreneurship. *International Journal of Entrepreneurship and Small Business* **1**(1–2): 1–20.

174. Peters, T. (1987) *Thriving on Chaos: A Handbook for a Management Revolution*. Macmillan, London.

175. Pinard, M. C., and Allio, R. J. (2005) Innovations in the classroom: improving the creativity of MBA students. *Strategy and Leadership* **33**(1): 49–51.

176. Pinfold, J. F. (2001) The expectations of new business founders: the New Zealand case. *Journal of Small Business Management* **39**(3): 279–285.

177. Porter, M. (1985) *Competitive Advantage: Creating and Sustaining Superior Performance*. Free Press, New York.

178. Ram, M. (1994) *Managing to Survive: Working Lives in Small Firms*. Blackwell, Oxford.

179. Redpath, L., and Nielsen, M. O. (1997) A comparison of native culture, non-native culture and new management ideology. *Canadian Journal of Administrative Sciences* **14**(3): 327–339.

180. Reid, G., and Jacobsen, L. (1988) *The Small Entrepreneurial Firm*. Aberdeen University Press, Aberdeen.

181. Ritzer, G. (2007) 'Inhospitable hospitality?' In: Lashley, C., Lynch, P., and Morrison, A. (Eds.), *Hospitality: A Social Lens*. Elsevier, Oxford.

182. Robbins, S. P. (2005) *Organizational Behaviour*, 11th ed., Prentice Hall, Upper Saddle River, NJ.

183. Robbins, S. F. (2001) *Organisational Behaviour*, 9th ed., Prentice Hall, New Jersey.

184. Rotter, J. B. (1966) Generalised expectancies for internal versus external control of reinforcement. *Psychological Monographs* **80** (609).

185. Russell, R., and Faulkener, B. (2004) Entrepreneurship, chaos and the tourism area lifecycle. *Annals of Tourism Research* **31**(3): 556–579.

186. Sainz, H. (2002). *Alimentos y bebidas con denominaciones de origen y distintivos de calidad, Balances y perspectivas*. Distribución y Consumo, July–August issue, pp. 58–73.

187. Satre, J. P. (1943) *L'etre et le neant*. Gallimard.

188. Schaper, M., and Volery, T. (2004) *Entrepreneurship and Small Business: A Pacific Rim Perspective*. John Wiley, Sydney.

189. Schein, E. H. (1985) *Organizational Culture and Leadership*. Jossey Bass, San Francisco.

190. Schumpeter, J. A. (1934) *The Theory of Economic Development*. Harvard University Press, Cambridge, MA.

191. Schumpeter, J. A. (1934) *The Theory of Economic development: A Inquiry into Profits, Capital Credit, Interest and the Business Cycle*. Harvard University press, Cambridge, MA.

192. Scott, and Bruce. (1987) Five stages of growth in small businesses. *Long Range Planning* **20**(3).

193. Selwyn, T. (2000) An anthropology of hospitality. In: Lashley, C., and Morrison, A. (Eds.), *In Search of Hospitality: Theoretical Perspectives and Debates*. Butterworth-Heinemann, Oxford.

194. Shane, S. (1995) Uncertainty avoidance and the preference for innovation championing roles. *Journal of International Business Studies* **26**: 47–68.

195. Shane, S. (2003) *A General theory of Entrepreneurship, The Individual Opportunity Nexus*. Edward Elgar, Basingstoke.

196. Shane, S., and Venkataraman, S. (2000) The promise of entrepreneurship as a filed of research. *The Academy of Management Review* **25**(1): 217–226.

197. Shanker, M. C., and Astrachan, J. H. (1996) Myths and realities: Family businesses.

198. Sharma, P. (2004) An overview of the field of family business studies: current status and directions for the future. *Family Business Review* **17**(1): 1–36.

199. Shaw, R. (2002) Successful succession transfers take prudent financial planning, Hotel and Motel Management, http://www.hotelmotel.com/hotelmotel/article/articleDetail.jsp?id=37172, retrieved February 29, 2008.

200. Sheldon, P. (1993) Destination information systems. *Annals of Tourism Research* **20**(4): 633–649.

201. Shelton, L. M. (2006) Female entrepreneurs, work-family conflict, and venture performance: new insights into the work-family interface. *Journal of Small Business Management* **44**(2): 285–297.

202. Sherringham, C., and Daruwalla, P. (2007) 'Transgressing hospitality: polarities and disordered relationships'. In: Lashley, C., Lynch, P., and Morrison, A. (Eds.), *Hospitality: A Social Lens*. Elsevier, Oxford.

203. Shrimpton, D. (2002) *High divorce rate points to stress among managers*.Caterer and Hotelkeeper, Jan. 10, p. 7.

204. Sirmon, D. G., and Hitt, M. A. (2003) Managing resources: Linking unique resources, management and wealth creation in family firms. *Entrepreneurship Theory and Practice* **27**(4): 339–358.

205. Slattery, P. (2002) 'Finding the hospitality industry'. *Journal of Hospitality, Leisure Sport and Tourism* **1**(1).

206. Smyrnios, K. X., Walker, R. H., Le, H., Phan, M., Vuong, T., and Young, P. (2003) *The Boyd Partners Australian family and private business survey 2003*. RMIT University.

207. Statistics New Zealand. (1999) *Enterprises, Geographic Units and Full-time*.

208. Statistics New Zealand (2005). *Enterprises, Geographic Units and Employee Count*, Retrieved May 20, 2006 from http://www2.stats.govt.nz/domino/external/.

209. Stevens, M. J., and Campion, M. A. (1994) The knowledge, skill and ability requirements for teamwork: implications for human resource management. *Journal of Management* **Summer:** 503–530.

210. Stewart, K. (2006) Recipe for failure. *The Listener* **203**(3439): 26–27.

211. Storey, D. J. (1994) *Understanding the Small Business Sector*. Routledge, London.

212. Stromback, T., and Malhotra, R. (1994) *Socioeconomic Linkages of South Asian Immigrants with their Country of Origin*. Canberra, BIPR/Australian Government Publishing Service.

213. Sullivan, A., and Margaritis, D. (2000) Public sector reform and indigenous entrepreneurship. *International Journal of Entrepreneurial behaviour & Research* **6**(5): 265–275.

214. Sweeney, M.. (2008) *An Investigation into the Hosts Connection with the Commercial Home*, PhD thesis, Queen Margaret College, Edinburgh.

215. Sweeney, M., and Lynch, P. A. (2006) Explorations of the Host's Relationship with the Commercial Home, *14th Annual Council for Hospitality Management Education Hospitality Research Conference Proceedings*, Nottingham Trent University.

216. Sweet, S. (2001) Strategic value configuration logics and the ''new'' economy: a service economy revolution? *International Journal of Service Industry Management* **12**(1): 70–84.

217. Tacoronte-Acentejo. (2006). Bodegas y sus vinos. Retrieved March 23 2007 from http://www.tacovin.com/dota/espanol/bodega0.htm.

218. Tannenbaum, R., and Schmidt, W. H. (1958) How to choose a leadership pattern. *Harvard Business Review* **36**: 95–101.

219. Tayeb, M. (1994) Organizations and national culture: methodology considered. *Organisation Studies* **15**: 429–446.

220. Telfer, E. (2000) The philosophy of hospitableness. In: Lashley, C., and Morrison, A. (Eds.), *In Search of Hospitality: Theoretical Perspectives and Debates*. Butterworth-Heinemann, Oxford.

221. Thomas, R., Friel, M., Jameson, S., and Parsons, D. (1997) The National Survey of small tourism and hospitality firms: Annual Report 1996–1997, Leeds: Centre for the Study of Small Tourism and Hospitality Firms, Leeds Metropolitan University.

222. Thomas, R., Lashley, C., Rowson, B., Xie, Y., Jameson, S., Eaglen, A., Lincoln, G., and Parsons, D. (2000) *The National Survey of Small Tourism and Hospitality Firms: 2000 – Skills Demands and Training Practices*. Leeds Metropolitan University, Leeds.

223. Timmons, J. A. (1999) *New Venture Creation: Entrepreneurship for the 21st Century*. Irwin/McGraw Hill, Singapore.

224. Trewin, D. (2002) Small Business in Australia 2001, ABS Catalogue Number 1321.0.

225. Tucker, V. (1999) The myth of development: a critique of a Eurocentric discourse. In: Munck, R., and O'Hearn, D. (Eds.), *Critical Developmental Theory: Contributions to a New Paradigm*. Zed Books, London.

226. US Census Bureau(2005) *Establishment and Firm Size 2002 US Department of Commerce*. Economics and Statistics Administration p. 10.

227. Volery, T., and Schaper, M. (2004) *Entrepreneurship and Small Business: A Pacific Rim Perspective* **Vol. 10 (5):** John Wiley and Sons Ltd., Australia pp. 191–197.

228. Vyakarnham, S., and Leppard, J. (1999) *A Marketing Action Plan for the Growing Business*, 2nd ed., Kogan Page, London.

229. Waldinger, R.D., Aldrich, H., and Ward, R. (Eds.) (1990) *Ethnic Entrepreneurs: Immigrant Business in Industrial Societies*. Sage, Newbury Park.

230. Wanhill, S. (1997) Peripheral area tourism: a European perspective. *Progress in Tourism and Hospitality Research* **3**(1): 47–70.

231. Ward, J. L. (1988) The special role of strategic planning for family businesses. *Family Business review* **1**(20 (Summer)).

232. Ward, R., and Jenkins, R. (Eds.) (1984) *Ethnic Communities in Business*. Cambridge University press, Cambridge.

233. Wennekers, A. R. M., Noorderhaven, N. G., Hofstede, G., and Thurik, A. R. (2001) Cultural and economic determinants of business ownership across countries. *Frontiers of Entrepreneurship 2001*. Babson College, Babson Park, MA.

234. Werbner, P. (1990) Renewing and industrial past: British Pakistani entrepreneurship in Manchester. *Migration* **8:** 7–41.

235. White, R. (2007) *Plan Before Your Leap: An Entrepreneur's Guide to the Feasibility Study*, Retrieved December 2007, http://www.whitehutchinson.com/leisure/articles/74.shtml.

236. Wickham, P. A. (2001) *Strategic Entrepreneurship: A Decision-Making Approach to New Venture Creation and Management*, 2nd ed., Pearson Education Limited, Edinburgh Gate.

237. Williams, A. M., and Shaw, G. (2004) From lifestyle consumption to lifestyle production: changing patterns of tourism entrepreneurship. In: Thomas, R. (Ed.), *Small Firms in Tourism: International Perspectives*, pp. 99–113.

238. Yammarinow, F. J., and Danserau, F. (2002) Individualized leadership. *Journal of Leadership and Organizational Studies* **9**(1)**:** 90–99.

239. Yukl, G. (2006) *Leadership in Organizations*, 6th ed., Pearson Prentice Hall, Upper Saddle River, NJ.

240. Zeppel, H. (1998) Selling the dreamtime: aboriginal culture in Australian Tourism. In: Rowe, D., and Lawrence, G. (Eds.), *Leisure, Sport: Critical Perspectives.* Hodder Education, Rydalmere, NSW, pp. 23–38.

241. Zimmerer, T. W., and Scarborough, N. M. (2002) *Essentials of Entrepreneurship and Small Business Management*, 3rd ed., Prentice Hall, Upper Saddle River, NJ.

242. Zimmerer, T. Z., and Scarborough, N. M. (1996) *Entrepreneurship and the New Venture Formation.* Prentice-Hall International, Upper Saddle River, NJ.

243. Zimmerer, T. Z., and Scarborough, N. M. (2005) *Essentials of Entrepreneurship and Small Business Management*, 4th ed., Pearson Prentice Hall, Upper Saddle River, NJ.

Index